ESSAYS IN PUBLIC FINANCE AND FISCAL POLICY

Essays

in PUBLIC FINANCE

and

FISCAL POLICY

by GERHARD COLM

with the editorial assistance

of HELEN O. NICOL

New York · OXFORD UNIVERSITY PRESS · 1955

TO ALVIN JOHNSON

'Unconsciously, he had absorbed into himself
the brave spirit of America.' (Alvin Johnson
about Robert La Follette.)

Preface

THIS BOOK presents a collection of essays written during the years 1934 to 1954. These fateful two decades covered periods of vast contrasts: the Great Depression, World War II, the period of demobilization and reconstruction, and the period of partial mobilization in a world of tension. Each of these periods also presented different tasks for public and fiscal policy. It may be of value for the reader to see how the ideas of a student of public finance and fiscal policy developed in response to these different situations.

There was a temptation to rewrite some of the essays included in this collection. Thereby the author could perhaps have advanced his standing as a prophet, but the educational value of the essays would not have been furthered.

The essays selected for this volume center around the contribution that public finance and fiscal policy can make toward national objectives such as restoring or maintaining high-level employment, raising the standard of living, and establishing full or partial mobilization. The writing of these essays was largely motivated by the feeling that a basic reorientation in the conventional approaches of economics and public finance is needed if they are to make the fullest possible contribution to the solution of the problems of our time. No system of 'new' economics or 'new' public finance is offered. At best the reader may find an opportunity to participate in the author's groping for a reorientation in public finance.

Of the eighteen essays combined in this volume, three (Chapters 11, 12, 13) have not previously been published in English. The last essay, 'Setting the Sights,' was written for this volume.

Some of the essays have been shortened to avoid repetition or to leave out parts that the editor believed were no longer of sufficient interest. Also, many footnotes of the original articles have been omitted. Apart from this, the editing has been confined to changes in language and the clarification of the original meaning. The author has added footnotes to point out instances in which he has changed his views or where he wishes to remind the reader of the circumstances in which a statement was written. The footnotes added by the author for the present publication are printed in brackets.

Dr. Helen O. Nicol took the initiative for this volume. She selected and edited the material, prepared the index, and performed all the chores connected with the publication of this collection of essays. My greatest obligation is due her without whose effort this book would not have been published. The author also wishes to acknowledge the many helpful suggestions of C. Lowell Harriss of Columbia University, R. A. Musgrave of the University of Michigan, and Arthur Smithies of Harvard University.

G. C.

Washington, D. C.
October 1954

Table of Contents

List of Illustrations

Foreword

THE AUTHOR of these essays on Public Finance and Fiscal Policy, Dr. Gerhard Colm, has succeeded over the years in gaining an ever-widening reputation as an outstanding economist. He has accomplished this during a period when economics has become an increasingly important subject in our country and is destined to become even more important.

I look upon the study of economics as an inquiry into how wealth-creating activities affect the welfare of the community; and in reviewing the history of economics three main periods come to my mind:

I. The period of inquiry with efforts concentrated on understanding the working of the economic system.

II. The period of admiration, when the system was regarded as self-sufficient and as needing no interference. Economists concerned themselves more with what governments should *not* do than with what could wisely be attempted.

III. The period of critical awareness, when economists were

less negative and began to give definite advice about what could be done, though at times—some say—contradictory advice.

It is during this last period of critical awareness of the short-comings of our economic system and of the need for corrective measures that Dr. Colm's essays have been written. During one stage of this period, particularly during the Great Depression, policy makers in business and government urgently requested advice from the economists who were themselves often groping in the dark as they sought answers to the complex problems that confronted us.

Those were the days when deficit financing was looked on by many as unforgivable, and when several conscientious economists were accused of trying to wreck our country, whereas today a responsible citizen may well object to an unbalanced budget but certainly does not regard its proponents as unpatriotic.

This, in turn, gave rise to debates about the ethics of the profession. Many people thought that economists should not make constructive suggestions but should confine themselves to giving technical advice on the economic effects of specific steps proposed by the policy makers. They felt that the economist might properly recommend the choice of *means* but not the choice of *ends*.

I have always believed that the only limitation to be imposed on an economist is that he must give advice which is appropriate to, and compatible with, the existing economic system or the kind of system desired by the majority of citizens. If he goes beyond that and knowingly recommends steps that put the economic boat on the rocks or force us later to adopt a different economic system, then he violates the ethics of the profession.

To live up to this standard was difficult at times, because many citizens were confused about what they really expected of our economic system. To avoid any such misunderstanding, an economist can protect himself by frankly expressing his interpretation of the premises which form the basis of economic discussion and of the desires expressed by the majority of the citizens.

During the period under review, it became increasingly obvious that nineteenth-century laissez-faire notions were no longer

xiv

practical. The laissez-faire period of economics may be likened to the period in sports when gentlemen merely used their spare time for tournament play. As soon as one of these amateur sportsmen gave up his work and in effect became a full-time professional, the other amateurs had no choice but to give up the game or become professionals themselves.

Similarly, when some countries or policy makers—perhaps by necessity—began to approach national and international problems from an entirely professional angle, other countries were compelled in self-defense to make the corresponding readjustments in their attitudes and practices.

It was in the course of such efforts that, in the early 'forties, I took part in a study for the National Planning Association, entitled 'National Budgets for Full Employment.' We tried to work out how the American economy would look at a given future date, not with a view to crystal gazing but in order to ascertain the consequences of projecting past and present relationships and magnitudes of economic factors into the future. We felt that even if we could not expect to give an exact picture of the economy at a future date, we might succeed in providing business and government policy makers with reasonable projections of future possibilities which could serve as the basis for intelligent decisions.

In the course of this study, in which many prominent economists took part, I had for the first time the pleasure of working with Dr. Colm. Subsequently, I had occasions to talk with him when he was the Budget Bureau representative in the preparatory work which resulted in the Employment Act of 1946. Later, I met him frequently when he was with the Council of Economic Advisers. I have often derived great profit both from his deep knowledge of economic theory as well as from his practical judgment as a working economist of the specific problems of business and government.

Throughout these many meetings I felt that Dr. Colm was not satisfied with merely giving technically correct but essentially unproductive advice, but that he recognized, as I did, that an economist placed in a high and responsible position must do his utmost to give unbiased but constructive advice.

To give unbiased advice is one of the most difficult tasks for an economist, because often, perhaps subconsciously, he starts out with a bias. The result will be that while he is working on his data he is all the time subconsciously trying to prove the validity of a preconceived notion.

After working with Dr. Colm for many years, I am convinced that he is one of the few who is able to approach a subject with an unbiased mind. If we add to that ability his great knowledge and skill, we can understand why his conclusions are generally of such nature that policy makers do well in paying attention to them.

It was this feeling about the character of Dr. Colm's advice and work, and recognition of its increasing importance to business and government policy makers, that prompted, in the spring of 1952, the offer to Dr. Colm of the position of Chief Economist of the National Planning Association. In this position he has free scope to work on the issues he considers of the most immediate importance to our nation, to the end that agriculture, business, labor, the professions, and government may all benefit from his efforts.

During the last two years, Dr. Colm together with us in the National Planning Association has emphasized the importance for our nation of what we call *economic preparedness*.

One of the important contributions to this end is his recent study entitled *The American Economy in 1960,* in which he outlines the problems that will face us over the coming years in the event that defense expenditures can be gradually reduced.

Another study, which has been published recently, deals with the problem of how, if necessary, we could increase our defense expenditures with as little harm as possible to our present and future economy.

Viewed against this background, I spent some delightful hours in reading Dr. Gerhard Colm's essays covering the period from 1934 to 1953. They have interested me from three angles.

First, they give a picture of many of the various problems and measures that have been discussed over the last twenty years in an effort to make our economy more stable and resistant. This affords many a busy person the rare opportunity of obtaining a really clear summary of several of the economic events of the last two decades.

Second, they show how, under the stress of circumstances and the facing of many perplexing problems, a man of Dr. Colm's caliber has avoided becoming entangled in specific technical details and has grown with the size of the problems and learned by taking cognizance of the mistakes that we as a nation have made in the past.

Finally, they have interested me because of the development of his careful thinking on the subject of economic ethics.

In his last essay 'Setting the Sights,' he points the way to more 'constructive economics' which can give practical guidance to private and public actions.

We need more economists like Gerhard Colm, and we need an increasing number of people in business and in government who are willing and able to understand the work of such economists and to use it constructively.

To that end this collection of essays will, I trust, serve a useful purpose.

H. CHRISTIAN SONNE

Part
-I-

INTRODUCTORY

1

Why Public Finance?

(1948) *

AN APOLOGY

A methodological article usually starts with an apology—for good reasons. In general, it is more important to contribute to the solution of a burning problem than to investigate whether there is a problem. Nevertheless, the author feels intellectually disturbed by the fact that we are publishing books on public finance, conducting academic courses in public finance, devoting magazines to public finance—when the present trend (1948) in economic thinking seems to suggest that there is really no longer any *raison d'être* for such a separate field in the social sciences. Are we, in treating public finance as a separate field of study, perhaps carrying over a concept that had its justification in the past but that has become submerged in present circumstances? I intend to defend public finance as a special field of study, but

* 'Why Public Finance?' *National Tax Journal,* The National Tax Association, 1 (3), September 1948, pp. 193-206.

in my defense it may turn out that I propose some modifications in the traditional approach.

To make sure that we are not setting up a straw man, I shall outline briefly some of the arguments that seem to invite the conclusion that there is no longer any reason for dealing with problems of public finance as a separate field of study and training.

THE CASE AGAINST PUBLIC FINANCE? [1]

Nobody doubts the need to study tax problems or debt problems or the financial aspects of defense expenditures, public works, or any other government functions, but is there any justification for treating these problems as parts of *one* field? Tax problems are most directly related to income and price problems; government expenditures for flood control invite treatment in connection with natural resources; social-security problems are closely related to employment and wage problems. Government debt management is related to general questions of credit and banking. Government receipts and expenditures are related to the flow of national income and employment. In all fields of general economics there are many opportunities to deal with various types of taxation, government expenditures, and debt problems. There is a strong case for treating the effect of government action wherever it occurs in the economy.

But what is the reason for pulling these various government actions together into one field? The traditional answer to this question is, of course, that all these fields of public finance are related to the budget; and that the budget, which represents a 'national program . . . our work plan,' [2] is a unifying concept and a unifying institution in the area of public finance. This is, I believe, a valid answer, but before accepting it we must

[1] This discussion is limited to problems of public finance on the national level. The conventional approach is more justifiable with respect to state and local finance.

[2] President Roosevelt in the budget message of 3 January 1941, *U.S. Budget for the Fiscal Year 1942*, p. xiv.

consider that it has been challenged by rather forceful arguments.

The traditional reason for dealing with the budget as a unit, embracing expenditures of the government as well as revenues, was the belief that taxes have the prime purpose of providing the money needed to pay for expenditures, and that in deciding on a feasible program of expenditures the availability of tax revenue should be a major consideration.

For the sovereign government with access to central bank credit, however, tax yields do not limit the amount of money the government can spend if it decides to do so. From this A. P. Lerner, for example, draws the conclusion that taxation has the sole purpose of seeing to it that the people have left in their hands just the right amount of money that enables them to buy the possible output of goods for sale.[3] Since the amount of expenditures is one of the factors that influence how much money people have in their hands, an increase in government expenditures may create a condition that requires an increase in taxes too in order to avoid inflation. But the need for an increase in taxes may also result from an increase in private business investments or net exports; or, if the increase in expenditures occurs at a time when private investments happen to decline, then there is no reason for increasing taxes. Thus, according to this approach, there seems to be no more relationship between government expenditures and government taxes than there is among all other elements in the national and international economy. This reasoning may appear to lead to the logical conclusion that a budget which compares proposed expenditures and revenues no longer has any significance as a guide for policy.

[3] See, for example, *Economics of Control,* New York, Macmillan Co., 1944, chap. 24. Reference is made to Lerner because the position he takes in the chapter referred to is the most uncompromising and therefore particularly suitable for an argument about the principles. Lerner has indicated elsewhere that he recognizes that taxation has other specific purposes but he believes it can never be justified solely by the government's need for money. See also various statements by Beardsley Ruml, such as, '. . . our taxes should be as low as they possibly can be without putting the value of our money in danger of inflation' (*Proceedings of the National Tax Association,* 1944, p. 167).

The limited validity of this idea is recognized when fiscal policy is considered not merely within the frame of the government budget but within the frame of the nation's economic budget. Here government expenditures as well as tax collections are viewed in their interrelationship with consumer income, expenditure, and savings; business profits and investments; and international transactions. Yet we intend to demonstrate later that this consideration of public finance within the frame of the national economy as a whole should supplement rather than supersede a consideration of government expenditure, revenue, and debt problems as a unified field of interrelated economic and social phenomena.

HISTORICAL ORIGIN OF PUBLIC FINANCE

Are we justified in still treating public finance as a separate field of study? Let us look at the rather strange historical origin of this science.

Public finance has two main roots. One of them was the cameralism of the sixteenth to eighteenth centuries. Cameralism was developed by the advisers and panegyrists of kings and princes and by the teachers of prospective public servants of these kings and princes. It embraced all economic, social, and financial facts pertinent to the management of government affairs, and practically all such (economic, social, and financial) facts were believed pertinent. In the thinking of these writers there was no distinction between the private and public sphere of economics.

The writings of the classical school and its followers formed the second root of public finance. These men treated government activities largely as an outside, non-economic factor which modified price and income relations in the economic system of private enterprise and exchange. The philosophers of the classical school did not deny the importance of state activities, but their scientific interests were aroused by the ideal of a self-regulatory exchange economy. While the cameralists believed in the divine origin and mission of the monarch, the classical writers were inspired by the belief in a divine power which controls the *ordre naturel* of the economic system just as it controls the movement of celestial bodies and the growth of vegetable and animal life.

In analyzing this self-regulatory system, the effect of taxes on income distribution and prices was treated as a disturbing factor. Thus the classical school contributed directly to the analysis of shifting and the incidence of taxation. Equally important, however, was its negative contribution: by failing to give adequate attention to government transactions classical doctrine forced the development of a special science of public finance.

Public finance was thus developed as a special field by writers who grew up in the conviction that the analysis of the self-regulatory economic process was the main topic of general economics, but who also recognized that the economic and financial affairs of the government required a special and systematic treatment in the literature and in academic teaching. Public finance was the product of a strange marriage between cameralistic and classical economics.

These origins are still reflected in many textbooks and curricula in public finance. The emphasis is on factual, institutional information (carried over from the cameralistic tradition) with a somewhat unrelated analytical treatment of shifting and incidence of taxation (taken over from the classical tradition). No genuine theory of the role of government within the economic process is presented because it is tacitly assumed that the only possible theory in economics is that of the self-regulatory process. This is the theory treated in general economics.

It is perhaps significant that recent progress in the economics of public finance has been made largely by writers in the field of general economics rather than by specialists in public finance. The influence of such men as Wicksell, Pigou, Keynes, Hansen, and Simons on public finance is outstanding but they are by no means the only contributors.

Today the treatment of general economic problems is no longer exclusively concentrated on the working of the self-regulatory process, as more attention is given to its limitations and to the government's positive role in the economic system. To that extent it appears that at least the negative reason for the development of public finance as a special science no longer

7

exists. On the other hand, the economists who treat government influences on the economy have largely neglected the essential institutional and procedural aspects of government action. That is why their analyses and recommendations are often characterized as utopian and unrealistic by the specialists in public finance. There is a wide gap between the textbook treatment of public finance and the actual legislative, administrative, and sociological processes of public finance. Thus there still seems to be a need for study and training in public finance that gives equal emphasis to its theoretical and its institutional aspects. What, then, is this particular institutional aspect of public finance?

Organizing Principles in the Private and Public Economy

Classical and neoclassical thinking tended to explain all economics in terms of one set of principles such as is implied in the labor theory of value or in the theory of marginal utility. The area of public finance presented an annoying problem to the pure theorist. He either regarded public finance as a disturbing external factor of basically non-economic origin or tried to explain that phenomenon away by forcing it into the general mold of value theory.

Contrary to such a 'monistic' explanation of the economy, I believe a more valid theory will recognize that there are three organizing principles in our economic reality: that of the family or household economy,[4] the self-regulatory mechanism of supply and demand relations (in short, the market principle), and, third, the principle of the public economy (in short, the budget principle). Both the market mechanism and the budget principle are forms of organization that determine the development and use of resources (labor, material, land, technological and managerial knowledge) and the distribution of the product.

The market mechanism works through the interplay of millions of individuals as producers and consumers. Production is

[4] The principles of the household economy, which are predominant in peasant economies and still have some significance as an element even in the industrial society, will not be elaborated in this article.

8

determined by profit expectations which in turn depend on demand. Demand is determined by the income derived in the process of production. The market principle is an organizing principle of such usefulness in a complex society that if we had not inherited it, its inventor today would be honored as one of the great benefactors of mankind.

Useful as it is, however, the market principle has its limitations and defects if viewed in the light of the requirements of the general welfare. It is not completely applicable to some important areas of activity (e.g. road construction, multi-purpose projects of resource development); in some areas sole reliance on the market principle would be undesirable (e.g. education); in other areas its operation, under modern technological and social conditions, has undesirable consequences requiring corrective action (e.g. business fluctuations, monopolistic tendencies, concentration of property and income distribution, economic insecurity).

The market principle therefore requires supplementary and corrective action by governments. Such actions are largely organized according to the budget principle. The essence of the budget principle is that the services in this sphere are determined not by profit expectations and the willingness of individuals to spend their money for the purchase of such services, but by decisions reached through political and administrative procedures and based on common social objectives. The benefits from these services are not necessarily allocated to those who pay the taxes to finance them; that is, the revenues may or may not be collected from those who are the beneficiaries. The distribution of the tax burden as well as the decision about what services should be performed and who will benefit from them is a political decision.[5]

An appraisal of the performance and results of market operations, and of the character and need of supplementary and corrective government programs, is possible only if there are at least general ideas concerning the broad economic and social objectives of the society. In other words, it is necessary for each gen-

[5] The meaning of the term 'political' in this context is the same as in 'political science' and is only indirectly related to 'politics.'

eration to work out a concrete concept of the requirements of the general welfare. This relation to economic and social objectives does not mean that the whole area of public finance is 'controversial'—most of these objectives are taken for granted at any period of time. Only a relatively small though important fringe is controversial.

The interplay between the economic processes determined by the market principle and those determined by the budget principle is one of the main subjects that requires study. Any attempt to analyze government transactions as if they were determined in the same way as private transactions omits the essence of the public operations and makes it impossible to analyze the interaction of the two principles. Any useful treatment of the problems of public finance must be based on recognition of the fact that the determination of public finance transactions is distinct from the determination of transactions of households and private businesses. The distinction follows from the political objectives and methods by which the government transactions are determined and executed.

It may be useful here to distinguish between a legal principle and an economic principle in defining these spheres in our economy, as is illustrated by the following diagram:

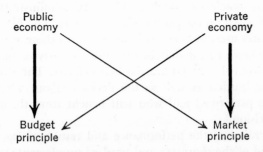

Fig. 1. The Budget Principle and the Market Principle

The difference between the public and private economy is primarily a legal distinction. The distinction between the budget principle and the market principle is a distinction between the methods of economic organization. It is true that in the public

10

economy the budget principle is predominant; in the private economy the market principle predominates. But it is also true that we have in the public economy government-owned and operated enterprises that are guided by the market in a manner quite similar to the way the management of private enterprises is guided. Then we have private educational institutions and philanthropic agencies, churches, and other private associations which, in their activities, follow the budget principle to a greater extent than they do the market principle.

Nevertheless, it can be said that the public economy, which is the subject matter of public finance, is dominated by the budget principle. Even in the case of government-owned and operated enterprises, there is some public responsibility and some element of control which distinguish them from private enterprises. The political nature of government decisions does not, however, place them beyond economics. Government expenditures result in competing claims for national resources. Tax policies aid in shifting resources from private to public use. The distribution of benefits and the method of taxation affect the distribution of real income. The interplay between expenditures, revenue, and borrowing, moreover, affects the whole level of economic activity. Therefore, government actions are not outside the economic field but are part of it. They affect the general level of resource use, the allocation of resources to various competing usages, and the distribution of the product. We do not have a public economy superimposed on a private economy, but we have several organizing principles which, in their interplay, form our economic system.

Public finance then has to do with the operations of government as they are organized under the budget principle. In this respect it is a field comparable to business management. But, as the general economist deals with the role of business in the economy as a whole, he will also deal with the role of government. It is the proper concern of general economics, or, may we say, of the science of political economy, to deal with the way in which government operations supplement, correct, or distort activities under the market system, and particularly with the way in which the two principles may be combined and integrated to accomplish the economic objectives of the nation as a whole.

TREATMENT OF EXPENDITURES AND PROGRAM FORMULATION IN PUBLIC FINANCE

Conventional textbooks of public finance have discussed expenditures mainly on an historical basis. Expanding government activities were treated as data demonstrating the growing size of the task of government financing and that task was regarded as the real subject matter of public finance. More modern textbooks may show the influence of Adolph Wagner's social theory of public finance or Pigou's welfare economics. They make at least some reference to the reasons why government services, under certain circumstances, increase the 'social net product' as distinguished from the 'private net product,' and why the public sector of the economy at times tends to increase in absolute and relative size. Also the debate concerning the effect of taxes on the distribution of incomes has been broadened from mere analysis of the shifting and incidence of taxation to include also consideration of the effect of government services (e.g. education) and payments (e.g. social security and interest payments) on the distribution of money and real incomes. Under the influence of the Keynesian school and its predecessors and successors, the effect of government expenditures, as well as of taxation and borrowing, on the level of employment has been treated in recent textbooks of public finance. It was found that even the incidence of an additional tax or a tax reduction cannot be fully analyzed without consideration of related changes in expenditures.[6] Thus there has been a growing recognition that expenditures and revenues deserve equal attention in public finance, and that the one cannot be fully dealt with without the other.

The treatment of expenditures has been limited, however, largely to the compilation of historical facts, discussions of so-

[6] For an attempted proof of this proposition, see my article 'Public Revenue and Public Expenditure in National Income,' in *Studies in Income and Wealth*, National Bureau of Economic Research, New York, 1937, vol. I, particularly pp. 185-91; and chap. xxv, 'Social Accounting and Public Policy.'

cial philosophy, and, more recently, to an analysis of economic effects. Very little systematic work has been done on the development of practical criteria and procedures for appraising the justification, urgency, and priority of government programs for which expenditures are contemplated.[7] Modern economics has had a very wholesome effect on recent texts in public finance —but in embracing the economics of public finance, we run into the danger of neglecting the specific problems related to policy formation, management, and operation that follow from the public character of public finance.

The determination of government programs is a political procedure and, as such, is carried on in a milieu, usually called 'politics,' which includes vote gathering, pressure by lobbies, logrolling, and competition among political rivals. The political nature of these decisions has induced many scientists to conclude that the development of any rational standards and procedures would be a hopeless undertaking.

It would be quite wrong to assume, however, that from the standpoint of the nation's economic development the decisions of private enterprise are wholly rational, while those of government represent a sordid compromise among self-seeking politicians. There is perhaps a presumption, but no certainty, that the investment decisions of entrepreneurs result in an expansion of the nation's productive plants which, according to tempo, location, and characteristics, approximates the best interests of balanced economic expansion.

Through the development of budgeting and other planning procedures, we have made it possible for 'political' decisions concerning government programs to be based more completely on

---

[7] A famous French engineer and economist wrote in a study on 'The Measurement of the Utility of Public Works': 'The legislator has prescribed formal procedures by which certain works can be declared of public utility; the science of political economy has not yet precisely defined the conditions that such works must fulfill in order to be really useful; at least the ideas that have been uttered on the subject appear vague, incomplete, and often inexact.' This was written in 1844. It would still be an understatement today —more than 100 years later. (Cited in 'Jules Dupuit et Son Oeuvre Économique,' École Nationale des Ponts et Chaussées, Paris, 1945, p. 18.)

13

economic considerations. Nevertheless, continuing analysis of past errors and future objectives must contribute to further improvement of standards and procedures for the most rational determination of public programs. It must also be recognized, however, that the degree to which objective criteria can be used differs greatly according to the type of program.

Programs that by their very nature are interrelated with other economic developments can be tested to determine their role in a growing economy. An irrigation program, for instance, can be tested with respect to its place in a comprehensive land and water utilization program, which in turn must be related to long-range national and regional objectives for agricultural output and power production, industrial developments, and other bench marks of economic development.

The question whether an investment will 'pay' for itself is of only secondary importance in the public domain. Nevertheless, there are many functions for which the benefits can be expressed in monetary terms and in which methods for cost calculations and cost comparisons can be of use. This is especially true for expenditures related to the development of natural resources, transportation, or power.

Policy is concerned not only with the formulation of meritorious programs but also with the tempo and timing of their execution. Assume that a large program, say a five- or ten-billion-dollar program for the development of river basins, has been formulated and approved on its own intrinsic merits; then the tempo of execution must be decided. Will the program be planned to be completed in five, ten, or twenty years? This is the point at which program planning and budget planning converge. The decision requires at least a tentative concept of the sustainable size of the budget total and of reasonable allocations to various competing programs. Budget planning demands a movement from bottom to top, as well as from top to bottom. It starts from tentatively formulated detailed programs, sums them up, and then looks at the result as a whole. It also moves down from the formulation of a reasonable total and sets limits

14

to detailed programs in a way that fits in with the budget target.

Expenditures that serve mainly social or political [8] purposes (in a narrower definition) are not as easily measured by rational yardsticks. The main effort with respect to these programs is to demonstrate their economic and social costs in terms of the alternative use that could be made of the same resources. It must be asked whether these programs exceed the magnitude that is compatible with existing policies and with existing economic organization; the analysis of economic and social costs includes an appraisal of the measures of government controls that may be needed if very large additional programs are considered.[9]

Besides the development of standards for appraising expenditure programs, there is the need for devising procedures of policy formulation and policy execution. These must be political procedures; that is, they must take account of legitimate interests of the people directly and indirectly concerned, and they must establish clear political responsibility for those who participate in the decision. At the same time, procedures must be devised that assure that objective standards are applied to the greatest possible extent.

Not only are procedures to guide the formation of policy required, but also methods for checking on its execution. To serve

[8] It is annoying that the term 'political' has different though related meanings. All government programs are political because they are formulated and adopted by political procedures. Political purposes, as distinct from social and economic purposes, are those directly related to the preservation or extension of the power of an organized nation or group of nations—purposes related to foreign policy, defense, policing, and administration of justice. This category may also include measures such as tax administration and general administrative overhead, which are a means without which none of the other purposes of organized society could be fulfilled.

[9] Recent analyses of the economic impact of foreign aid and defense programs may serve as illustrations (e.g. see *The Impact of Foreign Aid upon the Domestic Economy,* Council of Economic Advisers, Washington, D. C., October 1947). Such analyses are not intended to suggest conclusions whether and to what extent these programs are desirable or necessary. They are intended, however, to give the legislators and the public an objective appraisal of economic and social costs, which are an important factor in the formation of these programs. By such objective analysis the area of political controversy can be limited.

the interests of the administration, the legislature, and the people, progress reports, auditing reports, and other methods of program control and supervision are essential.

In the private market economy, profit expectation of business and buyers' demand provide guidance in the allocation of resources for productive undertakings. Actual profit accounts are regarded as proof of success or failure in business planning and business operations. A considerable portion of the nation's business, however, depends on public action that is determined by political process and not by profit expectation. When the public sector was small and the main dynamic forces were carried forward by private business, it was not too costly even if 'politics' was permitted to shape the actions in the public sector to a large extent. Under present circumstances, such a course would be fatal.

Though there is no way to determine political decisions 'scientifically,' systematic appraisals can and must play an important role in policy formulation. For this task, appropriate yardsticks and procedures must still be developed or improved. The same applies, of course, to problems of taxation and debt management.

In spite of this emphasis on economic considerations, other aspects should not be neglected. Particularly in programs that imply the use of compulsion, such as tax legislation or measures of regulation and control, public acceptability and fairness are standards at least equal to criteria of a purely economic nature.

RULES OF PUBLIC FINANCE

The unity in government operations, discussed thus far, is of an institutional and procedural character. As government expenditures, revenues, and debt management are determined by political decisions, similar problems as to criteria of rational action and appropriate administrative and legislative procedures must be solved. What about substantive unity, the interrelationship between government expenditure, revenue, and debt policy?

The era of laissez-faire ideology developed a rather simple set of rules with respect to the interrelationship of expenditure and

16

revenue policies of the government: (1) the lowest level is the best level of expenditures (the 'necessary evil' dogma); (2) revenues should *always* equal expenditures (the 'balanced budget' dogma); (3) taxes should be levied in a manner that affects existing economic relations as little as possible (the 'economic neutrality' dogma).

These rules have been questioned by unorthodox writers since they were first developed, and they have been more honored in the breach than in the observance. Nevertheless, they were widely regarded as yardsticks for appraising public-finance policies. Today the validity of these rules is questioned by most economists, and many doubt that any rules can be developed in place of those that have been discarded.

Are there any such rules other than those that say that expenditure policies as well as revenue policies and debt management should be conducted in accord with economic requirements? If there are, then expenditure and revenue policies would each still be related to economic facts, but there would be no particular relation between expenditure and revenue policies; in other words, the budget would lose its significance.

Nevertheless, serious attempts have been made in recent years to develop new guideposts for public-finance policy that could take the place of the discarded dogmas. These new guideposts, however, are not proposed as rigid rules but rather as working hypotheses.[10]

Only working hypotheses, rather than iron-clad dogmas, can constitute the basis of public finance, because public finance has to do with means or tools for attaining objectives that lie outside its own field. One may be dogmatic about an objective, but the suitability of a means is judged by expediency. Public finance is a means serving the government in fulfilling its various obligations of international and domestic policy, including particularly the promotion of balanced economic expansion.

---

[10] An interesting and encouraging contribution in this respect is the publication of the Committee for Economic Development entitled *Taxes and the Budget: A Program for Prosperity in a Free Economy*, New York, November 1947.

While we might say that the various aspects of business administration serve the profitability of the enterprise,[11] there is no comparable objective such as 'prosperous' public finance. Thus there can be no strictly endogenous rules of public finance. The question is rather whether, assuming given objectives, it is possible to develop certain working hypotheses or rules of thumb for public finance that will be conducive to attaining the objectives.

Policy objectives and economic assumptions give a working hypothesis for appraising and formulating public-finance programs. The study of the Committee for Economic Development (CED), referred to above, proposes that long-range budget planning should aim at a moderate budget cash surplus under conditions of full employment. This implies that under conditions of sustained full employment long-run business investments will tend to exceed the sum total of business saving plus consumer net saving.

We may quarrel with this particular working hypothesis. Some people may believe, for instance, that, after the end of a restocking and reconstruction boom, business intentions to invest, even if encouraged by appropriate tax revisions and other policies, may lag somewhat behind the amounts business and individuals may wish to save under conditions of a sustained high level of production and income. Under that assumption, we may reach the conclusion that the government as well as business should finance some of its regular expansion by security issues rather than out of current revenues.

The CED working hypothesis concerning the desirable moderate budget surplus does not mean that there must be a budget

[11] Speaking of profitability as a unifying standard of the various aspects of business management is, of course, an oversimplification. Business has learned that its profitability largely depends on general economic conditions, and that general economic conditions cannot be regarded only as a datum beyond its control. In an economy of partly 'administered prices' and 'administered investments,' business management has to take into account the effects of its action on general economic conditions as well as its direct effect on profits. To that extent, business management too transcends its conventional limits and becomes interrelated with economic policy.

18

surplus each year, or that there must necessarily be a budget surplus even over the period of a business cycle. In the short run, government expenditures and revenue are among the tools of the government for counteracting the business cycle. The CED program rests mainly on the automatic anti-cyclical effect of government expenditures and revenue. It relies on budget fluctuations which occur even without changes in government programs or in tax laws. As soon as a downswing develops, certain government expenditures, such as disbursements for unemployment insurance or farm price-support payments, increase automatically, while revenue, particularly from progressive income taxes, promptly begins to drop. Thus the budget surplus will be replaced first by a balanced budget and then by a deficit in case of growing unemployment. This deficit will then act as one of the reflationary forces helping to restore a high level of economic activity.

In case of a severe depression or any other emergency, the CED program would, however, not rely exclusively on this 'built-in flexibility.' In case of a severe depression, emergency action, particularly a reduction in taxes, would be needed. A temporary increase in taxes would be called for in case of an extraordinary inflationary boom. The CED recognizes that fiscal measures are only one among several necessary devices designed to aid in ironing out business fluctuations.

This proposal is a very important step toward replacing the traditional dogma of public finance by an approach that offers a rule of thumb for long-range budget planning as well as short-run budget adjustments. In detail it is not likely to be the last word. We cannot be sure, for instance, that the variation in expenditures and receipts resulting from the built-in flexibility of the budget will suffice to counteract even 'normal' fluctuations in private business investments and consumer expenditures. It may be doubted that keeping expenditure programs at the same level, irrespective of the cycle, is correct policy from the aspect of a rational allocation of resources. Aside from the purposes of counter-cyclical policy, it is obvious that the relative usefulness of a government program increases when it can be undertaken without bidding resources away from private use. It is a prescription not only of a counter-cyclical policy but also of merely good management that deferrable government programs should be postponed when labor and material are scarce and relatively expensive, and that government programs should be speeded up when labor and materials are idle and less expensive.

Whatever finally emerges from the present groping for a reformulation of the rules of public finance, it is clear that programs of expenditure and revenue must each be planned with respect to their economic effect. But it is equally necessary to take the quantitative and qualitative interrelationship between expenditure and revenue programs into account. The schematic figure below illustrates this interrelationship.

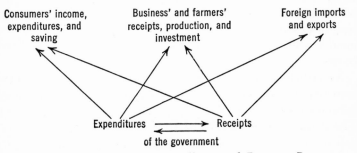

Fig. 2. Interrelationship of Expenditure and Revenue Programs

Though it is true that government expenditures and revenues must be planned in relation to the nation's economic budget, it is also true that the government budget is a significant component in the nation's economic budget. And it is with this component that public finance is concerned.

PUBLIC FINANCE A BORDERLINE SCIENCE

Public finance deals with the manner in which government objectives are pursued through the means of government expenditures, revenues, debt management, and related transactions. Specifically, it deals with the way in which decisions are reached in the public sector of the economy and how they are executed and controlled. It cuts across the lines of a number of traditional sciences.

As we have seen, decisions in public finance are reached through political procedures and are determined by the interplay of the political and social forces in the society. Thus its analyses fall into the field of political science and sociology. On the other hand, the objectives are largely economic in nature, and all public-finance transactions take place in the medium of economics and have economic repercussions. Essentially, public finance is the science that tries to strike a balance between politics and economics.

The fact that public finance necessarily encroaches on so many fields may lead to the danger of dilettantism. This danger seems to be invited by the fact that in public finance we are compelled to cover aspects of political science, public administration, sociology, management, planning, accounting, and economics within the covers of one book or within one academic course.

Nevertheless, the fact that an analysis of psychosomatic problems requires knowledge of psychology as well as of physiology is no reason to forego an analysis of these borderline problems. The character of borderline problems makes them perhaps more difficult for our conventional approaches but they are no less urgent. Furthermore, a field that happens to be located on the border line of several sciences need not cover more territory of knowledge than one that falls entirely within one of the conventional subdivisions of knowledge. The figure on page 22 illustrates this.[12]

Our scientific approach to a problem must be guided by the character of that problem. It is the nature of public finance that it is *political* economics; it requires a consideration of political procedures and of the forces that determine political processes, administrative procedures, and accounting procedures peculiar to this area, as well as of economic problems.

[12] The fact that public finance appears in the center of the figure is due less to egocentric thinking in public finance than to the exigencies of a two-dimensional presentation.

It follows from the borderline character of public finance that an adequate treatment of economics has to deal too with the effects of government expenditures, taxes, and debts. It also follows that the science of management cannot exclude problems of government and financial management, but none of these specialized treatments of economics, management, and others can do justice to the problems of public finance in their entirety and interrelationship.

Fig. 3. Public Finance in Relation to Other Sciences

Economists have made considerable contributions to the development of public finance, but it is also true that economists dealing with the public sector of the economy are not likely to give full weight to the procedural problems and therefore may often be unrealistic in their conclusions.

I should like to suggest that public finance is not simply a branch of the broader field of economics as conventionally defined. It definitely transcends economics in its narrower definition. It is a branch of economics only if economics is once again defined as the science of the *political economy*. This involves more than a reshuffling of labels—it involves a modified approach. We need a consideration of the problem of public finance in the context of general economics, political science, and public administration, and, in addition, a pulling together of these various pieces into a systematic treatment of the government's expenditures, revenue, and debt transactions, their procedure and management, their integration into the whole of the political, social, and economic life of a nation.

Public finance is a necessary major field of training for government service, but it is also highly useful as at least a secondary field of training for general economists and business managers who need some knowledge of its nature and processes.

Part
-II-

THEORY OF
PUBLIC EXPENDITURES
AND TAXATION

2

The Theory of Public Expenditures

(1936) *

THE modern science of public finance has its roots in the cameralist and the classical traditions. Two quotations may illustrate the attitude of these two schools of public finance with respect to government expenditures. Said the German writer Lorenz von Stein, who grew up in the tradition of cameralism: 'One state may be good because of great expenditures and another bad because of small expenditures.' This positive attitude toward the state is contrasted with J. B. Say's 'golden maxim' of classical public finance: 'The very best of all plans of finance is to spend little.' It should be the task of public finance in our time to reconcile these points of view—the recognition of the productive function of government and the concern for the necessities of the market mechanism.

In this respect the study of public expenditures is equal in importance to the study of taxation. It may well be that the

* 'Theory of Public Expenditures,' *Annals of the American Academy of Political and Social Sciences*, CLXXXIII, January 1936, pp. 1-11.

fundamental problems of taxation and public credit cannot be solved without an underlying theory of expenditures.

PUBLIC AND PRIVATE, ADMINISTRATIVE AND MARKETING ECONOMICS

The modern economic system consists of two sectors which are interwoven with each other: the private and the public sectors. Production and services in the private sector of the economic system are rendered by *enterprises,* in the public sector by administrative *departments* and public *institutions* (for instance, public schools). The public sector is distinguished by the fact that it rests on authority and, if necessary, even on compulsion, while private relations rest on contract. Production in the private sector is incited by the profit motive and directed by market conditions. In the public sector services are ordered by the responsible organs of the national government or the municipalities, by the parliament and the chief executive, or whoever else may have the constitutional right or factual power to determine public activities. This political or administrative purveyance requires appropriations which authorize and limit the different purposes of public activities. Private economic activity is steered predominantly by the *market mechanism,* public economic activity by the *budgeting method.* Thus it may be said roughly that there is a fairly close relationship between public economic activity and the budgeting principle, and a similarly close relationship between private economic activity and the marketing principle.[1]

Public purchases require special safeguards against graft and political favoritism on the one hand, and against an uneconomic or unfair price policy on the other hand. Auditing and special supervising methods, various regulations for bidding, specifications and standards, centralized purchasing agencies, although

---

[1] This is, of course, a simplified description, which intends to elaborate certain typical differences without pretending to grasp all the mixed phenomena of the reality.

[1954 Fn.] See the preceding chapter for a more detailed discussion of this relationship.

not unknown in private business, play a different role in the public administration. The main reason for this difference lies in the fact that public administration lacks the automatic elimination of inefficient management which is essential for the profit system of free competition. With the increasing size of private enterprises and with tendencies toward monopolization, some of these differences between private management and public administration decrease.

Within the public sector the planning, execution, and supervision of expenditures differ among public departments, public institutions, and public enterprises. The methods applied by a public enterprise are similar to, although not identical with, those of corresponding private enterprises. A public enterprise, even if it strives for profit, is an agency of the government, and in its wage and purchasing policy it can never neglect the government's social policy, price policy, or stabilization policy. Public expenditures are not only a means for hiring employees or buying material but are also simultaneously a means for the execution of social and economic policy.

PRODUCTIVE-UNPRODUCTIVE EXPENDITURES

The most popular way of distinguishing between private and public activities is to call the one productive, the other unproductive. But there exists the greatest confusion about what is meant by the term 'productive.' From a purely economic point of view, no judgment is possible concerning the final ends of production and services. It is impossible to say whether the production of liquor is preferable to the improvement of public education, or whether the production of books is preferable to the increase of the army.

In the marketing sector of economic activity every production is acknowledged as a part of the 'social product' if it can be sold at a profitable price.[2] In this sphere, therefore, the market —within the limits of the law—authorizes production and serv-

[2] A price is profitable if the product is sold at a profit larger than any other profit that could be made with the same capital, or at a loss less than the loss that would occur by another or by no use of the same capital.

ices. Public actions, however, are authorized by the budgetary appropriation of means for the purposes in question. Criticism of whether or not the consumers use their income in a 'good' way, or whether or not the politicians decide 'objectively' on the urgency of different private or public needs, requires a more comprehensive approach than a mere economic one. Nevertheless, for such criticism even a restricted distinction between productive and unproductive expenditures may be useful. Three different interpretations of the 'productivity' of public expenditures may be distinguished:

(1) Sometimes expenditures for *self-liquidating* projects are called 'productive.' The possibility of selling governmental services may indicate that these services are required, but it does not prove that there is less need for other non-liquidating projects. The construction of a road may be as urgent as the construction of a bridge, although the latter may be financed by a toll. The question whether or not the execution of a project is urgent and the question how it may be financed are both important but should not be confused with each other.

(2) A somewhat broader criterion of 'productivity' includes also expenditures which indirectly induce an increase in taxation or other revenue. Expenditures for road construction may increase automobile traffic and thereby the revenue from gasoline taxation. But this *'fiscal productivity'* criterion, as I propose to call it, also fails to say anything about which governmental activities are the most urgent; it is important only from the point of view of fiscal expediency, which is not the most important aspect of the problem. For determining the line of demarcation between public and private activities this criterion is not decisive.

(3) The most important, although the most problematical, criterion is *'economic productivity.'* According to this gauge public expenditures are productive if the activities for which they are made result indirectly in an increase in the productivity of labor. Expenditures for such purposes as flood control, professional education, transportation, and business statistics may in the long run increase the productivity of the nation out of

proportion to the costs. Expenditures for an art museum, for example, or for military purposes may be called non-productive in most cases. Under normal conditions, that is, when it may be assumed that there is no exceptional unemployment, such activities divert means of production from the marketing sector to the public sector and thereby decrease market production; and the tendency of productive expenditures to provide some compensation is absent. But again we must emphasize that this non-productivity alone is no decisive argument against such expenditures, provided their non-economic purposes are regarded as more important than other needs which could be satisfied at the same cost.

A government which increases the field of public activities either assumes new tasks which were not undertaken until that time or engages in certain activities which were formerly the concern of private firms or institutions. Thus it may be useful to distinguish 'additional' and 'transforming' expenditures. If, for instance, the government establishes public schools, which take the place of private schools, or if it erects houses, thereby restricting the demand for private construction, then a private service has been transformed into a public service. Concerning the 'productivity' of such measures, it must be asked whether in these cases public or private management is more efficient and which form of management best protects the public interest. Such a transformation will usually change the distribution of the benefit derived from this kind of services. In this respect transforming expenditures are similar to the transfer expenditures which bring about a redistribution of capital or income.

THEORY OF SUBJECTIVE VALUES

Many theorists, chiefly of the Austrian and Italian schools, try to analyze public and private economics with the same fundamental concepts. They represent a 'monistic' theory of economics applicable to both sectors and try to reconcile the differences between the administrative and the market economy by emphasizing that government activity, like private production, supplies certain benefits. They interpret taxes as just another kind of

31

price. Said Graziani,[3] 'We know that the tax tends to take away from each and all that quantity of wealth which they would each have voluntarily yielded to the state for the satisfaction of their purely collective wants.' The whole basis of such an argument seems to be invalid. In the market economy the one who pays the price acquires the right to receive the benefit. That is the principle of *special correspondence*, or equivalence, which is fundamental in the marketing exchange. In the public economy the distribution of services and the distribution of the tax burden are not related to each other in such an essential way.[4] How far they are connected in special cases, how much those who enjoy the benefits of a service have to pay for it depends entirely on the decisions of the responsible organs of the government. The principle of equivalence may or may not be applied. In so far as the government attempts to correct the existing distribution of wealth, it will attempt to impose the burden on other groups of citizens than those who benefit from public services.

Economists who apply the theory of subjective values to public finance offer a solution for this problem by saying that in public finance each individual has to sacrifice equally for the same benefit, just as in the market each individual pays the same price for the same good. *Equal sacrifice* involves the payment of a higher tax rate by those who have higher incomes. From this theory postulates could be derived for how taxation ought to be organized, but the theory offers no explanation of facts. The principle of equal sacrifice and equal benefits may or may not be applied in reality. There is in actuality no automatic tendency whatever to equalize benefits and sacrifice for the individual. Every 'monistic' theory, every theory which tries to explain the administrative and the market economy by the same principle, encounters failure. The fundamental difference between these concepts must be made clear before their interrelationship in a modern economy can be understood. A theory

[3] A. Graziani, *Istituzioni di Scienza delle Finanze,* Torino, 1897, p. 301. Quotation from F. Y. Edgeworth, *Papers,* vol. III, p. 81.
[4] [1954 Fn.] See also the preceding chapter, p. 20.

of public finance which attempts to eliminate the specific political factor that distinguishes this field from the private market economy fails to grasp the essentials of the problem.

INDIVIDUAL, COLLECTIVE, AND POLITICAL NEEDS

Another approach (often combined with the theory of subjective value) tries to separate the sphere of private economy from the sphere of public economy by stating that the one has to satisfy individual needs and the other collective needs. We may call national defense or the requirements of foreign policy collective needs, although 'political' need may be a better term. But what is education? It is undoubtedly an individual need. A good education for the individual is also, however, of political, cultural, and economic value to the community. In the same way we may say that good housing and nourishment of the individual are of political, cultural, and economic interest to the community. The whole distinction between individual and collective needs seems to be barren, and it is not possible, as many writers have attempted, to erect on this distinction a system of public finance and to use it to limit the field of public activity.

How may we describe the fields of public activities? Bearing in mind the various differences between public and private tasks, we may distinguish political needs from the needs of the people. Even if we believe that the ends of the nation are ultimately identical with the needs of individuals, we must accept the fact that there are political tasks which are related only indirectly to the needs of individuals. Every organization must perform certain tasks necessary to the organization's existence. Expenditures for the organs of the government, for national defense, and for foreign policy may be understood as expenditures for the political organizations as such, without which expenditures it could not exist. It is a political question how far these activities ought to be extended.

In the totalitarian philosophy of the state, these political ends represent values superior to any others. Expenditures for them are limited only by the necessary concern for individuals as the

33

material with which the state must be built. From a humanitarian point of view, expenditures for the political ends of government are justified only in so far as they are a necessary means with which to pursue the human ends of government. These human ends of government are individual and collective at the same time.

FILLING THE GAPS IN THE MARKET SYSTEM

The police system and the administration of justice help to protect the authority of the government and satisfy thereby primarily political ends. But they also help to protect the life and property of individuals and to guarantee the functioning of the market exchange. Though this protection is of vital importance for the market process, it could not be supplied by an application of the market principles. A system can perhaps be conceived in which those who call the police in an emergency would have to pay a fee for using their services. But it is the very nature of these activities that the people who benefit the most from them never use them directly. The people who never have anything to do with the police and the courts are best protected by them. The fundamental condition of market exchange, namely the specific correspondence between benefit and payment, could not be realized even if the costs of these operations were paid for by charges for the services. The government may collect fees if the people are able to pay for the use of the services and institutions, but this can be only a secondary principle. The bulk of the expenditures of this nature must be met by general revenue.

Nor, under modern conditions, could the price mechanism be generally applied for the use of roads. It is technically impossible to collect a price from every pedestrian crossing the street; there are only exceptional cases—toll bridges or toll roads—where the price principle is feasible and is applied.

The price mechanism of the profit economy fails further in the management of services which must be planned a long time in advance. No land reclamation project, no flood regulation, no investment in slow-growing trees can be immediately profitable, because the fruits of such investments cannot be gathered for many decades. The market economy has to calculate compound interest, which means a decreasing present value with increasing length of the ripening period. All kinds of measures for the conservation of natural resources belong in this field, and only an administrative economy can take care of such needs for the distant future.

CORRECTING THE MARKET SYSTEM

There are other tasks assumed by the government that could technically be assumed by the market system. Schools can be and are managed by private enterprise according to market principles. The application of the market system, however, involves certain implications. Education managed by private enterprise is a luxury which is distributed according to the distribution of purchasing power. If the government for political, cultural, or economic reasons desires to have a certain minimum standard of education, then this field must be separated from the market mechanism and shifted to public administration. Thus we have public education, public hygiene, public recreation, even certain attempts at public housing, because we wish to avoid the implications of the market distribution in those fields. Here, more than anywhere else, the line of demarcation between public and private tasks is a flexible one which changes with changing public opinion and with changing weight of interests and political groups.

The social tasks of government may also be understood as an attempt of public bodies to counteract the failures of the market system in procuring a minimum of economic security. Classical theory explained economic failure as a deserved punishment for laziness and inefficiency. The realities of modern life have refuted this interpretation to a large extent and urged all governments to aid those who are the victims of a malfunctioning in the market system.

There are, finally, many cases in which the government leaves production and distribution to private business but interferes through such measures as tariffs or wage regulations or restrictions of private monopolies. These government activities belong to the sphere of public finance only in so far as their administration requires expenditures or yields revenues (customs duties). Otherwise they belong to the field of economic policy.

PUBLIC EXPENDITURES AND INDUSTRIALIZATION

Adolph Wagner [5] formulated the famous law that public activities tend to grow faster than private activities. He derived his statement from historical experience and from his conviction that there were many urgent tasks of government to be performed in the future, even though they had not yet been performed in his time. Another method of verifying this law is to compare the expenditures of countries or districts with different economic structures.[6] This method proves that there is a tendency for government expenditures to increase with expanding industrialization and urbanization. Moreover, expenditures for war preparation rise with technical development, because there is almost no technical invention which will not be applied to the improvement of war equipment, thereby increasing the costs of the armed forces. The demand for vocational training, for social and sanitary services, for communication, and for protection increases almost inevitably with industrialization and urbanization. The reasons for such increases are not only economic and technical but also sociological. With progressive industrialization and with higher standards of living, there is greater pressure on the government to render services of higher quality, to construct more beautiful public buildings and parks, and to cure the shortcomings of the market system. Other conditions being equal, the greater the wealth and the more abundant the tax resources, the more successful this pressure will be. Here we may observe the rather paradoxical fact that social expenditures are relatively larger in wealthy communities where the objective need is less than in poor communities.

[5] Adolph Wagner, *Grundlegung der politischen Ökonomie*, pt. i, vol. ii, Leipzig, 1892-4.
[6] Cf. 'Public Expenditures and Economic Structure in the United States,' *Social Research*, iii, 57, February 1936.

We must distinguish from the number and quality of increased services the *cost* that must be paid by the government for performing a service of a certain quality and quantity. The costs of certain services are relatively high in rural districts of the lowest density and also in metropolitan districts of the highest density of population. In districts of the lowest density, school and office buildings often cannot be used to capacity; bus service must be provided for the school children; mail delivery is expensive. In districts of highest density, on the other hand, underpasses and superhighways must be built to cope with traffic congestion; high rents must be paid for government office space. We may therefore construct a U-shaped curve of 'governmental overhead cost' which will be highest in the districts of the lowest and the densest population.

Public Works

During the postwar depressions, public works have been suggested as a device for filling gaps in the market system. Three different theories of expenditures for public works may be distinguished.

(1) Public-works projects have been advocated to mitigate the harmful psychological effect of long-lasting involuntary idleness. Seen thus they are a type of relief expenditure that is more expensive than direct relief, at least for the moment.

(2) Public works are recommended as a means for 'priming the pump.' The deflationary tendency of the depression should be overcome, according to this theory, by public expenditures. If these expenditures are met by borrowing, the idle credit reserves are transferred into actual purchasing power and actual demand, thus stimulating production of consumers' goods and indirectly private investment. The economists who recommend this procedure expect that after the revival of private investment and production in the capital-goods industries, the public-works programs can be stopped; that workers engaged in public works during this transitional period will be re-employed in the capital-goods industries; and that artificial recovery will turn into prosperity.

37

(3) Many industrial countries during this depression have found, however, that although public works stimulated the consumer-goods industries, they did not induce the recovery of private investment. The reasons were very much disputed. Some believed that a lack of confidence, which arose from this policy of public spending, hindered private investments. Others believed that the capital-goods industries had been overexpanded in the preceding boom period. Some believed that the earlier periods of economic expansion had been stimulated by the era of industrialization, such as construction of railroads, electrification, and agricultural mechanization; and that the deepest root of the present [1934] depression is a lack of opportunities for large investments.

It has been suggested that the government may compensate for this lack by public works such as huge housing programs and by plans for the development of natural resources. Such programs, however, need to be planned not only for a brief period during a depression but possibly for decades. This would mean that the dynamic forces derived by capitalism from private initiative would be diverted partly to government planning. A large segment of the nation's capital would thus be directed by public activity.

PUBLIC EXPENDITURES AND THE SOCIAL PRODUCT

Attempts to draw a line of demarcation between the public and the private spheres of economics have often been based on statistical calculations of the relation between public expenditures and the social product. In Germany public opinion was alarmed when it learned from official sources that public expenditures amounted to half the total social product. From these statistics the conclusion was often drawn that half the economic process was 'socialized.' It has similarly been said in reference to the United States, 'We have 25 per cent socialism in the United States today.' [7] But such statistical calculations are

[7] Ray E. Untereiner, *The Tax Racket*, Philadelphia and London, Lippincott, 1933, p. 42.

misleading if they do not distinguish among the different kinds of expenditures.

The schematic chart below illustrates the various relations between the social product and public expenditures; it is based on ratios derived from German statistics for 1928-9.

Chart I. Social Product and Public Expenditures

Social Product			
Private Production		**Public Service (net)**	
Area of Indirect Public Regulation		**Public Expenditures**	

Private Production for Private Consumption of the Producers (50)	Reparation Payments (3)	Relief, War Veteran Pensions, Debt, Service, Subsidies (16)	Public Administration	
			Purchases of Materials (8)	Salaries and Wages (8)
			Public Enterprises	
			Purchases of Materials (7)	Salaries and Wages (8)

The 50 per cent of the social product required for public expenditures in Germany included the expenditures of *public enterprises,* such as the railroads and publicly owned utilities, which are directed primarily by the price mechanism of the market economy. It included also (16 per cent of the whole) domestic *transfer expenditures,* through which the taxpayer's money is transferred to people on relief rolls, to war veterans, to holders of public securities, and to subsidized firms.[8] These

[8] For this classification of public expenditures cf. Gerhard Colm, *Volkswirtschaftliche Theorie der Staatsausgaben,* Tübingen, Siebeck, 1927, and A. C. Pigou, *A Study in Public Finance,* London, Macmillan, 1928. The inclusion of debt services under the transfer expenditures has been questioned. Limited space does not permit discussion in detail of this problem. The terms 'transfer' and 'exhaustive' expenditures are not entirely satisfactory. I use them in order to avoid confusion with new terms.

transfer expenditures do not necessarily diminish the amount of private production for private consumption, but they do affect the distribution of income. Another 16 per cent of the social product was required for public services such as the administration of justice, public education, and the army. They are called *exhaustive expenditures* because they represent the public demand for labor and the products of labor. One half of these exhaustive expenditures are disbursements of the administration for material from private firms. They represent private production for public use. Even in Germany, with her extensive area of public activity, 92 per cent of the social product was provided in these years according to the market principle, even though produced partly under government ownership or for government use and regulated indirectly in many ways by governmental interference with wages, prices, and interest rates. For several of the other countries of Europe the corresponding percentage is even higher.

LIMITATIONS OF PUBLIC EXPENDITURES

It is impossible to set a rigid limit for the expansion of public expenditures. Not scientific calculation but the political struggle defines this line of demarcation and defines it every day anew. Some factors may be mentioned, however, which limit this dynamic process:

(1) The individual limitation. The individual usually thinks more of the taxes he has to pay than of the benefits he derives from public services. There exists in every situation a certain psychological limit of taxation which cannot be exceeded without strong reactions. Where this limit lies depends on the tax system and on the political and economic conditions, but not predominantly on the kind of expenditures that are met by the taxes. An individual often refuses to pay taxes even if an equivalent amount of money is returned to him in one or another form of public service or disbursement.

(2) The social limitation. Exhaustive public expenditures normally reduce production for the market and the consumption of market products, at least in the short run. A minimum stand-

ard of living cannot long be denied without undermining the economic process. The maintenance of such a minimum standard of living involves also a minimum amount for investments. In this respect the nature of the expenditures is decisive. Exhaustive expenditures, transfer and transforming expenditures, productive and non-productive expenditures, in the sense defined above, must be distinguished. Productive expenditures may often result in a decisive increase in the 'social product' and the standard of living.

If during a depression public expenditures are met by borrowing, it may happen that labor and machines will be employed which would otherwise remain idle. Then public expenditures do not involve a reduction of the production for the market but, on the contrary, may stimulate it. For the problem of the debt burden which must follow later, it is very important whether the public works consist of projects that are economically or fiscally productive, or of projects that are self-liquidating or non-productive (for example, for defense).

(3) The marketing limitation. Public expenditures may disturb the market mechanism in other ways than by removing funds from private use. For example, if a public relief system grants payments that are equal to or above the wage level of certain labor groups, then the labor market may be thrown into confusion. The same holds true with regard to subsidies, which may hamper necessary reorganizations under certain conditions. Moreover, by inefficient methods of taxation or by an inefficient administration of public departments, institutions, or enterprises the private sector of the economy may be curtailed more than the public sector gains. The opposite, however, may occur too; the government may deliberately try to restore a disturbed market mechanism. Some of the New Deal activities were at least supposed to function in this way.

LOCAL DISTRIBUTION OF EXPENDITURES

It is part of the democratic concept of self-government that each local administrative unit should have as much responsibility as possible in financial matters. As an ideal it was recognized that each governmental unit should raise the money that it was going to spend. The result was, however, that the quantity and quality of public expenditures varied from state to state, from county to county, and from township to township. Communities with wealthier populations and richer tax resources could fulfill their social duties much better than communities in which the need for government support was greatest. The financial implications of local self-government and of the social tasks of the local communities conflicted with each other. Two different methods of solving this problem have been tried in various countries. One is the centralization of certain functions in larger units which encompass both wealthier and poorer communities. The transfer of some functions to special districts, counties, or states, or to the federal government compensates for some of the inequalities among local units. Another method is the appropriation of grants-in-aid for local units by a state or the federal government. If these grants-in-aid are distributed according to the need for government expenditures in specified fields, they again overcome some of the local discrepancies. This method has been criticized because it enables local jurisdictions to spend money that is not collected within their own boundaries. But this criticism fails to take into account the fact that each community is committed to a legal or social minimum of expenditures; and for the portion of expenditures that is not larger than this minimum, grants-in-aid are not unsound. Only the local expenditures beyond this minimum and factually at the disposal of the local legislature should always be met by revenue collected within the boundaries of the community.

Some differentiation in local tax rates may be quite advisable for an efficient geographical distribution of industry. Higher business taxes in districts with greater need for social expenditures may in the long run result in a move of industry to rural districts, perhaps diminishing thereby the nation's aggregate need for social expenditures.

The Growing Responsibility of Government

We do not know how far the expansion of public activities will go, but even today public expenditures have reached a size that implies the greatest economic responsibility for the government. The methods by which persons are selected for public service and by which salaries and wages of public servants are fixed have become factors of utmost importance for the labor market. Governments have become the biggest buyers of certain products and the greatest employers in the construction business. The methods and conditions of public bidding are becoming the rule of economic standards. The government has become the greatest banker, and the situation in the national credit market depends entirely on successful co-operation between government and banks. As long as public expenditures formed only a small percentage of the social product, it was not very important how the government spent this money; but with this proportion increasing, public spending becomes a decisive factor in economic policy. Public expenditures today can no longer be considered from a merely fiscal point of view; they must be considered also from the point of view of the whole economic system.

3

The Ideal Tax System

(1934) *

In the present depression [1934] the relation of government to business has undergone a far-reaching change. Governments have had to assume new social and economic tasks. The passing of the depression is not likely to be accompanied by a simple restoration of the predepression relationships. Many countries, therefore, will have to reckon with the need for increased revenue for both central and local government. In connection with this the tax system will once more become the subject of heated controversies.

New points of view in the selection of taxes have been brought forward by the experience of the depression. The belief in the old criterion of justice, descended from the classical era, has been shaken and a demand crystallized for a tax system whose yield is less affected by cyclical fluctuations in business or which can be used to mitigate their violence. Hence the question arises whether the traditional criteria of an ideal tax system are still

* 'The Ideal Tax System,' *Social Research,* 1 (3), August 1934, pp. 319-42.

valid. The canons of taxation offer merely formal principles to be considered in evaluating any tax system, but the content of these principles and the relative emphasis placed on each of them must be debated anew in each historical era.

In this essay I attempt to analyze, in the light of the depression experience, the ideal tax system suited to the present stage of economic development. The criteria applied will be those of justice, fiscal productivity, and serviceability as an agency for mitigating business cycles. In this general discussion I must ignore the differences between the tax systems of national and local, or federal and state governments, however important and acute the practical and theoretical problems presented by these may be.

THE CRITERION OF JUSTICE

Eternal and historical justice

The economic and financial developments of the postwar [World War I] period raised the question whether the criterion of justice belongs in the theory of taxation. In insisting on fiscal justice the classical economists really defended the 'natural' right of the taxpayer against the arbitrariness of the state. In other words, fiscal justice reflected the eternal rights of the individual as against the historical demands of the state.

Influenced by Hegelian philosophy, German theorists of public finance attempted to eliminate this classical dualism which until then had been regarded as a part of the 'natural order' and the historically conditioned state. Adolph Wagner, for instance, derived the requirement of fiscal justice from the aims pursued by the state in a specific setting. He maintained that national purposes, and with them the meaning of justice, change with each historical era; the requirements of justice were thus given a concrete content, but their validity was limited to a particular period. Now, if the demands of justice vary with time and place, it seems to follow that they are the product of more or less arbitrary value judgments. These may be inescapable for statesmen but should be excluded from the consideration of scientists, just as the problem of the equity of the economic system is the concern of social philosophers and not of economists. A brief discussion of this problem will use Aristotle's concepts,[1] which have scarcely become outdated at the present day.

The first question is: Under what presuppositions would political justice actually lose its validity as a criterion of state action? 'Justice between master and slave and between father and child is not the same as absolute and political justice . . .' (v, vi, 8). Political justice rests on the polarity between the claim of the state to power and individual freedom. 'Political justice means justice as between free . . . persons' (v, vi, 4). A fundamental principle of the totalitarian nation is that the sphere of individual freedom is completely dissolved in the whole. Here, therefore, the meaning of justice has entirely changed; it is no longer political justice but 'domestic justice' —akin to rules that govern the relation between master and slave or father and child. Yet the totalitarian nation is only a limiting case never fully realized in practice, and the polarity between state and individual always exists in however varying a degree; hence political justice remains an essential criterion of all government actions, including taxation: 'the function of the ruler is to be the guardian of justice, and if of justice, then of equality' (v, v, 5).

'Equality' is the criterion of justice but only in a sense yet to be defined. For a nation of full communism, for instance, the rule is 'distributive justice, which gives to everyone an equal share, or more exactly a proportionate share' (v, iii)—'proportionate to his merits' (v, vi, 6) is the distributive principle mentioned once as an example. For a nation confronted not only with natural but also with economic inequality, the ruling principle would be 'corrective justice' (v, iv); this means not equality but equalization of disproportionate inequalities. The demand for equal treatment ('treating the parties as equal,' v, iv, 3) and for rectification of inequalities is the natural claim to justice presented by the individual to the state.

[1] Quotations in this article follow *Nicomachean Ethics,* tr. by H. Racken, London and New York, Loeb Classical Library, 1926.

It may be suggested that only such government discrimination among citizens is just as is based on their essential inequality within the sphere of public responsibility. For instance, the judge whose verdict is governed not only by the nature and circumstances of the crime but also by personal sympathies and antipathies is unjust. These sympathies are very important and legitimate differentiating factors in other social relations, but they are of no relevance to the government. Hence there is no point in objecting to equality as a criterion of justice on the ground that human beings are not equal. The question here is what differentiates men not as human beings but as objects within the sphere of public responsibility.

As further defined, the equality claim of justice is universally binding; it is valid for all ages and countries as long as there exists a sphere of individual freedom. Yet, Adolph Wagner was right in opposing to the universal rules of taxation of the classical school a concept of justice whose content varies with changes in the structure of the state. '. . . But in our world although there is such a thing as Natural Justice, all rules of justice are variable' (v, vii, 3). Now what precisely is the historically changing claim of the individual as against the 'eternal' or 'natural' claim? It is the change in individual inequalities that concerns the state—the varying configuration of the area which is politically relevant. Thus for the pure *Rechtsstaat* the only important difference between individuals is that between law breaker and law observer. With the increase in government responsibility for economic well-being, individual differences in the economic sphere, first in distribution and then in production, demand discriminatory treatment. Rules of justice vary therefore with a change in the lines of demarcation between the politically relevant and the purely private. The formal thesis that an equal treatment of equals and an unequal treatment of unequals is just varies in content, because it depends on the determination of which inequalities are to be politically relevant.

To define the boundaries of the politically relevant sphere is, however, not simply a matter of ascertaining a historically given

47

fact. Here too there are a norm and deviations from it. The measuring rod is the historical purpose of the state in each situation. '. . . The rules of justice ordained not by nature but by man are not the same in all places, since forms of government are not the same, though in all places there is only one form of government that is natural, namely, the best government' (v, vii, 5).

These considerations lead to the conclusion that a recognition of the historical relativity of rules of justice does not at all signify an abandonment of the rigor and binding force of the universal claim to justice. Also, the historically conditioned rules are not arbitrary but subject to the test that in each historical situation there is only one mode of conduct, one government that is best.

The task of our time is therefore not to eliminate the criterion of justice as a canon of taxation but to fill it with a new content. How far is fiscal science competent to undertake this task? Certainly the student of public finance cannot presume to define the purposes of the government with reference to a particular era. But he can arrive at rules of taxation corresponding to a particular delimitation of the sphere of state responsibility. Furthermore, he must decide to what extent taxation is a proper instrumentality for the realization of particular state purposes. Even if he believes, for example, that the government should favor a definite denominational policy and thus discriminate among its people on the basis of church affiliation, he may hold that taxation is not the appropriate means for the implementation of this policy. The use of the taxing power in the service of acceptable government purposes which, however, cannot be promoted thereby, is an injustice and a nuisance. A judgment about the justice of a tax or tax system presupposes therefore a historical-political interpretation of the existing state and society. The science of public finance must then deduce its special rules of tax justice from the given general content of political justice. If 'the chief task of economists at this hour is to distinguish afresh the Agenda of Gov-

48

ernment from the Non-Agenda,'[2] testing the old rules of just taxation in this light is a pressing task of fiscal science.

The rules of justice in the different stages of capitalism

I shall present four different concepts of the state in a capitalistic era to establish their bearing on the content of tax justice. None of these concepts has been fully realized in an existing government structure in any historical period; in every capitalist era the actual state has been a combination of these concepts, although with a varying emphasis. This creates difficulties, for the shift in emphasis follows not any objectively ascertainable criteria but is rather the result of a conflict of social forces and ideologies. Furthermore, it cannot be assumed that change in the concepts of justice 'causes' changes in tax systems; the latter are induced by fiscal and economic needs and shifts of political power. Yet there remains the necessity of justifying—up to a certain point—any tax system that rests upon the co-operation of taxpayers. Certainly there has never been a tax system that corresponded perfectly to the current concept of justice; but a recognition of the latter has always been a factor of importance in the evolution of public finance. Any interpretation of fiscal history, couched though it may be in terms of pressure politics or of interest groups, must therefore take account of the criterion of justice.

I shall outline four hypothetical types of state structure under capitalism, and investigate for each of them the corresponding criteria of justice.[3]

(1) During a period when the primary function of the public authority is generally interpreted as *protection,* the tax burden must be carried primarily by those who are the main beneficiaries of protection. In a 'night watchman' state, taxation based on the benefit principle fulfills the ideal of 'corrective

[2] J. M. Keynes, *The End of Laissez-Faire*, London, 1926, p. 40.

[3] In this I am following the tradition of the German science of public finance from Adolph Wagner to present writers; see for example H. Ritschl, 'Gestaltungsformen und Entwicklungsstufen der Staatswirtschaft,' *Schmollers Jahrbuch*, XLIX, 1925, and F. K. Mann, *Die Staatswirtschaft unserer Zeit*, Finanzwissenschaftliche Forschungen, no. 1, Jena, 1930.

justice.' The tax best adapted to the conditions and ideology of early capitalism not only from a technical fiscal point of view but also from the standpoint of justice was therefore the property tax. The real property tax appeared suitable to finance police and fire protection of real estate and was adopted just when land values increased owing to road building and other development measures of the government. Within certain limits the excise too followed the benefit principle; it could be regarded as a tax on sales in a local market protected by public authority. According to the benefit principle there could be no justification for income taxes. Differences in income result, according to the philosophy of this period, from differences in personal ability and effort and are proportionate to services rendered. Exponents of this point of view have characterized the taxation of incomes as robbery.

In the last decades many students of public finance have abandoned the benefit principle. They maintain that this principle contradicts the very essence of taxation, which is the idea of 'general correspondence' rather than of 'specific correspondence.' This argument, however, is not particularly convincing, because it is based upon an inexact definition of a tax. In the case of a purchase in the market, specific correspondence means that the buyer who has paid the price has a claim to the merchandise or, if the seller fails to deliver, to a refund of the money. But the home owner who has paid his tax has no claim for a refund of the tax if the state fails to protect him against burglary. A tax, even one levied according to the criterion of benefit, is a political payment not governed by market principles; a taxpayer *qua* taxpayer has no claim on the services of the government. Any principle may be used in the assessment of taxes, including the benefit principle. Moreover, in the modern state, whenever protective functions of the government redound to the benefit of particular persons, the use of the benefit principle is not unjust.

(2) The benefit principle could not be applied, however, where the imputation of benefits to individuals was impossible, as in

the case of war expenditures. Moreover, it proved theoretically inapplicable to the functions of the *social* state. These began with the provision of public schools and have reached a high point in the social security systems of modern governments. The ideology of the social state appears in two variants. One, which we shall call the *social-liberal,* regards the capitalist system of income distribution as just in principle, since income is proportionate to service rendered. The system suffers only from minor defects which should be corrected by such institutions as free instruction and social assistance, but there is no reason for drastic state intervention in the process of income distribution. The benefit principle does not hold in reference to the functions of the social state. Free schools, relief, et cetera, are not benefits for which the beneficiaries can pay in taxes; they are rather meant to rectify existing inequalities. (The elimination of injustice was not the 'cause' of the transition to the social state. The true reason was that injustices in capitalism impaired the vitality of capitalism and retarded its development. Adoption of more complicated production methods required a higher level of education among the masses than could ever have been achieved with schools on a commercial basis and without compulsory attendance for all children. The security of the state demanded measures that would eliminate the more shocking cases of poverty. Political and economic considerations may recommend a policy of leveling justice; all in all, the frequently formulated alternative between expediency and justice does not fit the fact.)

The second variant of the ideology of the social state, which we shall call the *social-critical,* goes farther. It does not merely seek to correct minor defects in an otherwise just capitalist system, but it blames the system itself for an unjust distribution of income and insists that the mitigation of this injustice should be a function of the government.

The principle of taxation that corresponds to the social-liberal ideology is that of ability, of equal, proportionate, or minimum sacrifice. Taxes should be so assessed as not to disturb the stratification of incomes, measured, however, not in money but in some kind of utility units.[4] The social-critical ideology, on the other hand, seeks to establish a tax system which, irrespective of the measuring rod used, taxes the rich more heavily than the poor. Despite their disagreement concerning the justice of capitalist distribution, the practical conclusions of the two ideologies are at present virtually identical.

For the social state the progressive income tax is regarded as conforming most closely to the demands of an ideal tax system. The other taxes are viewed simply as concessions compelled by fiscal or administrative requirements. That the differences in tax policy are not greater is due to two considerations. There is no objective quantitative measure for assessing taxes on the principle of equal sacrifice—however moderately the principle is applied. The use of units of utility or sacrifice involves a judgment of the utility of income at different income levels. This is a judgment that contains an element of subjective evaluation and reduces the difference between the 'equal sacrifice' point of view and the other, which admittedly aims at equalizing the distribution of money incomes. A difference might have arisen, however, about the degree of change desired in monetary income distribution. Here another factor is of importance in bringing the two schools together.

Equalization of income is possible under capitalism only within certain limits. Thus Marx, who certainly regarded capitalist income distribution as unjust, held that taxation can eliminate only minor injustices since income relations are rooted in the conditions of production and can be modified only with a change in the latter.[5] Others found the limit of progressive income taxation in the fact that large incomes are the source of capital as long as this mode of capital formation is not replaced

[4] On this insoluble problem see particularly the discussions of J. S. Mill, Edgeworth, Seligman, and Pigou.

[5] 'The relations of distribution which rest directly upon the bourgeois mode of production, the relation between wages and profit, profit and interest, rent and interest can at best be modified by taxation only at minor points, never fundamentally endangered.' (Karl Marx in *Neue Zeit,* xviii, Pt. 11, p. 570.)

by others, such as capital accumulation by the public authority.[6]

Thus it appears that in the present stage of capitalism the social-critical orientation cannot advocate an appreciably steeper progression than is demanded by the social-liberal ideology on the ground of equal or minimum sacrifice. Both consider the income tax as the ideal tax. Since, however, the limits of a single tax are narrower than those of a tax system, and since the needs of the public authority far exceed the revenue produced by the income tax, justification is also found for other taxes. These may be arranged according to the degree of their conformity to the criterion of justice in the social state. Progressive income and inheritance taxes are followed by taxes on luxuries of mass consumption. With the exhaustion of the latter, even taxes on wages, which burden the better-paid wage earners for the benefit of lower-wage groups or unemployed, appear to be justified.[7] On the other hand, taxes on necessaries and business or cost taxes that fall on production are unjust from the point of view of the social state.

(3) In a later stage of capitalist development it is recognized that the task of the state is not only to correct the distribution of income but to perform certain functions in the production process. Whereas formerly the state was the guarantor of property, it appears now as a *partner in production* side by side with capital and labor. For example, by building roads the state provides an important factor of production; it promotes business efficiency through industrial education, encouragement of technological research, economic and statistical reporting, et cetera; in undertaking recovery programs during depression, it attempts to reduce cyclical business risks. Thus the state enhances and assures returns from production. Having become to a certain extent an agent of production, why should it not,

---

[6] [1954 Fn.] Also the need to maintain adequate incentives should be regarded as a factor limiting the progressivity of income taxes.

[7] German Social Democratic labor leaders supported wholeheartedly the taxation of wages. See Herz in *Kapitalbildung und Steuersystem*, ed. by Gerhard Colm and Hans Neisser, vol. 1, Veröffentlichungen der Friedrich-List Gesellschaft, Berlin, Reimar Hobbing, 1930, p. 402.

like labor and capital, share directly in the output? Why should the share of the state pass first through the hands of entrepreneurs, financiers, and workers? The partner state therefore revives the benefit principle of taxation, although on a different basis and with different consequences. At this stage all types of business and cost taxes—from crude turnover taxes to the more refined forms of taxation on business capital, corporate profits, payrolls, et cetera—receive a theoretical justification.

The question still remains: What role should these business taxes play in the tax system and what base for levying the tax should be used? It should be observed that the productive services rendered by the state may be either of a general character, contributing to the more or less equal advantage of all branches of business, or of a special character, tending to favor certain industries more than others. The tax corresponding to the first type of service would be a general business tax that imposes an equal burden on every branch of industry. Actually, the problem of equality in tax distribution is insoluble because equality of income or income sacrifice can be expressed only in psychological terms incommensurable with the pecuniary terms in which taxes are levied. But in the sphere of production for the market, guided by the profit motive, equality may be adequately measured in terms of 'value added by manufacture.' [8] Most of the actual business taxes, however, for administrative reasons or because they are discriminatory in intent, are levied not on this basis but on gross volume of business, on capital, profits, payrolls, et cetera. Although in application to production for the market, as contrasted with the sphere of personal income, it is theoretically possible to achieve an equal distribu-

[8] I have attempted elsewhere to demonstrate this proposition and to indicate its limitations; see for instance, 'Das Mehrwertverfahren in der Produktionsstatistik,' *Weltwirschaftliches Archiv*, xx, 1924. It follows that from the point of view of the partner state a tax on business incomes must be proportional, not progressive; the latter would imply discrimination, which is not in accord with the aims of the pure partner state.

[1954 Fn.] For a modified view, see Chapter 5, p. 99, written twenty years later.

tion of the tax burden, virtually all existing business taxes involve a certain amount of discrimination.

Most of the productive services rendered by governments, however, are of the special type. The building of roads, for instance, is of particular benefit to the automobile industry and the consular service promotes the importing and exporting business. From the point of view of the pure partner state, special business taxes would be justified in such cases (witness the demand of railway companies throughout the world for an equalizing tax on trucks and buses). But the special productive services of the state can at best be only approximately compensated by special business taxes. Moreover, in many instances the government does not want full equalization, for the services are undertaken with the deliberate aim of aiding particular industries. Because of the discriminatory incidence—whether intended or unforeseen—of the productive services of the government and of the taxes that go with them, the government becomes more than a mere partner of business. It develops into a force which shapes the economic structure. This again extends the scope of government responsibility. The partner state thus assumes functions of the control state.[9]

(4) As the last conceivable function of the state under a capitalistic system we shall mention the stage at which the state not merely participates in production but actually dominates it to a greater or less extent. Here we speak of the *control type of state*. In this state, which in contrast to the protective state assumes responsibility for economic development, new economic differences among individuals become politically relevant. For instance, could such high exemptions for life-insurance premiums as are allowed in the British income tax be accepted from the

[9] Although I ignore throughout this article all questions related to the geographical distribution of the tax burden, it may not be amiss to point out that, since discrimination may be interlocal as well as interindustrial, it is legitimate to ask whether in the regions with higher local expenditures for schools and social services, for instance, business taxes should be higher as well. If the costs of public services at least in part become costs of production, they will influence the location of industry as effectively as other local differentials in production costs.

point of view of the older criteria of justice? The German income tax, too, enumerates a whole series of favored uses for income. What happens to the criterion of justice when in some countries income derived from government securities, premiums on life-insurance policies, gifts to foundations, or expenditures by business concerns for purposes of national defense (e.g. building of bomb shelters) receive preferential standing? This is justified only if the government considers certain types of expenditure better than others as measured by some political, economic, or cultural norm and favors those taxpayers who spend their net income in these preferred ways; it is an application of the idea of 'corrective justice.'

Much more important than the above is the discriminatory intervention in the sphere of production. Here belong the fiscal preferences granted to agriculture,[10] the favors extended to 'new' industries, heavier taxation of larger types of enterprises (e.g. department and chain stores) or of speculative business. All these are discriminations that should be of no importance to the government which leaves the shaping of the economic system to the free play of market forces. Just as the differentiation among the various types of expenditure must be determined by a political, cultural, or economic norm of the 'best' use of income, so the differentiation among various branches and types of production must be governed by a concept of the ideal economic structure. Thus when technological improvements depress the economic position of agriculture as compared with industry, and these developments run contrary to the ideal of economic structure held by the control state, the latter will seek to equalize the standing of the two in the market through discriminatory taxation. It is by an appeal to the 'corrective justice' that taxes on life necessities, the yields of which are to be used for the benefit of farmers, have gained acceptance in the United States; taxation of this type, which in the social state would be looked on as the acme of fiscal injustice, is adopted at present because it is

[10] For instance, exemptions of farm products from general sales taxes, in many cases.

designed to give agriculture a more appropriate place in the economic structure.[11]

While they open new possibilities for the realization of justice, the control functions of the state also carry the danger of gross injustice. Where does the equalization of market opportunities stop and the creation of new inequalities begin? To be just, the state must furnish substitute employment to the victims of destructive taxation of a particular industry. When the government assumes exclusive responsibility for a particular economic sphere (perhaps through nationalization of certain branches of production), its action is subject only to the criteria of political, cultural, or economic expediency; individual responsibility and freedom, the bases of the criterion of justice, cease to exist. An elimination of these may be demanded by the advocates of 'distributive justice' who wish to do away with the injustice rooted in capitalist production. Thus the control type of state lies on the boundary line of the capitalist system and sets a limit to the application of the criterion of political justice in the sphere of production. Only such a state, in assuming responsibility for the production process, may in all fairness raise this type of discrimination to the level of a general taxation principle. But since the modern state, except in Russia, does not assume full responsibility for production, these discriminations pass easily from a form of higher justice into a manifestation of rank injustice.

Rules of justice and the current problems of tax policy

The problem confronting all capitalist nations at present is that of the proper weighting of the protective, social, partnership, and control functions of government. The gulf that has appeared between the functions of the state and its tax system poses important problems for tax policy. Because of the depression, the functions of government in many countries have grown very rapidly while the more unwieldy tax system has lagged be-

[11] [1954 Fn.] This paragraph refers to the processing taxes, established by the Agricultural Adjustment Act of May 1933. They were declared unconstitutional by the Supreme Court in 1936.

hind. Thus in three countries of advanced capitalism, the United States, Great Britain, and Germany, economic and political necessities present the governments with more or less similar tasks, but their tax systems are radically different.

The United States has passed rapidly from a stage of mainly protective functions into the second, third and, to some extent, the fourth stage. The government which only yesterday disavowed any social tasks except education [12] was entrusted almost overnight with an extensive program of social and economic measures. Obviously, neither the administrative apparatus nor the tax system could be recast with the same speed. The American tax system and tax ideology still conform more closely to the protective type than those of any other capitalist country. In no other capitalistic nation does the property tax, especially the tax on real estate, play so prominent a part in the state and local tax systems; nowhere else is the benefit ideology so pre-eminent in the public consciousness. The fiscal consequences of the recovery program have been forestalled through the policy of public borrowing, but they cannot be avoided indefinitely.

In Great Britain, where the social state (of the social-liberal type) is represented at its purest, in the tax system as well as in all other functions of the government, the predominant role is played by the income tax, inheritance tax, and consumption taxes on luxuries. The principle of taxation according to ability in all its nuances and refinements and the view of the income tax as the ideal tax constitute here the basis of popular and learned discussion.

In Germany, business and cost taxes (turnover tax, industry taxes, etc.) are represented more strongly than elsewhere; their

[12] We cannot enter here upon a discussion of the reasons for this curious lag in the United States as compared with other countries. Attention must obviously be centered on such features of the American scene as the more rapid economic development, which seemed to offer opportunities even to those who were temporarily down and out, the importance of private philanthropy, the fact that the government is more firmly rooted in the consciousness of the masses and that therefore the pressure for a social policy is less compelling.

development was compelled by the need for larger revenue at a time when the productivity of income and consumption taxes was exhausted. The rising ideology of the partner and control state afforded them a certain degree of justification, and the belief in the income tax as the ideal tax was decidedly shaken. In Germany, both fiscal practice and fiscal literature favor particularly a policy of discrimination. In practice, taxation is used to expedite and retard certain economic developments. The Papen Plan,[13] for instance, was a very ambitious though unsuccessful attempt to regulate cyclical movements with the aid of discriminatory taxation.

German economic and tax policy is confronted above all with the problem of the extent to which control functions and responsibilities should be developed and taxation used in the service of these functions. In no other country is the validity of the criterion of justice as much in question, not only in practice but also in theory.

The United States undoubtedly faces the most difficult tax problem of all. It suddenly shifted from the protective to the partnership or even the control type, but the stage of the social state cannot really be passed over, for state functions typical of a later stage are an accretion to, and not a replacement of, the protective and the social functions. R. M. Haig is, therefore, entirely right in concluding his discussion of the rules of taxation for the United States by asserting that 'all of these interpretations . . . lead to a justification of progressive taxation and the weighting of the burden against the wealthy.' [14] Correct as this proposition is, the general thesis which follows it, viz., 'the historical trend is . . . definitely in the direction [of taxation] of net income,' is debatable. It is possible that in many countries, like Germany and England, this trend has already been surpassed and that general or specific cost taxes will assume in the future an increasingly larger place in the tax system.

[13] [1954 Fn.] For the Papen Plan see Chapter 4, footnote 14.
[14] In New York State Commission for the Revision of the Tax Laws, *Report*, Pt. II, Albany, 1932, p. 88.

THE FISCAL CRITERION

The traditional formulations of the fiscal principle require that a tax be not only 'sufficient' but also 'elastic'; the tax system should be capable of meeting fluctuations in the need for public revenue. Only in the present depression [1934], however, was the demand raised for a crisis-proof tax system. Whereas in the earlier depressions the effects of a decline in revenue could be reduced to tolerable proportions by temporary economies, a depression in the stage of the social and control state compels, on the contrary, an increase in expenditures. It was just such an increase in expenditures coupled with considerably reduced revenues that has produced in nearly all countries a deficit too large to be covered from savings. Thus the question was posed whether a reorganization of the tax system should not be oriented primarily toward strengthening its resistance to the effects of a decline in business activity.

Such a tax system can be achieved by increasing the weight of those taxes which are less sensitive to cyclical business changes. How is such a system to be organized? The empirical determination of the cyclical sensitiveness of various taxes is not a simple task. Since most tax rates have been altered during the depression in nearly all countries, the automatic responses of tax yields to changes in business are not visible to the naked eye. Nevertheless the following gradation of tax types may be offered as tentative:

(1) Poll taxes are the least sensitive, but with every refinement through graduation and exemption (such as were introduced in Germany), their sensitiveness increases.

(2) They are followed by consumption taxes on necessaries and, at a certain distance, by taxes on mass luxuries, particularly if the taxes are specific rather than ad valorem. Even in the present depression, because of price declines and unemployment relief, the consumption of necessaries remained relatively unaffected.

(3) Taxation of capital values—property taxes, capital taxes, inheritance taxes, etc.—is only a little more sensitive, for capital

values are affected not only by current returns but also by the anticipation of future yields. Even those property items which produce no returns in the depression still retain some value, although smaller than normal.

(4) Turnover taxes of all kinds, affected as they are not only by the physical volume of trade but also by the price level, are more sensitive and react more promptly to business changes.

(5) Income and profit taxes are still more sensitive because their base changes more rapidly than that of business volume and because of exemptions and graduation. Their sensitiveness is increased if losses from one source are allowed to be offset against profits from another and if deductions are permitted for capital losses.

(6) The most sensitive are the taxes on appreciation in property values, for such appreciation rarely occurs during depressions.

A tax policy that aims at stability in times of depression would increase the relative importance of the taxes mentioned earlier in the above classification and reduce that of the others. Raising poll taxes and consumption taxes on necessities, however, violates the criterion of justice. And raising capital-value taxation in order to reduce turnover and income taxes results in increasing fixed costs of production. When taxation reaches a level where taxes become important in cost calculation, an increase in capital taxes will make the entire economy more sensitive to cyclical changes; that is, fiscal stability will be achieved at the expense of economic stability. In the modern social and control state, which has assumed a considerable share of the cyclical risk originally carried by business, a tax policy of this type would be inexpedient even from a purely fiscal point of view; here the fiscal criterion is almost identical with the economic. The only taxes that can be raised in the interest of fiscal stability without violating at the same time economic and social canons are inheritance and luxury taxes, but in most countries, at least, the latter have already been increased to the very limit of fiscal productivity. In general, it should be said that a change in the tax system which is based on a social or economic criterion is likely to increase fiscal instability. It follows that if it is possible to make allowance for fiscal exigencies in some other way, fiscal stability should not be the guiding principle of tax reform.

Fiscal necessity can and must be provided for in a different way. As it is fully recognized now, budgetary surpluses of the prosperity period must as far as possible be used in meeting depression deficits. Two devices for accomplishing this have been proposed. In connection with the discussions of unemployment relief, it has been suggested that large funds be invested during prosperity and expended in depression. This proposal would apply to the public economy and is an arrangement well known in business. It may perhaps be applicable to the finances of municipalities. For a national government, however, it is preferable from both the fiscal and the economic points of view to borrow during depressions and to repay in times of prosperity.[15]

Public borrowing during a depression is, as has already been mentioned, a procedure subject to certain limitations, particularly for local governments. The experience of the present depression [1934] shows that it is impossible, particularly for local governments, to cover the entire budget by existing taxes and by borrowing. An increase in taxation has become inevitable, a fact that gives current significance to the old dictum that the ideal tax from a fiscal point of view is, among other things, a flexible tax. As distinct from the traditional approach, however, the present-day answer to the question of flexibility varies, depending on the stage of the cycle at which the tax increase is contemplated. The development of a cyclical theory of taxation becomes thus a new task for fiscal science.

Let us take the United States as an example. The depression deficits of state and local governments in this country are to a large extent covered by sales taxes; [16] no other tax can produce

15 This suggestion is similar to the proposal of the Columbia University Commission (*Economic Reconstruction,* New York, 1934) to accumulate during prosperity an unemployment fund in the form of sterile bank reserves and to utilize it as a basis for credit expansion during depression.

16 See R. M. Haig and C. Shoup, *The Sales Tax in the American States,* New York, Columbia University Press, 1934, pp. 100ff.

so large a revenue as quickly. But if such a tax is imposed while the general business trend is still downward, it accentuates the depression because production costs must be adjusted to the lower prices that result from a contraction of demand. This adjustment, always troublesome and difficult, is hindered by the imposition of turnover or other cost taxes. If added to the price such a tax will, in a period of general contraction, reduce demand even further; it cannot be absorbed in the profit margin, which is slim or non-existent; and if passed back to the cost element—wages, interest, or raw-material prices—the adaptation of costs to final prices becomes more difficult. The adoption of sales taxes under conditions of a depression therefore retards the restoration of equilibrium and intensifies or prolongs the depression.

During the time of revival, especially if bank credit is freely expanded, the same tax policy would have quite different effects. At this stage prices and costs rise, but on the whole costs lag somewhat behind prices; there exists therefore a profit margin which is capable of absorbing a certain amount of cost taxation. Also the shifting of the tax to wage earners would mean at this phase not wage cuts but slower wage rises. And its shift to the purchaser would not necessarily lead to a reduction of demand.[17] This example is sufficient to show that the incidence of a tax change depends on the phase of the cycle in which it occurs, that the requirement of flexibility must be qualified by cyclical considerations. If taxation must be increased during depression, it is safer to manipulate income and mass luxury taxes than business and cost taxes. Many problems still remain to be solved before fiscal science can undertake to formulate rules of the 'best' tax policy with reference to the business cycle.

It must be observed, however, that a tax and credit policy articulated in terms of the business cycle is more easily con-

---

[17] Which of these possibilities will materialize depends on the market situation for the commodity in question and on the way in which the proceeds of the tax are spent—'transfer' expenditures, e.g. relief, debt service, or 'exhaustive' expenditures, e.g. salaries of public employees, payments for materials.

ceived than executed, for in practice it is difficult to decide just what specific measure should be taken and how it should be timed. Since each cycle possesses peculiar complexities of its own, the ascertainment of the cyclical phase which characterizes the economy at a particular moment is no simple matter. A fiscal policy of this type presupposes therefore an advanced system of economic observation and diagnosis. We should also have to consider a whole group of problems which cannot be dealt with in this article. How radically must present fiscal legislation and administration be modified to conform to the tax policy which modern depressions compel? Should we not, for instance, enhance the discretionary authority of the administration to permit a more rapid adjustment to changing business conditions?

THE ECONOMIC CRITERION

In traditional fiscal science, the economic criterion of an ideal tax system is based on the assumption that the business system is to be protected from the disturbing intervention of the state, so that it may function smoothly. The present depression [1934] has shaken the confidence in the automatic character of capitalism, either because people have become skeptical of the classical doctrine of pre-established harmony or because its institutional presuppositions are thought to be lacking. The government has been entrusted with some tasks of economic regulation, and the tax policy has been placed in the service of these tasks. Now an ideal tax system is also supposed to contribute to economic stabilization. Can and should this new requirement be regarded as a canon of the rules of taxation in a period which is characterized by a mixture of elements of a social state and a control state?

The proposals to achieve greater cyclical stability by fiscal means, as represented in recent discussions, may be divided into three groups.

(1) According to one popular theory, in time of prosperity capital grows more rapidly than purchasing power and this results in a disproportion between productive capacity and the

64

size of the market for final goods. Following this theory, a tax policy that aims to prevent crises must endeavor to reduce capital accumulation during prosperity; the most effective means of accomplishing this is the progressive income tax.[18]

This theory appears to oversimplify the interplay of factors which disturb the dynamic equilibrium between investment, bank credit, saving, and consumption. In certain situations, a reduction in capital accumulation may be needed to maintain the balance, but in others just the reverse would be required. Moreover, the income tax is much too clumsy a tool for regulating capital supply. In general, if any government policy can supplement the automatic self-regulation of the market, it must be a series of measures influencing directly saving and investment. Again, it is questionable whether gradual, long-range reduction in capital accumulation—at the expense of economic progress— can result in greater economic stability. It must be borne in mind that saving by the upper income groups is only one source of new capital, and that if it fails, other sources, such as corporate saving, may acquire greater importance.

(2) Another type of cyclical tax policy is considered by Schumpeter [19] when he says that an increase of taxation in prosperity and a reduction in depression may act in the same way as a change in interest rates. From Schumpeter's allusion, it is not clear whether he has in mind the direct or the indirect influence of interest fluctuations. With the direct influence of interest changes, comparison applies only to business and cost taxes, not to income and consumption taxes. The direct influence of interest changes consists in stimulating or discouraging new investments; only a business or cost tax on new ventures could intensify this influence of interest changes. Taxation could become here an instrument of economic planning, especially if it were used to discriminate between various types of new investment. In certain situations, for example, taxation could favor new enterprises which provide additional employment and dis-

[18] I cite as an example H. M. Groves, 'Recovery through Taxation,' *Current History*, March 1934.
[19] *Economic Reconstruction*, op. cit. p. 239.

courage investments which displace labor; in other situations a reverse policy might be pursued. Yet, however great the theoretical importance of a planned tax policy, its practical significance is limited for the present because of administrative difficulties. But even now taxation can be used to expedite a desirable movement of economic groups, for example, through industrial decentralization, or through development of homestead settlements. Moreover, industrial reorganization may be aided by certain taxes or tax abatements.

(3) Schumpeter may also have been suggesting a similarity between the indirect influences of tax and interest rate changes. A high interest rate during prosperity may under certain circumstances cut short credit expansion, and a low interest rate in depression might conceivably mitigate credit contraction. A similar influence may be expected from higher taxes during prosperity and lower taxes during depression, if prosperity surpluses are used to repay debts, and depression deficits are met by credit expansion. The idea here is not unlike that which justifies public works financed by loans as a recovery measure.

Why is it necessary to incur new expenditures during a depression? Is it not sufficient to cover a part of the normal expenditures (which may even be reduced) by borrowing rather than by taxation in order to achieve the same effects on the volume of credit and purchasing power? The last question could be answered affirmatively if it could be assumed that the taxpayers, benefited by a reduction in taxes, would employ the funds thus saved in production. But while depression continues, many of them will use the savings to repay debts or will hoard them—thus neutralizing the effect of fiscal borrowing. For this reason a policy of tax reduction is insufficient; it must be combined with a policy of increased public expenditures.

In the present stage of capitalist development, the state must assume as a social state partial responsibility for mitigating the effects of the depression and as a control state partial responsibility for expediting recovery and for preventing a recurrence of depressions. Under the existing conditions, however, taxation is destined to play only a minor role in this connection. The old economic criterion is still valid; it requires that taxation interfere as little as possible with the economic operations, but that it support the economic policy of the government. True, in the control state taxation is a quite legitimate instrument for furthering economic policies. But economic stabilization cannot be made the supreme criterion of an ideal tax system; taxation must not be burdened with a mission to which it is not suited under present conditions. In combating cyclical instability, the government must place foremost reliance on instrumentalities other than taxation that affect the economic process more vitally.[20]

[20] [1954 Fn.] As articles written in later years indicate, today I should place greater emphasis on tax policy as an instrument of cyclical policy. This change in emphasis results largely from the fact that taxes today are so much higher in relation to national income; changes in taxes have therefore a greater effect on the economy.

4

Full Employment Through Tax Policy?

(1940) *

THE need for a complete reorientation in cyclical policy was felt during the Great Depression. When it was realized that variation of the bank rate—the traditional tool of cyclical policy—was not effective enough, many economists advocated a policy of public works, of 'pump priming' government spending, as the solution. Yet, in spite of the fact that this policy proved quite effective in several countries, it could not be regarded as a solution of the whole problem. Public opinion in general was skeptical and may even have underestimated the actual success of the policy. Irrespective of whether this skepticism was justified, the question was raised whether the same objective could not be achieved by means of a flexible tax policy rather than by a spending policy. It seems especially urgent to explore this question now with respect to the future post-defense adjustment, because when the defense program is terminated, a new spending

* 'Full Employment Through Tax Policy?' *Social Research*, VII (4), November 1940, pp. 447-67.

program would probably meet even greater resistance in many quarters.

Doubts of the efficacy of spending became pronounced when it was realized that the task of economic policy consists not only in restoring employment from the depression low to a high level, but also in maintaining it at a high and rising level. The idea that it is necessary only to inject purchasing power by deficit spending and that the additional money will then remain in circulation was based on a defective monetary theory. The hope that increasing business activities would bring about secondary effects by inducing new investments in many lines of production was justified, but the quantities of such induced investments were not sufficient to sustain a high level of employment without government outlays. The underlying causes of the depression are not removed by an injection of purchasing power, and a high level of income and employment cannot be maintained without a fundamental adjustment of the economic structure. Thus the focus of the discussion shifted from the problem of recovery to the problem of basic structural adjustments.

The question was raised of the role that fiscal policy could play in an effort to bring about a permanent adjustment of the economy. Those who regard the discrepancy between the propensity to save and the demand for capital as one of the fundamental maladjustments conclude that fiscal policy can play an important role with respect to structural adjustments. Such fiscal policy must either absorb savings through continued government outlays of borrowed funds or reduce savings by taxation. Spending would meet even more opposition as a permanent device than it would as a cyclical device. Therefore the question must be raised, with respect to cyclical adjustments and even more with respect to structural ones, of whether tax policy can accomplish the objectives that have been assigned to a spending policy.

THE REGULATION OF PURCHASING POWER BY TAX POLICY

Creation of purchasing power by tax reduction

When deficit spending was proposed as a means of creating purchasing power, it was suggested that a deficit brought about by tax reduction would have the same effect.[1] Those who object to deficit spending not because of the deficit and the increase in government debt but because of their dislike of increased expenditures, prefer a reduction in taxes to an increase in spending as a recovery policy.

A deficit that is brought about in a depression by maintaining the level of expenditures in spite of declining revenues has been called a maintenance deficit.[2] It prevents the downward spiral of the depression from spreading because it helps to maintain the incomes derived from government expenditures. Except in the case of a substantial decrease in prices and the costs of living, this policy cannot lead to an actual increase in purchasing power and to re-employment. It is a device for moderating the effects of the depression but not for bringing about recovery.

The situation is changed if a drastic reduction in tax rates is considered, depending on the types of taxes that are reduced. A reduction, for instance, of corporate income taxes in a time of depression would have little effect on the active purchasing power. The same probably holds true with respect to a reduction in progressive income and estate taxes.[3] The case is different, however, with respect to a reduction in consumer taxes. The lowering of sales-tax or payroll-tax rates may lead to lower prices and an increase in consumer purchasing power. This may

[1] See, for instance, *Savings and Investments*, Hearings before the U.S. Temporary National Economic Committee, pt. 9, Washington, 1940, p. 3553.

[2] See also Chapter 6.

[3] [1954 Fn.] It should be remembered that the federal individual income tax of the 'thirties was a different kind of tax from that developed during the 'forties; 7.6 million individual income tax returns were filed in 1939, compared with 53 million in 1950. In relation to the labor force, the number of returns filed was about 15 per cent in 1938, 88 per cent in 1950. Individual income tax payments absorbed about 1 per cent of total personal incomes in 1938, 8 per cent in 1950, and exceeded 11 per cent in 1953.

have an effect similar to that of an increase in purchasing power brought about by additional spending.

The respective efficacy of increased spending or reduced tax rates depends on the time lag existing in both cases between the enforcement of the measure and the actual increase in purchasing power. This time lag varies in different cyclical situations. A reduction in sales taxes or payroll taxes would probably not be very effective when some improvement in market conditions had already occurred. In such a situation it is likely that the tax reduction would result not in lower prices but in increased profits, and the active purchasing power would not rise until much later. Under the impact of a depression with its pressure on the price level, however, such a tax reduction may quickly result in increased purchasing power for the consumer. Consumers will react differently to an increase in purchasing power that comes from a reduction in prices than they will to one that is due to an increase in money incomes resulting from additional spending. The decrease in prices is probably more conducive to additional buying, but, on the other hand, additional government spending during the depression may place the purchasing power more directly into the hands of those who are worst hit by the depression.

During the Great Depression the federal government as well as state and local governments imposed many new consumer taxes (sales taxes, excise taxes, payroll taxes) [4] and thereby probably aggravated the depression. If our future defense financing should include the imposition of a heavy tax on consumers, such a tax should be eliminated or drastically reduced as soon as the defense expenditures are curtailed. This is not to suggest, of course, that the mere reduction of the tax would suffice to bring about the necessary post-defense adjustment. It would, however, be one important element in a comprehensive program.

[4] Gerhard Colm and Helen Tarasov, *Who Pays the Taxes?* Monograph 3, U.S. Temporary National Economic Committee, Washington, 1940, especially table XI, p. 29.

Limiting the increase in purchasing power by tax increase

Tax policy is even more effective in limiting or curtailing than in creating purchasing power. The objective of defense financing should be mobilization of all available productive forces so that the maximum defense effort can be combined with a maximum supply for civilian purposes. This aim leads to the recommendation of borrowing and of progressive income and profits taxation as the main methods of defense financing as long as unemployed men and idle facilities are available. With the exhaustion of idle resources, it becomes necessary to shift the emphasis to a method of financing by which the increase in purchasing power and consumption will be limited. Some type of consumption taxes will then become necessary.[5]

Such a restrictive tax policy may become necessary even before all the unemployed are absorbed. In the boomlet of 1936-7, bottlenecks in some types of labor and facilities developed into what could be called a production jam accompanied by forward buying and speculative inventory accumulation—at a time when there were still millions of unemployed. This led to restrictive fiscal policies and the ensuing recession. Such violent fluctuations must be remembered as an example of what to avoid in the defense effort. The use of flexible taxation designed to regulate the increase in purchasing power in accordance with the increase in production could help achieve such an objective.

In the defense effort it is quite obvious that a variation in spending is limited to the non-defense budget, and that the necessary variation must therefore be confined to the revenue side of the budget. The need for a flexible tax policy creates

[5] For such purposes either selective excise taxes or a kind of general consumption tax or both could be considered. A turnover tax, measured by 'value added,' with tax credit for federal and state payroll taxes, should be examined as a possible general consumption tax.

[1954 Fn.] Later during the war I recommended a general retail sales tax with a personal exemption on a minimum amount of purchases for each family. I thought that the tax exemption could be administered through a tax allowance on the withholding tax or a refund for those not subject to the withholding tax. I advocated a federal sales tax only as a war emergency measure to be repealed after the war.

a difficult but not an insoluble task for legislation and administration. It must be realized that a flexible fiscal policy must do the job that was assigned in classical economics to the central bank policy, but which a central bank policy was unable to accomplish alone. The more boldly fiscal policy is designed to mobilize all productive forces to strive for full employment, the more necessary it is to install an effective and smoothly operating brake in the economic system.[6]

THE REGULATION OF SAVINGS BY TAX POLICY

The problem of oversaving

Oversaving is one of the main problems in a maturing economy.[7] The saving-investment relationship is the feed line through which purchasing power is added to or leaks out of the economic process. If the gasoline line of an engine is clogged, the motor will not run properly. The interest rate does not keep savings and investments in such a relation that full and steady use of the productive forces is assured. An injection of purchasing power cannot result in increased production and employment if there are maladjustments in, for instance, the price-cost relationship. Of course, it is also true that an ample fuel supply cannot make the motor run if internal frictions are too great and the parts do not fit together.

When a country is in the early stages of its economic expansion, the level of incomes and therefore of savings is still low. Foreign capital is attracted and credit created; purchasing power is added to the income stream; the income level rises. Invest-

---

[6] Flexible tax policy is not recommended as the only measure for preventing a production jam. Training of workers, the stimulation of a far-sighted program of plant expansion, price and wage policies, and, if necessary, credit restriction on speculative inventory accumulation are examples of non-fiscal measures.

[7] The term 'oversaving' is misinterpreted as often as the term 'maturing economy,' to which it is related. It is not an adequate designation of the phenomenon but is used since no better term has been coined. It should be emphasized again that the theory of oversaving does not imply that technical progress is slowing down or that there is no room for further expansion.

73

ments anticipate demand and thereby create an increase in income. In the later stages of development, investments tend to increase in proportion to the rise in incomes, and savings increase substantially faster than incomes.[8] A tendency of savings to exceed investment must cause a deflationary movement unless it is absorbed by capital export. Such export of capital was part of Great Britain's solution for several decades and also reduced the problem in the United States during the 1920's. Other extraordinary factors, such as the realization of capital gains and an increase in consumer credit, augmented dissaving or the dissipation of savings in the 'New Era,' with the result that the problem of oversaving was temporarily concealed, although not solved.

For Europe, the last war [First World War] created an extraordinary investment demand first for armament and then for reconstruction, so that the problem was more one of undersaving than of oversaving. Fiscal policy was often used as an adequate instrument for stimulating individual and corporate saving. Now again [1940] armament and destruction are 'solving' the problem of oversaving for a large part of the 'civilized' world. Mankind has found most ingenious devices for conquering the problems of scarcity: can it find no other way of solving the problems of wealth than destruction of it? But granting that this continent will not be subjected to total destruction and that only a moderate portion of its savings will be absorbed by postwar reconstruction, then the problem of oversaving will appear again in its full weight. Post-defense adjustment must consider many dislocations in prices, costs, and production, but the main problem will be that a high-income level, corresponding to full employment, cannot be maintained unless all the savings expected at such a level are offset by dissavings or led into investments.

Fiscal and economic policy can affect saving and investment in many ways. The problem is so large that all available devices, fiscal and non-fiscal, must be applied so that the individual and

---

[8] The relation between saving and national income depends not only on the level but also on the distribution of the national income.

social benefits of thrift and foresight can be made compatible with the request for full and steady employment. Fiscal policy can aid in the solution in two ways: by absorbing savings for financing government outlays and by taxing funds which would otherwise be saved and using them to finance consumer expenditures.[9]

Once a high level of employment has been reached, only such government outlays as can increase the productivity of the economy should be financed by borrowing. It can be assumed that the federal, state, and local governments will have a substantial number of necessary productive improvements to be made and that it may be possible to finance these by loans without violating the rules of sound finance.[10] On the other hand, the whole problem probably cannot and should not be solved in this way. Corporate and individual savings, which are not otherwise fully absorbed, should also be curtailed by taxation and transformed into consumption by current government expenditures.

Curtailing individual savings

Progressive income and estate taxation has cut down individual savings. Is it possible to stiffen these taxes and thereby further cut down individual savings? There are still substantial loopholes in personal income and estate taxation, yet the use of this tax instrument for the curtailment of individual savings is not unlimited. In this context the problem arises of a scarcity not in the supply of capital but in the supply of the risk-factor in

[9] Financing social-security benefit payments by the usual sources of revenue, such as taxation of incomes, estates, or business funds would have such an effect to a great extent. A revised social-security plan may play an important role in post-defense adjustment.

[10] Sound finance requires a fiscal policy that does not imply constantly rising tax rates. In a period of full employment, debts should be regularly incurred only for fiscally productive purposes—for expenditures that cause taxable income and revenues to increase in proportion to the increase in interest payments. Tax rates will then be lifted to a higher plateau only if the government assumes additional functions. In a period of unemployment and unused capacities, however, the increase in national income may be so large, as a result of borrowing, that the increase in interest payments appears relatively insignificant, provided that a high level of income can be attained and maintained.

75

production. Changes with respect to this factor have by no means resulted exclusively or predominantly from tax policy, but tax policy has aggravated the problem.

Curtailing corporate savings

Corporate savings are as important as individual savings as a possible source of deflationary tendencies. The undistributed-profits tax was a device for curtailing one possible source of corporate savings by subjecting profits either to the heavy rates of individual income taxation or to a compensatory tax if the profits were retained in the hands of the corporation. An undistributed-profits tax of one type or another is a necessary complement to a stiff individual income tax.[11] As a device for curtailing possible accumulation of idle corporate funds, this tax was rather defective because it affected only one of the various sources of corporate accumulation of funds and it made no distinction between funds actually used for investment and funds kept idle. In addition, it happened to be enacted during a phase of the business cycle when such a curtailment of corporate accumulation was not desirable. Yet there may come again a time when it is held desirable to adopt a tax that actually curtails idle corporate funds, and it may be worth while to investigate whether such a tax can be devised.

A proposed tax on idle business funds [12] could be measured by the sum of profits and depreciation and depletion minus the amounts invested or distributed as dividends. The first difficulty arises with the need to define investments: Should they include the purchase of stocks of other corporations or of government bonds? It is proposed here that amounts spent for these purposes should not be regarded as investments in the meaning of such a tax law. Should the increase in inventories be regarded as investment? It may be advisable to discourage speculative accumulation in inventories, which is one of the main

---

11 Such a tax would not make superfluous a measure for bringing undistributed profits under individual income taxation.

12 [1954 Fn.] This proposal was first formulated by the author in connection with work done for the TNEC in 1939.

factors causing heavy short-run fluctuations. From this point of view, it might be recommended that only additions to inventories in proportion to the increase in business activities be regarded as investment. Investment would then be defined mainly as construction or repair of plant and addition or replacement of equipment.

A tax on non-invested funds, as here defined, would create great difficulties for enterprises that must accumulate depreciation funds over a period of years before they can spend money for replacement of plant and equipment. When they make such replacements, the expenses in a particular year are greater than the current accrual of funds. Therefore there must be a provision allowing a tax claim or credit to enterprises that in a specific year distribute or invest more than their annual accrual. These claims would not be payable in cash but would either be used to offset tax liabilities that had originated in earlier years or be carried forward to offset tax liabilities of later years. The tax should be constructed in such a way that its amount would depend on the length of the interval between the accrual and the investment of the funds. There would be no tax if funds were accrued and invested in the same year. The longer the period between accrual and investment, the heavier the tax should be.

Such a measure could be constructed in the following manner. A tentative tax of a given percentage, say for example of 30 per cent, could be imposed on the non-invested and non-distributed funds accrued in a specific year. Whenever the invested or distributed funds are higher than the accrued funds in any taxable year, the taxpayer acquires a claim *pro tanto* against the taxing authority. The tentative payments form a tax deposit for each taxpayer from which the tax credits are deducted.[13] The balance of the tax deposit will abate each year at a certain percentage. The annual rate of abatement could

[13] The fact that the tentative tax payments are regarded as additions to the taxpayers' deposits need not prevent the government from using the money immediately. The deposit is only a bookkeeping device for computing future tax liabilities.

be, for instance, 20 per cent of the deposit, which would then be the definite tax.

It may be objected that such a scheme imposes a hardship on those enterprises which by their very nature require a long period of fund accrual before they can replace their property. Such would be the case, for instance, with businesses that have a high proportion of assets invested in buildings. It would be easier to synchronize accrual and use of funds in the case of businesses whose assets consist to a great extent of machines that can be replaced piece by piece. Such a hardship could be eliminated by relating the rate of abatement for each taxpayer to his average rate of depreciation (depreciation as a percentage of depreciable assets of the enterprise). The rate of abatement could be, for instance, three times the average rate of depreciation of the enterprise.

If an entrepreneur erects a new plant with outside funds, he acquires a claim which may be carried forward as a tax credit against his liability on future accrual of funds. The tax claim, however, should abate at the same rate as the tax deposit.

There are still several technical details, such as exemptions, which must be worked out for such a tax. The plan is proposed not as a solution but rather as an illustration of one possible means of solving the problem of taxing idle business funds. There may be better and simpler methods of achieving the same objective.

Whatever the technique of such a tax, however, it should be handled in a flexible manner corresponding to the business situation. Although oversaving is considered a tendency characteristic of the present phase of economic development, it changes in degree and may even disappear temporarily—for instance, under the impact of an increased defense program or a large-scale program of reconstruction. If investments or dissavings (in Keynes's meaning of the terms) increase much beyond the expected level, a drastic curtailment of individual and corporate saving by taxation may not only be unnecessary but even harmful. On the other hand, if the curtailment of savings should prove very effective, even the financing of public improvements by taxation may become the appropriate policy at a future time. Under extreme conditions, however, it seems necessary to combine the two methods, the absorption of savings for public improvement and the curtailment of savings by taxation.

INCENTIVE TAXATION

Objectives of incentive taxation

The idea that the imposition of a tax or the offering of a specific tax exemption affects the behavior of the taxpayers and can therefore be used to bring about a desired reaction is much older than the term 'incentive taxation.' A tax on liquor has often been praised because it either produces revenue or deters people from drinking. Prohibitive tax rates have often been used for regulatory purposes. Tax exemption for government bonds was granted for the purpose of stimulating investment in such securities. The only new element in the proposals for incentive taxation consists in the fact that its techniques are now recommended for use in a recovery or re-employment program.

Incentive taxation appears in two forms, either as a punitive tax on behavior held undesirable, or as a tax exemption for those conforming to behavior held desirable in relation to the objective of employment. I propose to speak in the first case of 'corrective taxation,' in the second of 'tax inducements.'

Stimulation of employment

Proposals for incentive taxation can be classified according to whether they attempt to stimulate employment directly, or whether they act indirectly by increasing demand. Plans of the first type advocate imposing a corrective tax on entrepreneurs who do not make full use of their facilities and dismiss employees, or granting a tax inducement to those who make full use of their facilities and increase the number of their employees. Examples of such schemes are the Papen Plan,[14] the

[14] See Gerhard Colm, 'Why the Papen Plan for Industrial Recovery Failed,' in *Social Research*, I, February, 1934, pp. 83ff., and Kenyon Edwards Poole, *German Financial Policies, 1932-39*, Cambridge, 1939.

individual reserve system in unemployment insurance (the Wisconsin Plan), or one part of Hazelett's proposal.[15]

Some of those who propose incentive taxation of this type think in terms of a somewhat naïve psychological interpretation of the depression. 'Incentive taxation is a tax on ignorant selfishness' or 'Incentive taxation is a proposed law of mutual service which is the law of love' or 'Incentive taxation requires that we shall be "good stewards." ' [16] According to such views depressions are caused by entrepreneurs who fail to produce with all their facilities. As far as the entrepreneur is concerned, the incentive to make profits by production and the penalty of high overhead costs should suffice to make him interested in full employment. Most manufacturing entrepreneurs produce for their customers, and production cannot be stimulated by low wages or by tax inducements or by any other means unless the demand is highly elastic. It is a fallacy to believe that a depression can be overcome by stimulating production and that production then creates demand, in accordance with J. B. Say's law of the market. In reality the causal nexus proceeds for the most part in the other direction: demand must be activated first and production will follow.[17]

Stimulation of demand

Tax proposals designed to increase production and employment indirectly by affecting demand appear much more promising. Experiences of foreign countries show, for instance, that the provision to allow a deduction in income taxation for money spent on the redecoration of a house or for salaries paid to servants was quite effective. Tax privileges granted for the pur-

---

[15] C. William Hazelett, *Incentive Taxation, A Key to Security*, 3rd ed., New York, Dutton, 1939.

[16] Ibid. pp. 191, 192.

[17] It is, of course, not denied that additional production often anticipates an expected increase in demand, and then leads to the creation of purchasing power and an actual increase is achieved.

[1954 Fn.] Business seems to be undergoing a change in attitude—toward using a more dynamic type of market analysis which may result in a greater role of demand anticipation.

chase of equipment or for new residential houses also belong in this category. It can be assumed that in such cases money will often be diverted from other use to the privileged use, but in many instances the taxpayer may be induced to spend liquid funds for these purposes. In these cases the tax incentive really can contribute to a moderate amount of recovery and re-employment.

As was pointed out above, a general reduction in taxes on consumption can be quite effective if enforced at the right moment. This is not a case of incentive taxation, however, but a way of increasing the consumers' real purchasing power.

Another method of stimulating demand consists in offering tax inducements for investments. The Canadian income-tax law may be mentioned as an example of this type of incentive taxation. It provides that 10 per cent of capital expenditures made within the taxable year on plant construction or extension and on modernization of machinery and fixed equipment be permitted as a deduction from profits. Such an inducement has an effect similar to that of a corresponding decrease in interest rates. It has been said that such an incentive may increase employment for the moment by stimulating the demand for building materials and equipment but very soon must lead to increased difficulties in a period in which there are already excess capacities; that consumer demand, not the demand for new productive facilities, should be stimulated. It seems to me that no entrepreneur can be induced to expand his productive facilities unless he expects an increase in demand. Such tax inducements would be effective if industry were deterred from making investments by an excessive interest rate, but in general this is certainly not the case in a depression. On the whole, therefore, such incentives are ineffective. Only in very specific cases involving high risks or other high-cost factors can a tax inducement help to compensate for these adverse conditions. If such costs, and not the potential lack of demand, are the obstacle, then tax inducements may have some influence.

The special amortization for investments in defense industries may be mentioned as an example in this context. Another example is the proposal to exempt from federal taxes that part of the profits of ship operators which is deposited in an approved construction reserve fund and will later be used for approved ship construction. Such tax inducements can hardly be considered as a general recovery device; their justification and effectiveness must be weighed in each particular case. It must be made certain when such exemptions are granted that they will not then become an established right which may be retained long after the situation giving rise to them has disappeared.[18]

A further method of stimulating demand consists in the imposition of corrective taxes on idle funds, not in an effort to absorb such funds through taxation but as an incentive 'designed to promote the circulation of money so that it may earn interest for the owner.'[19]

A tax on demand deposits with the intention of driving liquid funds into 'productive' investments has been proposed several times. None of these suggestions solves the problem of how currency holdings can be taxed effectively. In addition to this technical difficulty the proposal rests on the theory that there is a lack of supply of capital in the depression, while in reality the lack is much more in the demand for capital. Furthermore there is already quite an incentive for investors to prefer 'productive' investments like stocks to hoarding. It can hardly be assumed that a tax, at least of a moderate rate, can achieve what the substantial difference in yields, which already exists, cannot accomplish.

Influencing 'marginal' decisions by taxation

Generally, it cannot be expected that an entrepreneur will be induced to produce when he has no orders, or to expand when there are still idle facilities. Yet there may be some less ambi-

[18] The classical example of such a case is the special depletion provision granted as an inducement to stimulate discovery of new oil and gas wells during World War [I]. This provision remained on the books when the problem of the oil industry had become overproduction and a tax inducement was in full contradiction to other measures of government policy.

[19] Hazelett, op. cit. p. 66.

tious objectives which can be pursued by a policy of incentive taxation.

A tax incentive may induce an entrepreneur not to increase production but to distribute a given or expected volume of production more evenly over the year. The individual reserve plan of unemployment insurance cannot bring about re-employment and recovery, yet such measures may assist in mitigating seasonal fluctuations. A tax advantage to be obtained by maintaining greater continuity in employment may help to reduce dismissal and rehiring of workers. Tax considerations may become one of the factors determining a corporation's location of a new plant or methods of financing (for example, equity *vs.* loan financing). Similarly, it can be expected that the tax on idle business funds discussed above may actually induce entrepreneurs to synchronize more effectively the accrual of funds and expenses for repairs and replacements. Even though only such repairs and replacements as are planned anyway are undertaken, the tax incentive may affect the timing in a way that may mitigate fluctuations.

Taxation may also affect the technique of production and thereby the volume of employment. A very interesting proposal with this purpose has been sponsored by Senator O'Mahoney.[20] In his bill 'To Reduce Unemployment,' Senator O'Mahoney proposes that the federal government levy a new tax on the 'labor-differential' income of profitable corporations. Labor-differential income is defined as gross income minus (1) costs of materials and supplies purchased and used during the taxable year, and (2) total payroll except remuneration above $3000 paid to any one individual. In other words, such 'income' includes mainly the sum total of profits, interest paid, taxes paid, rent, depreciation, depletion, and a few minor cost factors. On the other hand, corporations can claim a credit for the cost of labor, except for salaries above $3000. Such a labor credit will reduce

[20] See the Bill, S.3560, 76th Congress, 3rd Session, and the articles by Senator O'Mahoney and Karl Karsten in the *Journal of Electrical Workers and Operators*, March 1940.

the gross labor-differential tax, and if the credit exceeds the tax, the taxpayer will be entitled to an equivalent bounty. In a statement to the press Senator O'Mahoney said that it is the purpose of this measure 'to provide work for the millions who are now without it.'

A labor-differential tax, however, may slow down not only the introduction of labor-saving machinery but also the expansion of industries on the basis of current technical methods. Whenever a corporation calculates the capital costs of expansion, it must consider that thereby it increases the basis of this tax (although in this case it does not diminish the basis for the tax credit). The labor-differential tax thus has the same effect as a corresponding increase in the interest rates. It can be assumed that industries calculate much more closely in deciding on normal expansion than on the introduction of a labor-saving device. It is therefore quite possible that the tax might be more effective in curbing industrial expansion than in slowing down technical innovations. In any case, it cannot be assumed that this measure is an effective instrument for preventing technological unemployment. An efficient attack on the problem of technological unemployment should either directly regulate the introduction of labor-saving devices, which would be extremely difficult without far-reaching regimentation, or stimulate industrial expansion by increasing demand, which is the aim of many other recovery measures. This bill, however, would result in curbing the application of labor-saving devices and retarding industrial expansion, and thereby would partly defeat its own purpose.

A tax on the labor differential, which is substantially the 'value added' minus payrolls, could be recommended as an offset to the undesirable effects of payroll taxes, equalizing the burden imposed on firms with a capital-intensive and a labor-intensive type of production. Such a measure would eliminate the incentive to employ labor-saving devices and the advantages granted to capital-intensive industries, but it cannot be regarded as a means for achieving full employment.

84

Uses and Limits of Taxation in Employment Policy

By tax policy and by spending of the tax yield, the government can transform profits and incomes of the upper brackets into consumer purchasing power, which may help in the adjustment of the economic system. Such a policy is effective within limits. It cannot solve the problem of stabilizing our economy, but the economy probably cannot be stabilized without such a tax policy.

For the adjustment of cyclical fluctuations, a flexible tax policy should supplement a flexible spending policy. For a program of mobilization of all productive forces for the defense effort, a flexible tax policy is a necessity. Such a policy requires the development of legislative and administrative techniques, which need further exploration.

Incentive taxation may sometimes be useful in stimulating consumer demand and investments or in influencing the 'marginal' decisions of entrepreneurs, but it cannot be regarded as a very effective general instrument for promoting full employment. The main usefulness of tax policy in a program of economic stabilization lies in the fact that taxation can be instrumental in directing the flow of purchasing power, rather than in its punitive or incentive effect on the behavior of individuals.

5

The Corporation and the Corporate
Income Tax in the American Economy

(1953) *

LIKE many other good things in life, the corporate tax came into being through error and deception. When in 1909 a group of liberals of that day demanded a progressive income tax, its adoption was blocked by its supposed lack of constitutionality. As the nearest substitute Congress adopted a corporate-profits tax under the name of a 'corporate excise tax on the privilege of doing business.' That tax was levied at 1 per cent of corporate profits; its contribution to federal revenue was a modest one.

At that time, even the most imaginative tax student did not dream that this newly invented tax would become, within a few decades, one of the main revenue producers, especially during emergency periods.

* 'The Corporation and the Corporate Income Tax in the American Economy,' *American Economic Review*, XLIV, May 1954, pp. 486-503.

Three times within a lifetime the corporate income tax, rein-forced by an excess-profits tax, became a major source of war finance. In each war period it contributed roughly a third of

Chart I.

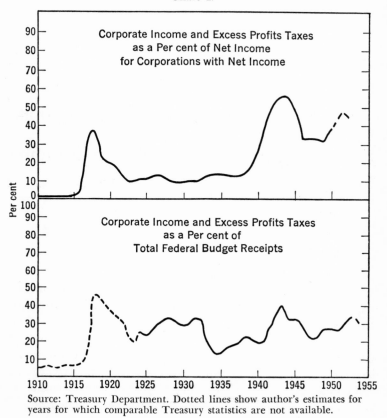

Source: Treasury Department. Dotted lines show author's estimates for years for which comparable Treasury statistics are not available.

total budget receipts (see Chart I, lower panel). After World Wars I and II, corporate tax rates were reduced but each time remained higher than before the war (see Chart I, upper panel).

Economists and tax philosophers, looking at this spectacular giant among tax sources, wondered with what kind of animal they were dealing. Like the small boy who saw a giraffe for the first time and cried out in dismay, some economists exclaimed: 'There is no such animal.' They felt that its creation was an error and there really should not be such a tax. Thus I realize that I have a difficult job when I undertake to demonstrate that the corporate tax has a place in the American tax system.

What is the Corporate Income Tax?

Economists are puzzled because the corporate tax does not quite fit into the conventional classification of taxes. They have been accustomed to thinking of a dichotomy between direct taxes on individuals, represented mainly by individual income, property, and estate taxes, and indirect taxes on merchandise, represented mainly by specific excise taxes. The corporate tax fits into neither of these categories.

Many students of public finance regard a corporate income tax mainly as a tax on individual stockholders. A few praise the tax because most of the dividends are received by individuals in the upper income brackets so that the tax is in effect progressive; more condemn it because it is 'double' taxation of the stockholders. On the other hand, there are many businessmen who believe that the corporate income tax is just another cost factor and that its effect is not much different from that of a sales tax. It is probably true that the majority both of economists and of businessmen, each for different reasons, believes that in principle there should be no tax on corporations *per se*.[1] They think either that the corporate tax should be integrated with the individual income tax or that it should be replaced by a tax on gross business receipts or some other kind of sales tax. Some of the most severe critics of the corporate tax do admit the justification of a corporate franchise tax of moderate rates.[2]

If the corporation is regarded merely as an instrument or agent of the stockholders, then only the individuals who own the cor-

[1] A remarkable exception to this point of view is found in Richard Goode's monograph 'The Corporation Income Tax,' 1951.

[2] See Beardsley Ruml and H. Christian Sonne, *Fiscal and Monetary Policy*, National Planning Association, Planning Pamphlet No. 35, 1944; also *Business Committee Report on Corporate Income Taxes*, National Planning Association, September 1944.

poration are real and can be taxed. It then follows that the corporate income tax is, by definition, a tax on the owners of corporations, that is, the stockholders. It seems to me, however, more realistic to conceive of corporate enterprises as social and economic entities with their own character and pattern of behavior.[3] The relation between the corporation and most individual stockholders is in the case of the public corporation only an indirect and ephemeral one. A few owners of concentrated stockholdings exert, as members of the Board of Directors, a direct influence on management; stockholding for most individuals, however, is just another form of investment. The corporation's financial independence is demonstrated by the fact that about two thirds of corporate funds are derived from internal sources, undistributed profits, and depreciation and depletion reserves. Furthermore, not all stock is owned directly by individuals. Corporations own stocks of other corporations and often form complex networks of affiliation. Investment trusts, insurance companies, universities, hospitals, and many other institutions hold stocks.

Walther Rathenau, forty years ago, spoke of the trend toward the 'autonomous corporation'—he envisaged groups of corporations owning each other with management becoming the determining factor. Berle and Means, twenty years ago, described in detail the structure and life of the modern corporation in which management and ownership are largely separated. These were simplifying exaggerations. Nevertheless, we may say that the corporation is a case where the whole is something different from the sum of its parts—directors, managers, workers, and stock-

[3] What do we mean when we say that the corporation is an economic and social entity? We mean that the corporation as such, like other social institutions, has a tradition, a reputation, a place in the economic process and in the community. The individuals who participate in the decisions of the corporation consider themselves to be acting 'in behalf of' the corporation. At the same time that they are shaping the corporation, they are influenced by the fact that they represent the corporation or work for it. It is said that individuals run the corporation but it can also be said that the corporation runs individuals. The corporation may well survive many changes of owners and management personnel. The corporation changes too, but its changes do not necessarily reflect the turnover of individuals who are in charge.

holders as individuals. This is particularly true of the public corporation, less true of the privately held corporation.

The corporate tax is a tax on corporate enterprise and not a supplemental individual income tax in disguise. The corporate income tax will be viewed in this paper as a tax on enterprise, which is a type of tax different from taxes on individuals or on specific merchandise.

Recognizing that the corporate tax is a tax on enterprise does not mean that the tax does not affect individuals. A tax on tobacco is a tax on consumption; obviously it affects those individuals who smoke. An excise tax involves double taxation in the sense that the same individual may be hit once by an individual income tax and once as a consumer of a taxable product. In the same way a tax on enterprise affects individuals, who are also taxed by several other taxes. There will always remain double or multiple taxation as long as we fail to adopt a single tax system.

Who Pays the Corporate Tax?

The corporate tax then is a tax on corporate enterprise. But how does the corporation respond if corporate taxes are either increased or reduced? Does an increase in corporate taxation result in lower dividends, curtailment of retained earnings, lower wages, or higher prices?

For individual income taxes and for excise taxes on specific commodities, there is at least a reasonable presumption concerning the immediate economic effects of a change in taxes. For taxes on enterprises *per se,* however, the effect depends on the steepness and suddenness of the rate change, on whether there is a simultaneous change in government spending, on monetary policies, on wage and price policies, and on other factors. Also, there may be a difference between the immediate and longer-range effects of a tax change.

Classical theory had a simple answer. The costs of marginal production determine the competitive price. There is no profit, and therefore no tax, on marginal production. Hence, the tax cannot enter into determination of the price. The tax is paid exclusively out of the profits made in lower-than-marginal-cost production. Similarly, in classical economics, wages are not influenced by profit and therefore cannot be influenced by profit taxation. In our world, which has little resemblance to the world of classical economics, we recognize that prices determined by the individual entrepreneur and wages determined by collective bargaining are affected, among other factors, by profits and profit expectations.

I believe it is impossible to obtain a satisfactory answer through the usual analysis of shifting and incidence. The usual analysis proceeds on the *ceteris paribus* assumption, that is, on the assumption that a specific tax measure is adopted but that nothing else changes. Taxes, however, will not be raised except when government expenditures rise too or when the tax takes the place of borrowing or of another tax. Thus a meaningful analysis of an increase in corporate taxes should take into consideration also the effect of an increase in expenditures or a reduction in other methods of financing.

Increase in corporate taxes

In search of some factual evidence we may take a look at the effect of corporate tax increases during the Second World War. At that time the average effective tax rate on corporate profits, including the excess-profits tax (for corporations with net incomes) reached 55 per cent compared with 14 per cent before the war (see Chart I, upper panel). During this period the profit ratio *before taxes* rose and the *after-tax* ratio declined in about the same proportion.[4] The after-tax ratio declined from 7.2 per cent in 1939 to 4.8 per cent in 1944 (see Chart II). *This suggests that during the war at least a large part of the increase in corporate taxes was not passed on in prices but reduced after-tax profits.*

This observation cannot be generalized since, during the war, there were direct controls which limited price rises. There was also the fact that investments in new construction and equip-

---

[4] Ratios of net income, before and after taxes, to 'gross compiled receipts.'

ment were limited by direct controls. This limited the inflationary pressure, facilitated price control, and again made it
harder for business to pass on corporate taxes.

Chart II. Ratios of Net Income, before and after Taxes, to Gross
Compiled Receipts

(for corporations with net income)

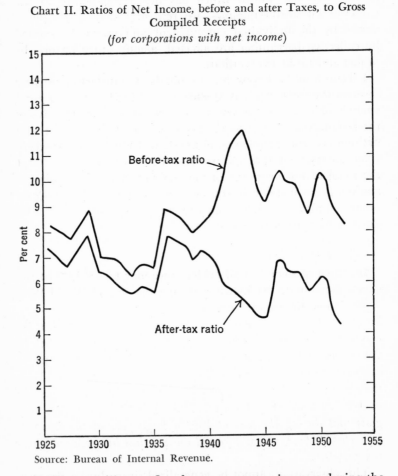

Source: Bureau of Internal Revenue.

Besides curtailing profits, the corporate-tax increase during the
war helped to make wage controls workable. It is simply a fact
of life that the wage control of World War II would not have
been possible without the simultaneous adoption of very drastic

92

corporate-profit taxation. It would not have been possible to persuade wage earners to limit their demands for wage increases if there had not been at the same time a definite limit on the profits that the corporations were permitted to retain.

Thus I conclude that the increase in corporate taxes during the war was, for the most part, not passed on, and that it actually helped to control inflation, working in conjunction with other taxes and direct controls of prices, wages, and investment.

If corporate taxes were to be increased to finance an additional government program without the simultaneous imposition of a broad program of direct controls, the effect might be quite different. An additional government program adopted under conditions of full employment would cause a price rise unless private demand were to be curtailed. It is not likely that such a price rise would be prevented by an increase in corporate taxation. The increase in corporate taxes would not curtail consumer demand. It would reduce corporate funds only as compared with what they would have been without the tax rise. Corporations—particularly larger corporations—could find ways to finance investments. In case of very high tax rates, business might even extend some activities which can be charged as current expenses. This would tend to offset what curtailing effect the corporate tax might have.

If an additional government program is adopted without curtailment in private demand, a price rise may ensue. Profits before taxes may go up and corporate funds available for distribution or investment be restored. The end result would be a shift of the tax. I believe, however, that this will be the result only when the sum of private and public demand exceeds available and forthcoming resources, when there is no comprehensive anti-inflation program, and when tax rates are raised so high that the stimulating effects offset what curtailing effects the tax may have. It is difficult to prove statistically that this actually happened in the United States in recent years. Nevertheless, it is remarkable that in 1953, in spite of the very high tax rates, profits after taxes were three times as high as those of 1939. If corporate taxes were borne fully by corporate profits, it would not be easy to explain why in recent years profits after taxes, and also investments, have been higher than ever before. I conclude from this that part of the high corporate taxes has entered the price structure.

It is immaterial whether this result is called 'shifting' or 'effect' of the corporate tax.[5] Even if corporate taxes are assumed to be treated as a 'cost' by corporate managements, it must be remembered that the price level is determined both by demand and by cost factors. If prices rise as a result of an increase in government spending which is financed by additional corporate taxes, it may be said that the price rise is due primarily to the increase in spending. It can be said also that the increase in taxes has not prevented the price rise; probably it has supported the price rise. Nevertheless, the shifting of the tax would not be likely to occur without the increase in active demand.

If the corporate tax were to be increased moderately when government expenditures also increase only moderately, the result would probably be quite different. Especially if the additional tax were imposed at a time when business's desire to expand is not very active, a price rise might not be possible. Under such conditions it would be more likely that the tax would result in a curtailment of corporate funds.

In summary, the effect of a large increase in corporate taxes for war finance depends largely on the way in which this measure is made part of a comprehensive program of anti-inflationary controls. The effect of a more moderate increase in corporate taxes depends largely on the size of the simultaneous increase in government spending and on the vigor of business investments.

If this analysis is correct, the tax has a sort of built-in safety

[5] I think a more meaningful distinction in tax analysis is one between the effect of tax changes (and the related changes in expenditures or other methods of financing) on the flow of funds and on demand and costs on the one hand, and the effects on the intentions, motivations, and behavior of business managers, capitalists, workers, and consumers on the other hand. Certain features of corporate taxation, such as carry-forward or carry-back provisions, have during periods of favorable business conditions only a relatively small effect on actual collections and therefore on changes in the flow of funds but may have a great effect on business motivation.

valve. When it reaches a rate that could impair an otherwise vigorous economic expansion, it may change its character. If the force of economic expansion is strong, prices and profits may rise, so that funds are restored for financing the expansion.

Reduction in corporate taxes

In regard to reduction of corporate-tax rates—in case of a decline in government expenditures—again the effects are likely to differ with varying economic conditions. When both tax rates and controls were relaxed after World War II, after-tax profits rose quickly. It is probable, however, that wage earners also gained from the corporate-tax reduction in that corporate management, experiencing such a rise in profits, put up relatively feeble resistance to wage demands.

In another climate, for instance, in a buyer's market when slack is developing in the economy—a condition which many economists expect to develop with the tapering off of the present defense program [1953]—there is the possibility that a corporate-tax reduction might facilitate price reductions or that it might make some wage increases possible in spite of a weakness in the market.

If a tax reduction should be designed primarily to strengthen mass purchasing power, a reduction in individual income or excise taxes would undoubtedly be more effective than a reduction in corporate taxes. If, however, a corporate-tax reduction is desired for the main purpose of strengthening management incentives, there could also be, as a desirable by-product, some favorable effect on mass purchasing power.

I cannot deal here with all aspects of the incidence and effects of corporate taxes in the short and longer run. I have not analyzed the differential effect the corporate tax may have on different types of enterprises. What I have been saying has already been sufficiently complex. Perhaps I could state what I have to say in even simpler terms: the effects of corporate taxes, as the effects of all general taxes on enterprise, depend on the circumstances.

WHAT JUSTIFICATION FOR CORPORATE TAXATION?

As I have said, probably the majority of economists believe that there is really no justification for corporate taxation. They urge us to move away from the corporate tax as fast as practicable—that is, as fast as government expenditures decline or a substitute source of financing can be found.

Here I will deal with the various criteria for the appraisal of taxation, discussing to what extent the corporate tax can be vindicated or should be indicted on the basis of these principles.

The 'cynical' rule of taxation

While economists and tax philosophers have been puzzled, the tax collector has learned to appreciate the corporate tax as a source which not only gives very high yields but which also permits collection at relatively low costs. In the fiscal year 1947, the only year for which we have such a comparison, the Bureau of Internal Revenue collected from the corporate tax 25 per cent (in fiscal year 1953, 31 per cent) of total gross tax receipts but used only 10 per cent of its man-hours on the collection of those taxes.

As a side remark it should be mentioned that a corporate tax is almost ideal from the point of view of the politician. There is no other tax which brings in so much money while making so few voters angry.

The fact that the corporate tax is relatively easy to collect and meets with less political resistance than most other taxes is in itself regarded as undesirable by those writers on tax and fiscal policy who believe that government programs and expenditures are evil and that their growth can be restrained only by the resistance of taxpayers. This opinion would lead to the conclusion that the most painful taxes are most likely to do the best job. If one believes, however, that a minimum of government is not necessarily the optimum, then it is an advantage if a tax involves relatively low costs of collection and low resistance on the part of the taxpayers. A tax source with these merits is given up or drastically reduced only if there are strong reasons against the tax on grounds of fairness, or strong evidence that it is damaging on economic grounds, or if there is a good candidate to take its place.

The criterion of fairness [6]

I do not regard the *ability-to-pay principle* as the main justification of a corporate tax; nor do I believe in the validity of objections made against the tax on the ground that it violates the ability-to-pay principle. At any rate, I do not believe that the fairness of our tax system as a whole would be improved by substituting another tax for the corporate tax as a revenue source. It is likely that corporate taxes have at least in part entered into the price and cost structure of the economy and also that they are reflected in the market valuation of stocks. It would be impossible to say today whose income has been affected by corporate taxes and who would benefit from their abolishment.

In the modern economy the government has become so involved in many aspects of the economic process and is forced to raise such large amounts of revenue that it would not be feasible to impose only taxes that are based on observance of the ability-to-pay principle in its strictest definition.

Corporate taxes might possibly be justified through reference to the *benefit principle of taxation*. Enterprises do enjoy many advantages which are provided by society in general and governments specifically. Production today could not be carried on without the skilled workers, engineers, and scientists who are educated in part at the expense of the general taxpayer. Without the legal arrangements of the centralized capital market, it would not be possible for corporations to obtain funds at costs which are relatively low compared with the costs of eliciting funds from local sources. These are just a few of the ways in which corporations benefit from the social environment in which they operate. We may add to these the government's pledge in

[6] For a more detailed discussion of the rules of justice in taxation, see Chapter 2.

97

the Employment Act of 1946 that it will endeavor to promote conditions of continuing expansion and economic stability. The fact that the government is committed to a policy of stabilization has substantially improved the longer-run outlook for business profits and generally reduced the risk that business may suffer severe losses during depressions.

Nevertheless, I prefer to limit application of the benefit principle to cases in which there is a direct correspondence between a specific tax and a specific government service as, for instance, in the case of automobile or gasoline taxes and the construction and maintenance of roads. Also, I believe that government contributions to the productive process, even if they were measurable, should not necessarily be used to determine the right amount of corporate taxes.

I think there is a broader principle of tax justification involved which, for want of a better name, has been called the *'partnership' principle*. This term is, however, subject to possible misinterpretation. As commonly understood, a partner has the right both to participate in the yield and in the management of an enterprise. But what those who refer to this tax principle have in mind is that the government is a sort of *'silent' non-voting partner* who shares in the profits and to some extent in the losses of enterprise.

This might be only a somewhat sophisticated expression of our 'cynical' rule of taxation according to which the government takes money where it can be found with the least effort and with the least resistance on the part of taxpayers. But the principle also implies a limitation. No partner—non-voting or otherwise—who knows his self-interest would take out of an enterprise amounts that would make it impossible to give adequate remuneration to the active participants in production, or that would make it impossible for the latter to conduct the business in an effective manner.

It is difficult to see why the government should be justified in taxing incomes received by individuals but not in taxing the yield of production before it has been distributed to the individual agents of production. The individual income tax grew out of the idea that the monetary counterpart of the product is distributed and that the government should tax these individual incomes progressively according to ability to pay. This permits some correction in the income distribution as it is determined by forces of the market, inheritance, and regressive excise taxes.

Not as a substitute but as a supplement, there is need and justification for taxes which give the government a share of income right at the source. It is hard to see why the total income from production should first be distributed and then taxed, and why some part of the yield should not be taxed before it is distributed to individuals. I cannot see why such a tax should be incompatible with the working of our economic system.

There is, however, a serious objection to this interpretation of the corporate tax which must be considered.

Why should a tax on enterprise be levied in the form of a tax on profits? Why should the government take a share only out of profitable operations and not out of non-profitable operations? Why should profits rather than total yield ('value-added') be the basis for such a tax at the source?

It is true that both profitable and non-profitable operations benefit from government services. A benefit tax in the narrower definition is usually paid by both profitable and non-profitable enterprises; trucks and buses pay a tax for the use of public roads irrespective of whether they operate at a profit or a loss.

A tax on enterprise *per se* could be based on any criterion of the business operation. Actually, we have taxes on sales, payrolls, business property, and other criteria. Some of these taxes are imposed by state and local governments, others by the federal government. Particularly for state and local governments, a case can be made for a tax on enterprise on a very broad base. In this connection, the recently adopted tax on value-added in the state of Michigan is very interesting. Only if we had *one* single tax on enterprise for federal, state, and local governments would a value-added tax be a logically superior choice.

For the federal government, a tax based on profits has decided advantages. A tax on business profits is much more flexible than a tax on a broader base, such as gross receipts or value-added. It does not add an additional fixed cost to doing business. Also, a corporate tax that allows for adequate carry-back and carry-over of losses does not substantially modify the chances and risks involved in a business venture, since the government participates in both gains and losses. For these reasons I feel that, from the point of view of tax philosophy, there is justification for using profits as a basis for a federal tax on corporate enterprise.

The economic criterion

Basically, taxes are designed to enable the government to utilize resources needed for the execution of government programs. If the government wants to purchase five billion dollars' worth of munitions, taxation can aid in curtailing demand for producer or consumer goods so that materials, facilities, and labor will become available for meeting the government demand. The same is the case when the government does not want to use resources itself but wants to transfer resources from one group of the population to another group. If the government decides to give one billion dollars to veterans or social-security beneficiaries, a tax will help if it reduces the spending of other consumers by one billion so that the goods which the beneficiaries want to buy will become available without a price rise.

In terms of this basic economic criterion, the corporate tax is probably less effective than other taxes. These examples, however, assumed full employment of a given amount of resources. Under conditions of growing resources or some slack in the use of resources, the government may adopt additional programs (e.g. the World War II or Korean defense programs) without necessarily reducing the private use of resources. In such a situation, it is not essential that the tax curtail private demand; it serves a function if it limits the rise in incomes and private demand. This the corporate tax is able to do.

There is another necessary qualification. We have spoken of the effect of one tax, the corporate tax. Before drawing conclusions we should analyze the effect not of one tax but of the tax system as a whole. Even if the corporate tax is not directly effective in curtailing or limiting private demand, it may do so indirectly. An increase in corporate taxes may make increases in the individual income tax in the lower and middle brackets more acceptable. Thereby it may indirectly contribute to a needed curtailment or limitation of demand.

Even assuming that the corporate tax would not substantially aid in redirecting resources from private to public use, it may still fulfill a useful function. If the tax does not curtail or limit effective demand, its immediate effect will not be very different from that of financing the same program by inflationary borrowing. With respect to the longer run, however, there still remains the difference for the federal budget and debt management between financing a program by borrowing or doing it by taxation.

Our defense of the corporate tax, therefore, is not based predominantly on the ground that it is a very effective means of directly rechanneling resources. But we must examine whether the tax is objectionable on economic grounds.

Objections on economic grounds

The main points in the economic bill of particulars against the corporate tax are that it discourages investment; encourages waste in corporate management; and promotes debt financing while discriminating against equity financing.

Enterprise is the engine that provides the motion of the economic system. Careful consideration should therefore be given to the claim that the corporate tax tends to stall or distort the operation of this all-important engine.

I have already said why I believe, on the basis of theoretical argument and observation in recent years, that high corporate taxes do not necessarily discourage investment when business is intent on modernization or expansion. Moreover, when individual income taxes are high, and particularly when capital gains are taxed at a lower rate, there is a strong incentive to retain earnings in the corporation and a premium is placed on investment in 'growth' corporations. Thus the curtailment of funds by the corporate tax is at least in part if not more than offset by the effect of other taxes. *The tax system as a whole has probably not been unfavorable to corporate development.*

There are more indications that bear out the indictment that a corporate tax with very high marginal rates invites extravagance in business management or, more cautiously stated, encourages expenditures which would not have been made with lower taxes. High corporate taxes and high individual income taxes have induced many corporations to grant their executives benefits which are charged as business expenses of the corporation but which are not taxed as income of the executives. It is also true that very high marginal rates induce liberal spending by business in advertising, in 'good-will' campaigns, and in 'investment' in the beautification of factories. Many corporate activities stimulated by high taxes, particularly expenses for research and development and contributions for philanthropic causes, are very desirable. Some of these activities which use scarce resources, however, are of doubtful value in a period of inflation. Therefore, as part of anti-inflation policy, high corporate taxes require strict disallowance by the tax authorities of 'unreasonable' expenses; otherwise, the anti-inflationary effect of high taxes is at least in part offset. That high marginal rates promote wasteful spending was a forceful argument against the continuation of an excess profits tax at the end of both world wars when direct controls of materials no longer limited business activities. It is much less an argument against a corporate tax with a proportional and more moderate rate.

We often hear the argument that a corporate tax promotes debt financing and penalizes equity financing. This argument is entirely logical. It is surprising, however, that there seems to be only a limited number of cases in which corporations have engaged in borrowing instead of equity financing clearly because of tax considerations. It seems that the method of financing is determined primarily by the kind of securities which find a market. Nevertheless, thought should be given to modifications in corporate taxation that would approximately neutralize the effect of taxes on the methods of financing.

Thus, looking at the economic bill of particulars, I find no convincing reason why this tax source should be abandoned or drastically reduced as long as moderate rates are used. What rates should be regarded as moderate cannot be determined with any precision. It depends in part on the relationship between rates and rate structure of the individual income tax and the corporate tax respectively. Even though I can only give an opinion without proof, I venture my personal impression that a corporate tax is harmful if its rates exceed 50 per cent except in an emergency when wartime controls are simultaneously adopted. I admit that fifteen years ago I would have put that limit at a lower figure.

Though I feel that a corporate tax of moderate rates has a definite and significant place in the federal tax system, some important problems remain unsolved. In the last section of this paper I will discuss what appear to me as the three most important of these problems.

THREE UNRESOLVED PROBLEMS IN CORPORATE TAXATION

The three most difficult interrelated questions with respect to the corporate tax seem to me the following:

(1) The line of demarcation between enterprises that operate in corporate form and enterprises that operate as individual firms or partnerships is entirely arbitrary. The more significant distinction is between what may be called the public corporation on the one hand, and the privately held corporation and the unincorporated firm on the other hand. Can tax law define and recognize this distinction?

(2) High individual income tax rates give a considerable incentive for retainment of profits by corporations. The present provision for a tax on 'corporations improperly accumulating surplus' (Section 102 of the Revenue Code) is criticized by some as undesirable, by others as ineffective for dealing with this problem.

(3) One of the main problems of economic stabilization at high and expanding levels of activity consists in reducing fluctuations

in business investments. What contribution can corporate tax policy make toward the regularization of business investment?

With respect to each of these three problems I shall make a few remarks without claiming that I know the solution for any one of them.

Corporate and unincorporated enterprises; public and private corporations

In exploring the first problem we ask what justification there is for a different tax treatment of corporations and unincorporated enterprises. Profits of the individual firm or partnership are taxed by the individual income tax. The individual income tax does not make any distinction between the profits the individual withdraws from his unincorporated enterprise and the profits that stay in the enterprise. As far as individual entrepreneurs and partners are concerned, a part of the individual income tax could be interpreted as a tax on the enterprise. Individual enterprises and partnerships have no problem of double taxation but they have a very serious problem in that business profits are taxed in accordance with rates for the income bracket in which the owners happen to be. By the use of the corporate form, the enterprise is able to have the undistributed profits taxed at the rate of the corporate tax, which is often lower than the marginal rate of the individual income tax paid by the owners of the enterprise.

By far the largest number of corporations are by the nature of their business much more similar to unincorporated enterprises than to the relatively small number of what we may call public corporations. Does it make sense that a corner grocery store is in the same category as U.S. Steel or General Motors as far as legal form of organization and taxation are concerned?

How would it be possible to make a distinction between what we may call the private corporation and the public corporation? In some countries there is a distinction based on whether the owners have no liability or limited liability for the debts of the corporation. Other countries make a distinction according to

104

the number of owners. Years ago a proposal [7] was made to establish two different types of corporate charters in the United States—one for private corporations and one for public corporations—the distinction being made in accordance with the method of financing the corporation elects to use.

Private corporations would have all the traditional rights of the corporation except that, unless they were specifically certified as institutions for small-business financing, their stocks or obligations could not be traded at the stock exchanges or bought by financial institutions. On the other hand, public corporations would have access to the public capital market, including the privilege of trading their securities at the various stock exchanges and of selling securities to all kinds of financial institutions.

The public corporation, so defined, would be taxed by the corporate tax, while privately held corporations could elect to be taxed either as corporations or as partnerships; that is, the partners could include in their individual incomes their shares in profits, distributed or undistributed. In the latter case the penalty tax of Section 102 would not be needed.

This proposal would remove the so-called double taxation for those corporations in which management and ownership are typically one, or are intimately related, and in which ownership does not change hands frequently. These are the corporations most vulnerable to double taxation. Only if these corporations found it more advantageous to pay the corporate income tax would they do so.

It would be desirable if all private corporations could be taxed as partnerships. This would, however, not be feasible under the present individual income-tax rates which reach a maximum effective rate of 88 per cent in the highest brackets. As long as we have these very high top rates, I think taxation as partnerships should remain optional for corporations in this category. This means that the penalty tax of Section 102 would have to be continued.

[7] See *Proceedings of the Annual Conference on Taxation, Final Report,* Committee on Federal Taxation of Corporations, National Tax Association (San Francisco, California, meeting), September 1939, especially p. 559.

Over the long run I think it would be desirable to lower the top bracket rates on individual incomes. This could be done by shifting part of the tax burden of high-income taxpayers from the income tax to a broadened and strengthened estate tax. Such a shift in emphasis would probably also somewhat reduce undesirable effects on work incentives. With lower top-bracket rates, the profits of all privately held corporations could be taxed as individual income. I personally see merits in this proposal but I do not know whether it would be practicable. Still, I recommend it for consideration.

Retained profits

The retained profits of corporations have long been recognized as a major problem of taxation, even by those who do not admit that there is a justification for taxing enterprises *per se.* The fact that a large proportion of corporate profits does not become individual income and is not subject to the individual income tax appears undesirable to those who regard only the individual owners of the corporation as *real* taxpayers.

Another group of tax students has been concerned on the economic ground that the tax system grants an incentive for the retention of earnings. These are the economists who fear that, with a rising standard of living, the people's desire to save may at times tend to outrun business's desire to invest, thus creating a recessionary force. Therefore, both on equity and economic grounds, many economists during the 'thirties searched for tax measures that would equalize the burden imposed on distributed and undistributed earnings.[8]

During the last fifteen years the economic concern has moved into the background. The inflationary pressure generated by defense and war spending and very high levels of business investment made undersaving and inflation a more urgent problem than the threat of oversaving and deflation. No one, however, can be sure today that the concern with oversaving will not appear again when personal incomes continue to rise and de-

[8] The National Tax Association's Committee report on Federal Corporate Taxation, cited above, presents an expression of this view.

fense expenditures and defense-supporting investments decline.

I have referred to the problem of retained earnings of privately held corporations. For what we have called the public corporation, there is less likelihood that the corporation will retain earnings exclusively for tax considerations if the stockholdings are widely distributed. We may say, however, that the preferential treatment of undistributed profits and capital gains has made it easier for corporations to retain the earnings that they can profitably use in business expansion. Only if the force of business expansion should begin to slacken may retention of earnings again become a problem of real importance.

If profits that are earned in periods of high-level activity and are not used for distribution or investment should be earmarked for future productive use in periods of an economic downswing, at least part of the concern on economic grounds would be removed. Therefore, this problem of retained earnings naturally leads over to the third problem, which we have identified as the problem of regularizing business investment.

Regularizing investments

Attempts to influence investment have been made by modification of the depreciation allowance—a rapid amortization allowance in the case of defense-supporting investments (in the United States), and the deferment of amortization for non-defense investment (in Canada). Sweden has experimented with the idea of building up tax-free investment reserves during periods of high employment for use in periods of economic slack.

I do not think that any tax device will be able to induce business investments at times when business would otherwise be unwilling to invest. There seem to be indications, however, that the thinking of business about economic fluctuations is undergoing a change. It appears that investment planning is increasingly oriented toward longer-range objectives of business expansion and that confidence is growing that recessions will be effectively counteracted before they develop into deep and long-lasting depressions. If such a psychology should become more prevalent, business may be inclined to take advantage of the

107

lower costs of construction and more ample financing in a period of slack. If an attitude of this kind is growing, it might be possible and advisable to strengthen it by tax incentives.

I believe it would be possible to devise methods that would make it advantageous for business to earmark profits and depreciation reserves accumulated in periods of high activity for use in periods of economic slack. Within the space of this paper I want only to raise the question whether development of an incentive of this type would be desirable, rather than to discuss technical details of such proposals as have been made or could be made.[9]

In any case, it seems to me that adoption of such a counter-cyclical device would be preferable to a policy of changing the corporate-tax rate in the cycle. Variation of the corporate-tax rate *per se* as an anti-depression measure is probably not very effective. It is also desirable, in the interest of long-term business planning, not to vary the corporate-tax rate frequently once it has been set at a rate which appears appropriate for peacetime.

SUMMARY

In summary, I consider it an error to regard the corporate tax as a substitute for or supplement to the individual income tax. It is not a tax that is primarily justified by the ability-to-pay principle. It is a tax through which the government partakes in the yield of corporate enterprise. At times the existence of the tax may reduce what the other partners in production—labor, management, capital—receive as their share. At other times, particularly when rates are very high and additional funds are needed to finance investment, it may result in rising prices or in keeping prices at a level higher than they would otherwise be.

The corporate tax *per se* should be imposed only on the public corporations which use the opportunities of the national capital market. Private corporations should be taxed if possible as partnerships.

[9] For a more detailed discussion of this subject, see Chapter 4.

In times of war or mobilization a case can be made for high rates of corporate taxation, including an excess-profits tax. Such a tax, however, is effective only if price, wage, and investment controls are also adopted. It will, in turn, make these controls more effective. High tax rates also make it necessary to have permissible expenses closely scrutinized by the tax authorities.

In normal times the corporate-tax rate should be set below 50 per cent. Management should not feel that half or more of any marginal expenses it incurs are borne by the government. What may be regarded as a normal peacetime rate depends, of course, on the total revenue need. The corporate-tax rate should be determined in proper relation to other taxes, particularly in relation to the individual income-tax rates. A reduction from the present rate to a future normal level should be so timed that it occurs when business is weakening and when the tax reduction would not only strengthen management incentives but also alleviate the effects of price declines or wage increases. Once a peacetime level has been reached the corporate-tax rate should not be changed too frequently. Other taxes are more suitable for anti-cyclical rate changes.

In my opinion the corporate tax—if possible an improved version of the present tax—has a definite place in the American system of enterprise and in the federal tax system. At least it can be said that this tax is a lesser evil than other taxes that have been suggested as possible substitutes.

Part
-III-

FISCAL POLICY

6

Public Spending and Recovery
in the United States

(1936) *

IN this study we shall try to answer the question whether and
to what extent the policy of public spending has helped to bring
about recovery in the United States. Before the Great Depression economists developed the theory of 'priming the pump' as
a device for overcoming depressions. They believed that additional public expenditures financed by credit would break the
deadlock of the depression and would produce *lasting* recovery

* 'Public Spending and Recovery in the United States,' Gerhard Colm and
Fritz Lehmann, *Social Research*, III (2), May 1936, pp. 129-66. (The part for
which Lehmann took major responsibility has been omitted.)

[1954 Fn.] The methods for measuring the economic effects of government
spending have been greatly refined since this article was written. Nevertheless, I believe, the basic approach of the article is still valid and some students may find the elementary methods of measurement used in this paper
more understandable than the mathematical formulations of more recent efforts.

effects. In the United States during the last few years, billions of dollars have been spent for fighting the depression, and recovery—at least a certain degree of recovery—has taken place. The economist, however, cannot content himself with the mere juxtaposition of spending and recovery. He has to find an answer to the vital question whether or not recovery is a *result* of public spending. Has the 'pump priming' theory stood the test of reality in this depression? Can it be recommended therefore as a remedy to be applied again in the next depression?

Economists have no laboratories for checking theories. Their laboratory is history; but historical facts are seldom staged in a way that permits a direct answer to whether or not the theory is verified by reality. In actual life a complexity of factors affect business and employment. To isolate the effects of one factor is almost impossible and yet economists cannot therefore abandon the attempt to verify the theory. This would mean to question every practicability of economic science.

In this essay we shall try to compare the actual facts with the economic development to be expected if public spending, and public spending alone, had influenced economic development in the depression. Such a method, of course, cannot render unmistakable proof of cause and effect, even if the constructed and the actual curve of recovery coincide, for this coincidence might occur by chance. Therefore, it is also necessary to discover whether or not other stimulating or hampering factors have existed by which the actual conditions of business and employment might have been influenced. In such a way the question could and should be answered with sufficient certainty. We cannot pretend, however, to present the definite answer in this preliminary study. Our attempt is rather to indicate in what ways the solution might be found.

STIMULATING EXPENDITURES, LIQUIDATING EXPENDITURES, AND THE MAINTENANCE DEFICIT

The 'pump priming' theory has been related to the policy of public works. In the United States during the last few years, public works have frequently been supposed to be the means of 'pump priming.' But the book of Gayer [1] and recent statistics of expenditures for public works show that in the United States during the depression much less was spent for public works than in the preceding years of prosperity. In the years 1927-9 the average annual expenditures of federal, state, and local authorities for public works was 2,933 million dollars; in the years 1933-5 it was 1,917 million dollars. Federal expenditures for this purpose did indeed increase from an average of 257 to an average of 897 million dollars, but this increase was more than offset by the decrease in state and municipal expenditures for public works. Can we therefore speak of 'additional' public works which might have 'primed the pump'?

J. M. Clark says that 'the important thing is the total amount of expenditures financed by expansionary borrowing rather than the amount spent in any particular way.' [2] If we measure this expansion by the amount of the deficits (debt redemption deducted) during the depression years 1930-35, we arrive at the figure of 14,300 million dollars incurred by the federal government alone. If we calculate as 'pump priming' only the additional expenditures for public works, then we may reach the conclusion that the device has not been tried at all. A brief theoretical consideration will reveal what expenditures we can regard as stimulating expenditures.

The 'pump priming' theory [3] contends that through public spending of borrowed money during a depression additional credit reserves are directed into active purchasing power, and that the increase in purchasing power and production, expressed for instance in the yearly national income, is larger than the additional amount spent by the government. Since idle labor

[1] Arthur D. Gayer, *Public Works in Prosperity and Depression*, National Bureau of Economic Research: Publications, no. 29, New York, 1935.

[2] J. M. Clark, *Economics of Planning Public Works*, National Planning Board, Washington, 1935, p. 87.

[3] An excellent restatement and refinement of the theory is given by Clark, op. cit. Compare also chapter XIV of Gayer's book, op. cit. Gayer quotes the earlier literature on p. 366, sec. XXX (4), XVIII (1).

and idle plant capacities are available in depression times, prices are not expected to rise to any considerable degree. Production and employment, and therefore the real income, are expected to increase.

This cumulative effect of public spending is not, however, unlimited. First, the process requires a certain time until the amount passes from one stage to the next—the speed of transmission, as J. M. Clark calls it. Clark suggests the positing of six cycles of secondary effects per year as a basis for calculation.[4] Second, not the whole amount is transferred from stage to stage. 'Leakages'—to use Kahn's apt term [5]—sooner or later dry up the flow of purchasing power.

In a period in which repayment of debts and increase in deposits do not increase bank loans (because there are no debtors), public expenditures do not necessarily create additional purchasing power but money thus spent may pass into a blind alley. The same holds true for taxes from increasing sales and incomes, since in such a period these amounts are more likely to diminish the borrowing of public authorities than to increase their spending. In agreement with Keynes, Clark estimates that 100 dollars spent will create additional income of 200 to 300 dollars. This would mean average leakages of between 50 per cent and $33\frac{1}{3}$ per cent—a 'multiplier' of between 2 and 3. He believes that in the course of recovery 'the percentage of "leakage" will decrease as industrial conditions grow better.' When, for instance, the consumers'-goods industries which have been revived through the effects of this 'pump priming' begin again to invest, we may speak of the 'tertiary' effects of public spending. We call tertiary effects all those business activities which, induced by the primary or secondary effects of public spending,

[4] The speed of transmission is not constant in all circumstances. If the community *believes* in the 'pump priming' theory and anticipates the secondary effects of public spending, the transmission will be speeded up considerably. This, however, means no more than a concentration in time; the total effect is not changed.

[5] R. F. Kahn, 'The Relation of Home Investment to Unemployment,' *Economic Journal,* June 1931.

involve either a demand for credit in addition to the credit used by the government or the use of idle bank balances.[6]

What are 'pump priming' expenditures in the light of this theory? Expenditures made by means of simultaneous taxation cannot in general [7] be regarded as having such a stimulating effect. In the main they may be regarded as a transfer of purchasing power from the taxpayer to the receiver of government payments. The same holds true of governmental borrowing that encroaches on private borrowers' demands and thereby replaces private investments which would otherwise have occurred. As long as there exists a huge amount of unused credit reserves, it may be assumed that governmental borrowing does not involve a reduction of consumption or the replacement of private investments. Therefore it seems best to start with the total *budget deficits,* as Keynes and Clark [8] have suggested. Two different factors, however, have brought about budget deficits during the depression: decreasing revenues and increasing expenditures.

As to the first, there may be two reasons for the decrease of revenues. It may be due to a reduction of tax rates or it may be due to a reduction of tax yields because of falling incomes, property values, and sales. We may neglect here the reduction of tax rates since what happened was quite the opposite: new taxes were introduced and tax rates were raised. A budget deficit caused by declining tax yields has no stimulating effect, because neither the state nor the taxpayer is thereby enabled to spend more, but it does mitigate the spreading of the deflationary process. To avoid such a deficit either taxes would have to be increased (thereby diminishing the purchasing power at the taxpayer's disposal) or public expenditures (and thus the income derived from public sources) would have to be curtailed.

---

[6] [1954 Fn.] What I called 'tertiary effects' is similar to the concept of the 'acceleration principle' in recent literature.

[7] The only exception is the taxation of incomes that would otherwise have been hoarded. For the sake of simplicity this exception may be neglected. [1954 Fn.] I should not subscribe today to the proposition that the income-creating effect of expenditures financed by taxes may be negligible.

[8] J. M. Clark, op. cit. p. 104.

We may call such a deficit the *maintenance deficit,* since it permits the maintenance of a certain level of public spending without further reduction of private purchasing power.

The second factor responsible for budget deficits is an increase in expenditures with no corresponding increase in tax receipts. The consequence of such a budget deficit, however, will depend on the nature of the additional expenditures. An example may serve for clarification. Federal land banks financed by the government granted mortgage loans to farmers to redeem the loans they had received from insurance companies and from joint-stock land banks, thereby preventing a breakdown of the credit and insurance system of the country. Private credit was replaced by public credit, but the actual purchasing power was not increased, at least not directly. We suggest calling such expenditures *liquidating expenditures.* It is not always, of course, easy to decide what expenditures should be regarded as liquidating.[9]

We have regarded as *stimulating expenditures* those additional expenditures, presumably met by borrowing, which are made for relief, agricultural relief, and work relief, for the Civilian Conservation Corps, and for public works of every kind, including expenditures for armaments, housing, and resettlement. The benefit payments of the Agricultural Adjustment Administration present a problem; so far as they were met by processing taxes and were included under the general accounts of the budget, they may be regarded as a shifting of purchasing power from the urban to the rural population. They created additional purchasing power in the agricultural regions. But from the point of view of the total economy, they may be regarded as a means of letting the agricultural population participate in the purchasing power created for the urban population through stimulating expenditures.

This classification refers only to the 'pump priming' theory in general. A more detailed analysis should draw distinctions, for

[9] We have included in this category loans, which if not granted by a governmental agency, were probably granted by private institutions, although perhaps under less favorable conditions.

instance, according to the industries or regions that have the first advantage from the spending. From the long-run economic and fiscal point of view, it is very important to draw further distinctions based on whether expenditures are for productive or non-productive purposes. The differentiation we have made between liquidating and stimulating expenditures refers only to the 'pump priming,' not to the long-run effect, and cannot be regarded as a rigid classification. Stimulating expenditures, through the leakages, also affect the credit market. Liquidating expenditures on the other hand, through reduced interest rates for example, may enable farmers, home owners, and institutions to spend more than they could otherwise have spent. A small portion of the farm and real-estate loans were used not for refinancing but for improvements. In such ways the liquidating expenditures may also have a slight direct stimulating effect.

THE MEASUREMENT OF RECOVERY

Our problem is the question whether and how much the policy of public spending may have influenced recovery. It is through the creation of purchasing power that recovery is promoted by spending. Relief distributed to the unemployed, for example, creates purchasing power because they receive an income derived not from other people's income but from additional borrowing, from credit expansion. Thus the first step is an increase in the nominal national income paid out. Part of the additional income will be spent. The spending will increase sales, production, and employment, thereby enlarging again the national income paid out, and this process will be repeated in widening circles. But an increase in the nominal national income paid out is not in itself an accurate measure of recovery. Higher prices may compensate higher nominal income figures. Table I shows that fluctuations in the national income have to a certain extent been offset by the price movement.

The figures for 'real' income have been calculated by reducing the nominal national income by the index of the cost of living. These figures show a recovery by December 1935 of about 40 per cent of the drop that occurred in 'real' national income

TABLE I. SYMPTOMS OF RECOVERY

	Nominal National Income * (in billions of dollars)	Cost of Living **	'Real' Income (in billions of dollars)	Industrial Production (1923-5 = 100)	Employment † (in millions)	Unemployment (in millions)
1929 (average)	78.6	100.0	78.6	119	46.2	1.9
Oct. 1929	82.0 ‡	101.0	81.2 ‡	121	47.4	0.9
1933 (average)	44.4	74.8	59.3	76	37.0	13.7
March 1933	40.3 ‡	71.8	56.1 ‡	60	34.9	15.7
1934 (average)	49.6	79.4	62.5	79	38.9	12.4
1935 (average)	52.7	83.1	63.4	90	39.7	12.2
Dec. 1935	56.0 ‡	84.8	66.0 ‡	95	40.7	11.4

* The Cleveland Trust Company. The estimates of the Cleveland Trust Company include federal relief under national income. [1954 Fn.] Under present-day national income accounting concepts, relief payments would be considered part of personal income but not of national income.
** Figures given by National Industrial Conference Board.
† Based on figures given by *American Federationist*.
‡ Calculated on annual rate.

between the peak in October 1929 and the depth in March 1933. Disregarding all doubts about the technical validity of these figures, we might nevertheless question whether the 'real' income adequately represents recovery. The 'real' income *produced* would probably show a larger increase during the 1933-5 period than do these figures for the income *paid out*. The development shown in the column of industrial production is not an accurate measurement of this increase, since other branches of production (agriculture) developed more slowly, but we have not yet the complete figures for production and for services during this period. Nor can our figures for employment and unemployment be regarded as an adequate index of recovery. The real degree of re-employment should be measured by the increase in the quantity of work, which in a period of changing hours of work per worker is not accurately expressed by the rise in the number of employed. Moreover, if there is any change in the productivity of the individual worker, even the total quantity of hours of work would not be an exact measure of recovery. And yet, although all single indices are objectionable, it is fairly safe to estimate that by the end of 1935 economic activities in the United States recovered about a half of their depression fall.

The problem is then to estimate how far this recovery may be attributed to the policy of public spending. Even though recovery is not accurately represented by the increase of national income paid out, the relative importance of the effects of public spending can be measured approximately by the relation of primary and secondary effects of public spending to the increase of national income.

The Maintenance Deficit, 1931-3

From the outset a practical calculation of government expenditures for 1931-3 is made difficult by the fact that there are sufficient financial statistics only for the federal budget, while the statistics for states and municipalities are available only up to 1932. Stimulating federal expenditures met by borrowing may be offset by the curtailment in state or local budgets or by new taxes introduced by these lower jurisdictions. In both cases the stimulating effect of the federal expenditures is countervailed by the contracting effect of the state or municipal fiscal policy. What remains could be regarded only as a maintenance deficit.

We regard the federal deficits of the fiscal years 1931 and 1932 as maintenance deficits, partly emerging from diminishing federal tax revenues, partly compensating the curtailment of state and local expenditures. More difficult is the treatment of the deficit in the fiscal year 1933. In this year relief expenditures from state and local funds increased but there was a much greater decrease in outlays for public works. In addition, many states introduced new taxes during this year, especially sales taxes. We may assume that states and municipalities curtailed purchasing power through reduction of expenditures or through the imposition of new taxes by three quarters of a billion dollars, thereby offsetting more than the whole amount of additional federal expenditures. Therefore, we regard the deficits of this whole period, 1931-3 (fiscal years), as maintenance deficits. If this assumption is justified, we cannot expect any stimulating influences from the fiscal policy in these years, but we may assume that during this period the process of deflation was slowed down through the maintenance of public expenditures.

The basic assumption is that the driving force of the deflation was the falling demand for durable goods, consumers' as well as producers' goods. This falling demand for durable goods was neither the single deflationary factor nor the ultimate one. The agricultural crisis, the waning expansion of consumers' purchasing power after installment credit had been expanded to the limit, the breakdown of the stock market, and the world market's sinking capacity to buy may be mentioned as probable primary causes. The contraction of bank credits, the 'buyers' strike,' the vanishing of confidence in the economic future certainly speeded up the process of deflation.

Measurement of the driving force of deflation by the one factor, falling demand for durable goods, is justified by the fact that it is through this falling demand that most of the causal factors of the depression affect the economic process.

Falling production of durable goods must engender secondary effects in the nature of falling prices and production in other spheres, a result comparable to the secondary effects of public spending or expanding investments. The amount of these secondary effects will decrease from stage to stage. The concepts of leakages and multipliers appear therefore to be applicable also to secondary effects in the process of contraction. A decrease in the secondary effects of a primary deflationary cause is due to negative leakages; in other words, the reduction of expenditures by business and households becomes smaller than the reduction of sales and incomes. A lower percentage of profit and income will be saved, and savings accumulated in the past will be drawn upon to meet current expenditures. Also imports of foreign goods will decrease. If no negative leakages existed, expenditures at every stage of production would be curtailed by the full amount of the reduction in receipts. In this event, assuming that the speed of transmission brings six cycles of secondary effects per year, the annual national income would shrink by six times the amount of the primary contraction. If, on the contrary, business continued to pay out the same amount of income as before, regardless of decreasing sales, and if the income receivers also left their expenditures unchanged, no secondary effects could appear. Neither of the two extreme cases (negative leakages of either zero or 100 per cent) is likely to happen. Business and households will reduce spending, but by less than the decline in sales and incomes.

For a first approach we may assume the negative leakages at 50 per cent, the multiplier for the total effect at 2. Table II,

TABLE II. NATIONAL INCOME ESTIMATES
(in billions of dollars)

	I Sales Value of Durable Goods *	II Fall in Sales Value of Durable Goods	III Secondary Effects of Falling Sales Value	IV Total Deflationary Effect	V Actual National Income Paid Out **	VI Actual National Income in 1929 Minus Total Deflationary Effect
1929	24.6				78.6	78.6
1930	19.9	4.7	3.1	7.8	72.9	70.8
1931	13.9	10.7	8.7	19.4	61.7	59.2
1932	8.3	16.3	14.5	30.8	48.4	47.8

* Figures are based upon Simon Kuznets' *Gross Capital Formation, 1919-1933*, National Bureau of Economic Research, Bulletin no. 52, p. 6. Deductions have been made for the estimated value of parts and servicing.
** *Survey of Current Business*, August 1935, p. 16.

computed in billions of dollars, contains in column I the estimated figures for the sales value of durable goods; in column II the differences between these figures and the figure for the basic year 1929, thus indicating the driving force of deflation; in column III the secondary effects, so far as they appeared in the year; in column IV the total deflationary effect (the sum of columns II and III); in column V the actual national income paid out; in column VI a fictitious national income, computed for each year by subtracting from the actual income in 1929 the deflationary effect estimated for that year in column IV.

123

The table shows that the actual figures for national income correspond approximately to the figures calculated. In 1930 and 1931, the actual income decreased less, in 1932 more, than the calculated income. This may be interpreted as meaning that the negative leakages were greater than 50 per cent in the beginning of the period and smaller than 50 per cent at the end of the period. This coincides with reasonable expectations. As long as a depression is considered no more than a temporary recession, people will see little reason for drastically cutting their expenditures and banks will not press for repayment of their loans. Later, expenditures have to be adjusted more and more to falling receipts, and the dwindling safety margin causes the banks to call in their loans energetically, forcing their debtors to pay them from a reduction in their inventories.

In order to estimate the effects of the public deficits on the national income from 1930 through 1932, we may assume that cutting down public expenditures would have had the same secondary effects as cutting down private purchases of durable goods. The deficits incurred by all public authorities, federal and local, in the calendar years 1930, 1931, and 1932 may be estimated at 0.3, 2.9, and 3.4 billion dollars,[10] or 6.6 billion for the three years. With the negative leakages estimated at around 50 per cent during this period, the secondary effects would have equaled this deficit. Thus the maintenance deficit contributed about 12 billion of the 183 billion dollars total national income from 1930 through 1932. It decreased the deflationary fall (the sum of the differences between actual incomes in 1930, 1931, and 1932, and the actual income in 1929) from 65 to 53 billion dollars, thus reducing by 20 per cent what might be called the pressure of deflation.

[10] The relative importance of these deficits may be demonstrated by a comparison with the figures for business dissaving: the difference between the income paid out by business and the value of its production and services. This dissaving—after deductions have been made for the depreciation of commodity stocks and the losses of financial institutions—amounted to approximately 3 billion dollars in 1931 and 5 billion dollars in 1932.

STIMULATING EXPENDITURES AND THE NATIONAL INCOME, 1933-5

The spring of 1933 was the turning point in the cycle. Up to that time the increase in federal deficit expenditures was offset by the fiscal policy of states and communities. After that time the stimulating expenditures of the federal emergency budget were no longer offset by other fiscal developments. These expenditures can therefore be regarded as accruals to the national income. If we can determine the amounts of these accruals, deriving only from the influence of public spending, we shall have a basis for measuring how much of the recovery may be attributed to this cause.

The accompanying charts illustrate an attempt at such a measurement. The actual development of the national income from

Chart I. The Development of the National Income and the Effects of Stimulating Federal Expenditures and of Additional Investments in Automobiles, July 1933–December 1935
(*Leakages calculated at 50 per cent*)

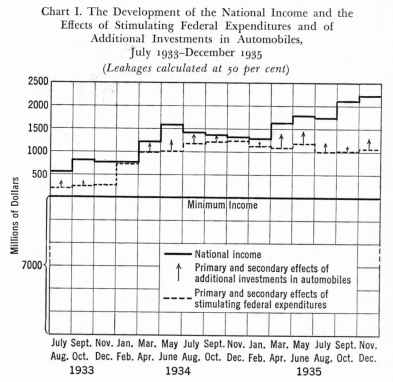

Chart II. The Development of the National Income and the
Effects of Stimulating Federal Expenditures and of
Additional Investments in Automobiles,
July 1933–December 1935
(*Leakages calculated as decreasing from 50 to 33⅓ per cent*)

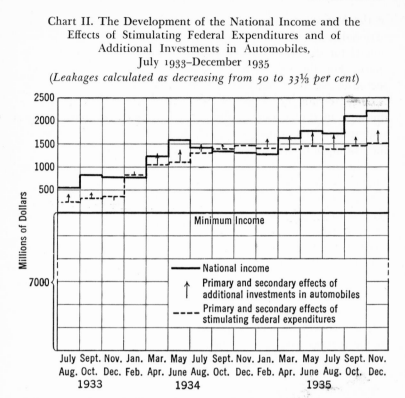

July 1933 through December 1935 is shown by the unbroken
line; the broken line represents our calculation of the development due only to the primary and secondary effects of public
spending; the area between the lines represents the influence of
other recovery factors.

The curve represented by the broken line was derived by adding the amounts of the primary and secondary effects of stimulating expenditures to a hypothetical minimum figure of the
national income, which may be regarded as the bedrock, the
basic stratum at which it may be presumed that the process of
deflation came to an end and which would have been maintained if no stimulating factors had existed. This low point
was reached in the first half of 1933; calculating on the basis

126

of the first six months of that year,[11] we assume the minimum national income to be 3.5 billion dollars a month, or 7 billion dollars for the two-month period we have elected to use in the charts. For the calculation of the secondary effects of public spending we have assumed, as explained above, that on the average income needs two months to pass from one stage to the next in the economic circuit. Chart I is constructed on the assumption that leakages amount to 50 per cent, Chart II on the assumption that they decrease from 50 per cent to $33\frac{1}{3}$ per cent in the course of recovery. These two assumptions mark the limits between which the true figures probably lie.[12]

Leakages in Chart II were estimated as decreasing from 50 per cent in July 1933 through June 1934 to 40 per cent in July 1934 through June 1935, and then to $33\frac{1}{3}$ per cent in July through December 1935; and, moreover, we added to the stimulating emergency expenditures 10 per cent of the liquidating expenditures.[13]

Thus it can be seen that under the assumption of Chart I, 66 per cent—under the assumption of Chart II, 80 per cent—of actual recovery must be attributed to the stimulating spending of the federal government and its secondary effects.

OTHER RECOVERY FORCES

Before we may trust such a hypothetical conclusion, we must also apply an indirect approach to our problem. We have to ask whether or not there might have been in reality other forces

[11] We have used figures slightly below the actual figures for this period, since the actual figures were still influenced by a certain amount of deficit spending. Our figure is slightly above the extreme low of March 1933, the month of the bank crisis.

[12] In our calculation we have used the whole amount of the bimonthly stimulating expenditures and, for the sake of simplicity, have disregarded the first leakage, which takes place before the amount spent by the government creates additional income (for example, the import of foreign steel for public works). This is taken care of in the leakages of the later stages.

[13] Liquidating expenditures are calculated not on the basis of the actual monthly figures but on the monthly averages for the fiscal years 1933 and 1934 and for the second half of 1935. We have included only the liquidating expenditures of the emergency budget, not those financed by guaranteed issues of the various agencies.

that could explain recovery. Were there any other forces that had an expansionary or, we may say, reflationary effect? The 'classical' explanation for recovery is that when the interest rate drops sufficiently, private entrepreneurs turn to anticipating investments, that is, investments which do not respond to an already existing actual demand but aim to meet a future demand. Construction of new railways, often in colonial countries, and construction of new houses may serve as examples. In this way idle credit is used again, additional purchasing power, with all its primary and secondary effects, is created, and recovery and re-employment are the result. It is not necessary to explain here why, in spite of low interest rates, these anticipating investments did not appear in this depression; it must suffice to state that they did not occur.

There was a little boom in the summer of 1933, anticipating expected effects of the NRA and other New Deal measures. This certainly explains why the national income increased far beyond what could be expected from public spending during this period. This anticipating boom could have established an independent factor of recovery if the volume and assortment of the additional production had corresponded sufficiently to the simultaneous increase in consumers' spending and in investing activities. The fact that commodity stocks were piling up indicates that these conditions were not fulfilled. The liquidation of these stocks in the second half of 1934 resulted in a conspicuous recession, which was mitigated, however, and finally overcome by the increased purchasing power created by public spending. Thus our national income figures show only a relatively small decline during this period.

Nor can the rising level of wage rates be acknowledged as a factor of recovery. On the contrary, it is not improbable that an increase of wage rates in the very first stage of recovery acted as an adverse factor, checking production and employment. But we should not exclude the possibility that the higher incomes, resulting from rising wage rates, pushed up the nominal national income more than it was pressed down by the decreased employment.

Can recovery be attributed perhaps to the success of the agricultural policy in raising agricultural prices and incomes? Certainly a correlation can be observed between the increase in agricultural incomes and the sales of industrial products in rural districts. And yet this cannot be understood as an independent factor of recovery. Whether the increased farm income was derived from increased prices or from benefit payments through processing taxes, it could be realized only through spending by the urban population. If the income of the urban population had not increased, the farmers' income could not have risen without a simultaneous decrease of industrial incomes. Then it would have been a mere shifting of purchasing power from one branch of the national economy to another. Both could expand at the same time only because there existed a source for increased urban purchasing power: public spending. Through the agricultural policy, the rural population was allowed to participate in the additional purchasing power created for the urban population through stimulating expenditures. Thus the agrarian policy cannot be regarded as an independent recovery factor [14] but rather as a means for a fair distribution of the recovery gains between the rural and urban population.

The revival of exports contributed in some degree toward recovery. In 1934, export values were about 450 million dollars greater than in 1933, and in 1935 showed a further increase of about 200 million dollars. But this influence was not extensive enough to constitute a decisive factor in recovery.

From NRA, AAA, and international trade, certain limited recovery influences may have arisen. There is, however, one important recovery factor which we can estimate: the 'investment' in automobiles. We assume that one third of the newly produced cars were bought out of current income, one third from existing liquid funds, and one third on installment. If deposits or other hoards accumulated during the depression are used for buying cars or if cars are bought on credit, this investment rep-

[14] An independent stimulant toward recovery could emerge from the agricultural policy only in so far as farmers bought additional equipment on credit, because of the improved economic situation.

resents a reflationary factor. We have tried to calculate the amount of this expansion and its secondary effects on the national income; the results are represented in the charts by the arrows. Here again leakages are estimated at 50 per cent in Chart I, and in Chart II they are assumed to decrease from 50 per cent to $33\frac{1}{3}$ per cent. Under the first assumption 12 per cent, under the second assumption 13 per cent of the increase in the national income can be attributed to additional investments in motor vehicles. We cannot assume, however, that such recovery factors as an increasing investment in automobiles and those in other durable goods are entirely independent of the strongest recovery factor, the stimulating expenditures. This can be demonstrated by the fact that after the bottom of the depression the registration of automobiles did not increase at the same speed in all states. The increase, to be sure, was stronger in those states in which registrations had decreased more than the average. But the correlation between the increase in registrations in the individual states and the improvement of economic conditions is closer than that between increased registrations in the respective states and the preceding decline. These investments, therefore, although they form a genuine factor of economic expansion, cannot be regarded as a cause of recovery entirely independent of the main factor, which is public spending.

The last recovery factors which must be mentioned are new investments in buildings and plant equipment. According to all statistics, these investments did not start in substantial measure until the second half of 1935. They, too, represent a genuine factor of expansion, but it is questionable whether they can be regarded as independent causes of recovery. As long as the income of the urban population did not increase sufficiently to raise apartment rents from the low depression level, as long as vacant dwelling space was abundant, no increase in building activities occurred. The index number for house rents did not show a substantial increase until early in 1935. We may conclude that these investments, as well as the new investments in certain industries, were not of the independent anticipating type but were rather the result of an increase in consumer purchasing power. Thus they may be regarded at least partly as tertiary effects of public spending.

If we bear in mind these subsidiary recovery factors, we can explain to some extent the main instances in Charts I and II where the curve of the actual national income has substantially passed the curve representing the effects of stimulating expenditures. On the basis of the facts that are known concerning these subsidiary factors, we believe that the assumption of leakages of 50 per cent, which we used in Chart I, is probably more realistic for the years 1933 and 1934, while the lower leakages, as assumed in Chart II, probably correspond better to the conditions of the year 1935. But we must emphasize how little we really know about these important facts we call leakages.

Adverse Factors

For the period 1933-5, the accruements in the national income that we calculated as the result of public spending and of consequent investment in automobiles are for the most part less than the actual accruements in the national income. Thus we may conclude that the effects of the recovery elements on which we based our calculation were not frustrated by 'adverse factors.'

Our charts show that in certain periods, especially in the second half of 1934, the hypothetical accruements in the national income were very close to the curve of the actual income; in Chart II, in fact, the estimated curve of spending effects surpassed substantially the actual curve of national income in this period.[15] But here we observe probably a reaction to the anticipating boom of the summer of 1933. During this NRA boom, which lifted the national income far above the effects we expected from public spending, stocks were piled up and a year later were liquidated with deflationary effects.[16]

[15] It is worth emphasizing again that Chart I, based on the assumption of leakages of 50 per cent, is probably more realistic for the years 1933 and 1934.

[16] The index of stocks in finished textile goods rose from 79 in May 1933 to 180 in November 1933, and declined to 159 in May and 119 in August 1934.

It might be said, however, that the adverse psychological factors cannot be adequately shown by the results of our calculations because they are already included in the assumptions on which these calculations have been based. Under conditions of very great optimism with regard to the effects of public spending, the transmission of these effects from one stage to the next can be accelerated, and thereby the whole process would be speeded up beyond our assumption of a 'speed of transmission' of six cycles a year. This acceleration, however, could have influenced only the distribution of the effects over the entire period and not the effect as a whole.

Optimism and pessimism among industrialists could also influence the factors determining some of our leakages. If industrialists do not believe in the permanence of the recovery brought about by public spending, their replacements of plant equipment will be postponed, and they will not spend their additional income but will save it for a recession which they expect to occur. It is probable that replacements were rather low in 1934 but increased in the second half of 1935, thereby diminishing industrial leakages. Psychological factors—a strengthened confidence among some groups after the Supreme Court's invalidation of the NRA, for example—may have influenced this upturn. But it is not necessary to resort only to psychological explanations. An upturn of this kind corresponds to theoretical expectations that in the course of recovery replacements will become increasingly unavoidable.

We have discussed only whether adverse factors affected the primary and secondary effects of public spending. There is at least the possibility that adverse factors may have delayed the tertiary effects in producers' investments. Might the delay in producers' investments have been caused by factors emerging from public spending? In this context two contentions should be considered: first, that public deficit spending destroyed confidence; second, that it exhausted the capital funds of the nation.

It is the general impression that the first period of confidence after the reopening of the banks was followed by a long period of uncertainty which did not end before the spring of 1935. This impression is confirmed by the behavior of stock prices. After reaching temporary heights in July 1933 and February 1934, they dropped in March 1935 to the low level of May 1933. Thus during a long period of public spending, confidence in recovery at least did not increase. But it would be wrong to infer from this that it was public spending which caused the lack of confidence. First, the upturn of stock prices as well as many other indices of business activity show that confidence grew after March 1935, although public spending was still continued. Second, if confidence had been shaken by public spending, the fear of inflation should have pressed down the prices of bonds in general and of government bonds in particular. But average bond yields (which express the general tendency better than bond prices) declined from 5.78 per cent in May 1933 to 4.41 in March 1935 and 4.11 in December 1935. The yield of Treasury bonds was 3.47 per cent in May 1933, 2.69 in March 1935, and 2.73 in December 1935. If there was a fear of inflation and if government obligations were regarded with distrust after the stabilization of the dollar, these feelings at least found no expression in the best symptoms available.

As to the second contention—that public spending exhausted the capital funds of the nation—the development of bond prices and bond yields leads to the conclusion that this also is not correct.

CONCLUSIONS

Summing up the results of a study such as this always involves the danger of drawing conclusions while forgetting that the findings were based on assumptions. Our positive results, especially the figures, must be understood more as illustrations than as exact measurements. This study has at least made clear the gaps in our information about facts that ought to be known for a definite answer to our question. The whole problem of leakages, for example, indicates a vast lacuna in our knowledge about fundamental facts in economic development. And yet we think that we can claim at least a certain probability for our assumptions. Therefore we venture to suggest a tentative answer to the question which we put at the beginning of this article about whether or not the 'pump priming' theory has stood the test of reality.

The 'pump priming' theory contends that stimulating spending results not only in primary but also in secondary increases in income and employment. A study of this recovery period shows that the upswing was not initiated by 'anticipating' private investments. Public spending filled this gap. And yet the recovery is not merely a reflex of the primary effects of public spending. The actual recovery can be explained only by taking into account the secondary as well as the primary effects of stimulating expenditures. With regard to this point we may say that the facts conform with the theoretical expectations.

The 'pump priming' theory also contends that after a certain period deficit spending can be stopped either by curtailing expenditures or by increasing taxes, without the danger of a new recession. With regard to this point it is much more difficult to draw any definite conclusions from our study. Stimulating expenditures reached their peak in the second half of the year 1934 and after that declined somewhat, while the nominal income and employment increased further. Thus we find indications—again in harmony with theoretical expectations—that a diminution in stimulating spending did not result in a new recession. We have attributed this fact to decreasing leakages, that is, to relatively increasing secondary effects of public spending and to beginning tertiary effects. These compensating factors, however, set in rather late and in a very limited degree. A more radical curtailing of deficit expenditures would probably have resulted in a recession. Why did these compensating factors not develop earlier and more strongly?

One kind of tertiary effect appeared rather promptly—investment in durable consumers' goods, such as automobiles and refrigerators. But investments in new houses or in industrial plants and other productive equipment started only slowly, in the last period of our analysis. A possible explanation for this delay is that deficit spending, though it brought about positive primary and secondary effects on recovery, nevertheless caused adverse factors which hampered the development of the tertiary effects. Such an explanation would be valid either if public spending exhausted the capital resources with which private investments could have been financed, or if confidence in the political and economic future was shaken by the deficits in public budgets. As to the first argument we can state rather definitely that credit funds available for private purposes did not decrease but, on the contrary, increased all through the period we have studied. As to the second argument there is no doubt that there existed some uncertainty in the political and economic future. This psychological factor alone is not sufficient to explain the delay in productive investments. Economic causes must also have existed.

Another possible explanation for the delay in tertiary effects is that in relation to existing idle capacities the stimulating expenditures were not large enough to lift the consumers' purchasing power up to the point where increased demand made new investments unavoidable, thereby overcoming even psychological hindrances. We must confine ourselves here to these few observations, for our material does not allow a definite answer to this problem. But this point—the transition from the secondary to the tertiary effects of public spending—seems to be crucial in explaining the slow recovery. It is also of the utmost importance to the problem of whether a more permanent public policy of stimulating investments (represented in housing projects, for example) should supplement the temporary policy of deficit spending.

7

War and Postwar Fiscal Policy

(1942) *

THERE are two approaches to problems of postwar economic re-construction. There is the need for preparing blueprints for action to be taken when peace comes. There is also the need for considering what measures can be devised to meet immediate wartime problems in a manner that also paves the way for postwar reconstruction. The present paper will deal with the latter.

What is meant by postwar objectives of present war policies can be easily illustrated by a few examples.

(1) The war policy of price stabilization has been justified on the grounds that it reduces the danger of a postwar price collapse and thereby facilitates postwar reconstruction. Such a policy, it is argued, also limits the increase in war costs and the national debt of the future, thus further reducing postwar difficulties.

* 'Washington Fiscal Policy: Its War and Postwar Aims,' with the assistance of Gerald M. Alter, *Fortune*, xxvi (4), October 1942.

(2) Forced investments in war loans, combined with progressive income taxes, has been proposed as a measure of war finance on the grounds that 'taxing the rich and borrowing from the poor' would tend to increase mass consumption in the postwar period and thereby help to reduce economic maladjustments then.

(3) The pending proposals for increased corporate income and excess-profit taxation are contested on the grounds that such taxes prevent corporations from building up reserves for postwar contingencies. According to this point of view, corporations survived the depression of the 'thirties fairly well because they entered that period in great liquidity. Under the impact of the presently [1942] proposed corporate taxes, it is argued, corporations will be prevented from building up liquid reserves and thus will have little resistance against a postwar depression.

These three examples show how postwar objectives may be cited in support of or in opposition to present-day war policies. They represent cases in which postwar planning is to be done now—not only by blueprints prepared for a later day but by present-day decisions.

Against any emphasis on the postwar aspects of present-day policies, it is claimed that in a war for survival those policies must be chosen that are best for the immediate purpose of winning the war. This objection is based on a misconception of the nature of government war policy. Postwar objectives cannot be ignored in devising fiscal policies to meet the war situation. If policies adequate to meet wartime needs can, in addition, aid in ensuring a solution to postwar problems, they are *better* war measures. The war is not an isolated episode separated from the past and the future. People fight today not only to win the war but to win the peace. Winning the war requires during the war the establishment of the conditions upon which a secure and free world can be built after the war. Obviously, if there is a conflict between the war and postwar objectives on any particular policy, the issue must be decided in favor of the former. It would be suicide to adopt, in the interest of postwar reconstruction, policies that actually impair the war effort. Thus, the three wartime fiscal policies cited above will be considered from this point of view to demonstrate the basic harmony between war and postwar objectives in three particular cases.

In our analysis of these postwar objectives we shall distinguish three phases of postwar development: the immediate phase of gradual demobilization; the intermediate phases of reconstruction; and the long-run phase of economic development.

THE CASE OF THE COST OF LIVING

The wartime cost-of-living stabilization program has been advanced as a measure designed to facilitate postwar reconstruction, the reasoning being that the stabilization of prices involved in this program will tend to avert a general postwar collapse in prices. The argument that an increase in prices during the war may lead to a collapse in prices after the war often seems to be so obvious that it needs no elaboration. Acceptance is based, first, on the belief that 'what goes up must come down'; second, on the experience of earlier war and postwar periods.

This much can be said: it is desirable to maintain prices during the war at a level that can be approximately sustained in the postwar period. If after the war we should be compelled to pay principal or interest on war bonds in terms of a lower price level than when the debt was contracted, we add to the relative tax burden. Furthermore, an inflationary price rise now is likely to bring about a distortion in the price structure, which would later require costly adjustments even if a general collapse in the price level could be averted. The more limited the war (or immediate postwar) increase in prices, the easier it will be in the postwar period to stabilize the price level and to adjust the economy to the international situation. Although some individual price adjustments adapted to lower costs will be desirable, the main attention can then be concentrated on maintaining effective demand for both capital and consumers' goods.

On the other hand, it has been said that rising prices and wages aid in the war effort, the former being conducive to an increase in production and the latter to an increase in the active labor force. If this view is correct, we should conclude that an attempt to stabilize prices and wages, though in line with post-war purposes, is in contradiction to an effort to increase production to the limit during the war period. If this is the case, adoption of the stabilization policy was a mistake. But is there really such a conflict between war and postwar objectives in this case?

It is certainly true that rising prices are conducive to or even necessary for increasing production in certain situations, but it is equally true that in other situations other incentives are more effective. Two quite different arguments are advanced for a price increase as an inducement to production. It is said, first, that higher prices permit larger profits, which, in turn, induce greater production; second, that increasing production, often accompanied by increasing costs, depends on increasing prices.

During the first period of the defense effort it was important to shift the economy from the low gear of depression to high gear. It was the time when war plans were still in the blueprint stage. It was thus desirable to use all facilities not yet directly employed in the war effort for stocking up with consumers' goods, particularly durables. A certain increase in prices, as well as increasing incomes, promoted such utilization. During this period it was necessary to control prices only of really scarce raw materials. At the same time, when an inducement to marginal production was desirable, increasing costs were met by paying higher prices. In the case of agriculture, prices of meat, dairy products, and other foodstuffs were permitted to go up, while the prices of corn and other fodder were held down in order to create the maximum incentive to produce meat and dairy products. The year 1941 brought a record in all types of production as well as in farm and business profits. The price-profit mechanism was thus adapted to the situation.

PRICE AND WAGE INCENTIVES BEGAN TO WEAKEN

The situation changed, however, with the end of the year 1941. With the United States directly involved in the war and with the rapid progress in procurement plans, the most drastic and expeditious conversion of all industries to war production became necessary. A general price incentive was no longer desirable. Government contracts could offer whatever price incentive was deemed desirable for direct war production.

It could even be argued that for the civilian sphere of production a downward pressure on prices might have made production unprofitable and created an incentive to maximum conversion. Experience has proved, however, that price deterrents are only partially effective as a steering mechanism when sudden and drastic turns in the direction of production are necessary. Only direct controls through the allocation of materials and organized conversion proved to be really effective.

The price incentive cannot be fully neglected in production for civilian use. Within the limits of available raw materials, manpower, and facilities, the greatest possible amount of civilian goods should be produced without impairment from a prohibitive price-cost relationship. All that is needed is a price sufficient to cover costs and permit a reasonable profit. No special incentive from constantly increasing prices was needed at this stage of the war effort.

During the year 1941, labor felt the effect of rising prices and, observing the profits of expansion, was all set for demanding wage increases that would not only make up for the increase in cost of living during the last year but, in addition, assure labor against the hazard of an anticipated further increase in prices. Thus, for another reason, price rises were losing their stimulating effect on production and became less effective as a means for curtailing consumption when the 'spiral' pushed up prices and wages in mutual causation.

Rising wages had a productive function, too, in the first period of the defense and war effort. In a great number of lines, wage rates increased more than prices of consumers' goods, so that an effective incentive for taking up work was created. However, it seems that from now on [1942] the incentive effect of rising wages can no longer be the main force in mobilizing the labor reserve. As long as the whole supply of civilian goods increased, an increase in real wages was still possible and indeed occurred on a large sale. With the reduction in civilian supplies, however, an increase in the spendable income of those just induced to take jobs must be offset by a reduction in consumption of those regularly employed. Thus, the use of higher wage rates to induce entry into the labor force must be strictly limited to substandard or inequitable rates. Appeal to patriotism, the pressure resulting from heavy taxes and forced savings, rather than the incentive of steadily increasing wages, must be relied on to increase the active labor force.

From the point of view of postwar reconstruction it probably would have been more desirable to stabilize prices and wages as of, say, spring 1941. Stabilization at that time, however, would have hurt the defense effort. It would have prevented the fullest possible use of labor and facilities during the initial period of the defense program. Price control of a selected number of scarce but essential commodities served as an adequate secondary policy during that period. Later price stabilization became the appropriate basic policy, as a general price rise with its spiraling effect no longer served a productive function. In cases in which the current price impedes a production otherwise possible and desirable, an adjustment should be made, either by permitting a carefully limited price or wage increase, or by paying a subsidy in certain cases. The subsidy is preferable in the case of services (like freight) that substantially affect the cost structure of many industries or in the case of life necessities (basic food), in order to prevent such a rise in the cost of living as would induce, in turn, demands for higher wages.

Thus it appears that in the case of price stabilization there is no real conflict between war and postwar objectives. A general price rise is no longer in the interest of the most intensive war effort, while price stabilization definitely is in the interest of postwar reconstruction. Price stabilization, along with all the implementing policies, contributes to organization of war effort by eliminating the futile race between prices and wages. It contributes to morale by reducing the injustice imposed by an accelerated price rise upon those in a weak economic position, and upon those who do not profit from rising prices and cannot adjust their income to the rising cost of living.

The Case of the Universal Savings Program

Keynes conceived the idea of financing a major part of the war expenditures by forced savings at a time when the deadly seriousness of the 'struggle for survival' was not yet realized. It is quite probable that he proposed the scheme because it seemed to serve equally well the needs of war finance and postwar reconstruction. In accordance with his interpretation of the Great Depression, Keynes expected that our economic system at higher levels of national income would suffer again from oversaving and underconsumption after the war.

The traditional policies of war finance—borrowing from the rich at increasing interest rates—would necessitate huge interest payments to the wealthy after the war and accentuate the economic maladjustments that were at least partly responsible for the gravity and duration of the last depression.

In the period between the wars, taxation of the wealthy, in combination with a desire to 'take the profits out of war,' was emphasized as an adequate measure of war finance. Though these policies were in accord with popular feeling, they contributed little to the immediate attainment of an adequate wartime fiscal program.

Heavy war taxes on the wealthy and forced borrowing from the poor was the ingenious proposal designed to meet at the same time the needs of war finance, the desire for a fair distribution of the financial burden, and the requirements of the expected postwar situation. War finance requires a drastic curtailment of private spending; and, in view of the modern concentration of expenditures in low- and middle-income brackets, a curtailment of the spending power of the masses above the subsistence level is necessary.[1] Such a policy, however, comes into apparent conflict with the requirements of a fair distribution of the war burden—imposing the greatest sacrifice on those best able to bear it. It is possible, however, to combine the need for the curtailment of mass purchasing power with the desire for

[1] About two thirds of consumer expenditures are made by people in the $1000 to $5000 income bracket [1942].

an equitable distribution of the financial burden, if (1) the im-
posts on the lower- and middle-income groups are levied partly
at least in the form of forced savings rather than completely in
the form of taxes, and if (2), in addition, effective progressive
taxes bearing heavily on the upper-income brackets are imposed.

Thus, it appears that again, as in the case of the price-stabili-
zation program, the proposed policy is justified because of its
merit as a war-finance measure. The postwar aspect can best
serve as an additional argument.

SAVINGS AS POSTWAR CUSHION

The forced or 'universal' savings plan has been criticized in
view of its postwar aspects. Two main arguments have been
leveled against it. The first is that the greatest possible portion
of war expenditures should be met by taxation in order to keep
down the national debt. Keynes or Hansen might answer that
the increase in postwar difficulties resulting from a larger national debt is more than offset by the wholesome influence ex-
erted by the additional stable spending power of the masses
enjoying interest receipts, and by the spending reserve that the
sale of bonds would represent in case of need. This leads, however, to a point of second criticism.

When Keynes recommended his plan he was certain that the
immediate postwar situation would be characterized by 'lack of
consumers' purchasing power and a redundance of saving.' At
that time nobody could imagine the full measure of destruction
that the war would cause in all continents and the degree of
conversion from peacetime to war production that is taking place
[1942] in all countries.

For the immediate postwar period we must expect a situation
of extreme scarcities of supplies in many lines of civilian goods
as compared with the demand that will be forthcoming. The
first postwar problem will not be too different from the war
problem: it will involve the conversion (or better, reconversion)
of industry and a restraint of consumers' demand. If millions
of people should try to cash in war bonds for financing purchases of new automobiles and other goods, which they were

143

not acquiring through the war years, the threat of a postwar inflation may be seriously aggravated. Of course, the war bonds will not all mature at the same time. Yet, it is conceivable that there will be tremendous popular pressure for permitting their immediate redemption after the war. Proper timing of such redemptions may be as difficult as was the proper timing of the payment of the veterans' bonus after the last war [World War I].

The postwar period of scarcity will be of a temporary nature only, though it is extremely difficult to venture any guess about the duration of that transitory period. This period will probably be characterized by two features, namely, scarcities with upward price pressures, on the one hand, and unemployment on the other hand. Measures to facilitate reconversion and public re-employment and retraining schemes, to cushion unemployment, will be necessary.

It is more difficult to predict the economic situation of the second postwar phase, or period of reconstruction. If the war should last very long and should cause more and more destruction on all continents, it may well be that civilization will have 'solved' the problem of oversaving and underconsumption for a long time to come. It may be that a large portion of productive forces will be absorbed by reconstruction at home and abroad, or that the standard of living will be able to recover only slowly from its wartime level. Strengthening mass purchasing power would not then be necessary.

It appears more probable, however, that in spite of the destruction ensuing from a long war, the need of outlets for the tremendous productive capacities will be experienced again very soon.[2] In such a situation full employment and economic development will again depend on an increase in mass purchasing power. At least in that situation—the third postwar phase of economic expansion—mass purchasing power strengthened by gradual liquidation of war bonds purchased in large quantities

[2] [1954 Fn.] When this was written (in 1942) it was not expected that world tension and a localized war would lead to partial mobilization soon after the end of World War II.

under the impetus of forced savings may be of great assistance.

The forced-savings plan thus poses not so much a conflict between the objectives of war finance and postwar reconstruction as a dilemma attributable to the different problems faced at different times in the postwar world. The expected scarcity of the period of economic demobilization and the expected opportunity for a tremendous increase in mass consumption in the later postwar period may call for a discriminating use of the reserve of mass purchasing power represented by war bonds purchased under a forced-savings plan. In view of the problems involved in securing such use, it seems reasonable to place the greatest emphasis on the war objectives of the forced-savings proposal.

Adoption of forced savings—or a system of voluntary saving through the payroll-deduction plan—makes it even more necessary, however, to prepare the public for the temporary continuation of some control measures, perhaps selective price control and rationing, in the immediate postwar period.

The Case of Corporate Taxes

It has been said that heavy corporate taxes during the war may aggravate the problems of economic demobilization and postwar reconstruction without being of much value as a war measure.

The main argument for corporate war taxes is of a merely fiscal nature. Most war expenditures become corporate receipts in one form or another. Corporate taxation is the most direct way of recovering for the Treasury a portion of these expenditures before they enter the flow of individual incomes in the form of dividends, management salaries and bonuses, and wages.

In addition to the fiscal argument there is the equity argument. Farmers cannot well be asked to forego the advantages of increasing farm prices and labor the advantages of wage increases if corporations are permitted to make high profits in a market where most of the risk is borne by the government. The argument that 'profits' can be taken out of the war by steep individual income taxes alone does not hold true because undistributed corporate profits escape individual income taxes (unless realized as capital gains).

Corporate taxation, though not a direct anti-inflationary measure, plays an essential role in an anti-inflationary program based on 'equality of sacrifice.' Corporate taxes assist in a policy designed to limit the increase in wage and farm incomes by making more acceptable a policy of curtailment of mass purchasing power.

On the other hand, there are limits to a policy of corporate taxation. In a fully developed war economy, the profit incentive is needed not so much to stimulate maximum production as to preserve economical management. It is not intended to discuss here the limits to corporate taxation beyond which the incentive to preserve economical management might be paralyzed; nor what devices, such as tax refunds, target prices, or management premiums, are available for maintaining a positive incentive even under heavy corporate taxation. In any case, it can be said that there are no arguments against heavy corporate taxes but only arguments for respecting a certain limit in corporate taxation.

But how about the argument that postwar considerations, if not war considerations, should also prevent us from imposing too heavy taxes on corporations? The argument is that corporations should be permitted to put a large portion of present war profits in contingency reserves, which can later be used either to make up for operating losses in the postwar period or for financing the reconversion of plants to peacetime production.

Earmarking a portion of profits as contingency reserves prevents their distribution as dividends. In that respect, the policy would be in accord with a wartime anti-inflationary fiscal program. The earmarking of a portion of profits as reserves does not in itself, however, determine for all time the use that will be made of these funds. A corporation might use the working capital preserved by such reserves for financing present plant expansion, for building up inventories, for accumulating bank deposits, for the purchase of stocks of other corporations, or for investments in government bonds. The present, as well as the postwar, effects of promoting the accumulation of corporate contingency reserves depend entirely on the use made of these funds.

War profits earmarked for contingency reserves and used for financing war-plant expansion or war-plant conversion cannot be used for financing reconversion or for paying wages in a postwar period. Such reserves may be used for writing off a capital loss without impairing the capital stock. The existence of such book reserves may be very useful, but their contribution to the problem of postwar reconstruction is limited. If reserves were so used, their establishment would not justify departure from a tax policy essential as a war measure.

The case is different, however, if the reserves are held in a liquid form either deposited in banks, invested in government bonds, or deposited with the government in other form. Such liquid reserves, used in a postwar situation, may actually offset deflationary tendencies. Again it may be useful to distinguish between the periods of economic demobilization, reconstruction, and long-term developments. Construction of war plants and conversion of industry were for the most part financed directly or indirectly by the government. How will industry finance the reconversion in the period of economic demobilization?

The Reconversion Problem

Reconversion might be financed by equity capital or the issue of obligations, bank credit, government credit (RFC type of financing may be used again for peacetime purposes), or by the corporation's own liquid funds. A great variety of methods for financing plant war conversion are used; probably an even greater variety of methods for financing peacetime conversion will be adopted. The use of the corporation's own funds appears especially desirable in cases in which the money is needed mainly for restoring a corporation's peacetime capacity. On the other hand, consider as an example a corporation that built a new war plant financed by the Defense Plant Corporation. The corporation intends to buy the defense plant after the armistice in order to convert it to peacetime use. The transaction would lead to an expansion of the productive capacity of the corporation beyond its prewar capacity. It would represent sound policy to broaden the capital basis for such a purpose. If the time should not be favorable for equity financing, a temporary financing by credit might be considered.

The case appears to be different, however, if a corporation rearranged its machinery and tools and adapted them to war production. By re-adapting its converted plant to peacetime use the corporation will only restore, not expand, its prewar capacity. To allow corporations to deduct from profits a contingency reserve up to an amount sufficient for reconversion of existing facilities and similar purposes might be worth consideration. Such a provision appears to be at least as justified as the special amortization provision for new war plants. Such a contingency reserve will serve its purpose, however, only if held in liquid form, or preferably deposited with the government with conditions attached to restrict its use to the designated purpose.

The case of reserves for reconversion is different from the case for postwar refunds of the excess-profits tax, embodied in British wartime tax laws and discussed in connection with the pending 1942 United States revenue bill. These refunds resulted from the attempt to reconcile wartime tax rates on excess profits of 100 per cent or approaching 100 per cent with the desire to maintain an incentive for economical war management. In attempting to use these refunds also as an instrument of postwar control, the British planned to make these refunds in accord with later government regulations in the interest of economic reconstruction. The conditional character of these refunds, certainly in the interest of postwar reconstruction, weakened their immediate purpose of promoting economical management. The British, therefore, moved in the opposite direction by making the promise for refunds more definite and thus weakened the postwar value of the measure.

The argument for establishing reconversion reserves is, of course, quite different from the 'rainy days' or 'cushion' argument. The 'cushion' argument is usually based on the experi-

148

ence of the depression of the 'thirties. It is said that corporations were able to weather the storm of the depression because
they had built up liquid reserves during the boom of the 'twenties. The existence of ample liquid reserves had, it is true, also
some effect on the economy as a whole. They enabled some
corporations, in spite of losses, to distribute deficit dividends
and to continue other payments without which the deflationary
effect would have been still more drastic. Yet this argument
should not be overemphasized. Part of these liquid funds, created not from reserves built up during the boom but from the
process of inventory liquidation that took place during the depression, reflected the forces at work during the depression. The
Great Depression taught us that these forces cannot be sup-
planted and depression overcome by confidently resting on corporate cushions.

Reserves for Rainy Days?

It is not intended to deny the desirability of earmarking a
portion of war profits as contingency reserves. In certain cases
such a policy should even be encouraged and could be facilitated and controlled by preferential tax treatment as discussed
above.[3]

The case for forced corporate savings (tax refunds) is quite
different from the case for forced individual savings. Forced individual savings may be, as we saw, an important factor in
strengthening mass purchasing power in a later postwar period.

Forced corporate savings or tax refunds may, on the other
hand, prove of value in the immediate postwar period of reconversion, but they will not be of great import for the long-run
period of reconstruction and economic development. The supply of funds for corporate expansion will probably not be the
most difficult problem of our future economic development. If
difficulties in future equity financing should occur, postwar revisions in the tax laws or the creation of appropriate financial

---

[3] The rehabilitation of firms that were forced out of production during
the war may also be a serious problem, one which cannot be solved by tax
provisions.

institutions can remedy such a situation. At least it must be assumed that these problems can be solved more easily than those involved in a steady expansion of consumers' purchasing power. These latter problems must be solved if full and steady use of our expanding productive facilities is to be made.

Thus we reach the conclusions that (1) corporate taxation during the war should be so limited that an incentive to economical production is maintained and so devised that corporations may be permitted to accumulate earmarked contingency reserves, for instance, in the form of deposits with the government for the reconversion of plants and similar purposes; (2) the present accumulation of corporate funds is not an effective safeguard against a possible postwar depression. The threat of a postwar depression must be fought by other means. If a steady growth in consumers' purchasing power can be assured, the difficulties in financing future expansion will not prove unsurmountable.

Our examination of three examples of financial war policies demonstrated that there is no real conflict between war and postwar objectives. In each case postwar arguments can be added for the support of a policy fully justified by consideration of the immediate war purpose. In the last two cases, however, different emphasis results from considering the immediate postwar period of economic demobilization, the intermediate period of postwar reconstruction, or the long-run period of economic development.

By pursuing the most effective fiscal war policies we at the same time contribute to the solution of postwar problems. It should, however, not be concluded that we need not worry about postwar problems as long as we pursue an effective war policy. The best war policies will reduce but by no means solve the many serious postwar problems. Despite the urgency of planning current war policies, it is also necessary to plan postwar policies. To make planning for war meaningful, we must also plan for peace.

8

Fiscal Policy and
Economic Reconstruction

(1945) *

THE PROBLEM

The wide acceptance [1] of fiscal policy as an instrument of economic policy can be attributed to a combination of two factors. The first is a deep-rooted skepticism about the ability of the free-enterprise system to assure automatically, without the support of government, full and steady employment of all avail-

---

* 'Fiscal Policy in Economic Reconstruction,' in *Economic Reconstruction*, ed. by Seymour E. Harris, New York, McGraw-Hill, 1945, chap. xiv.

[1] Cf., for example, writers coming from such different camps as those of Beardsley Ruml (see his speech 'Fiscal Policy and the Taxation of Business,' before the American Bar Association in Chicago, 11 Sept. 1944); and Raymond Walsh (address on 'Taxation and Fiscal Policy in the Postwar,' before the National Tax Association conference in St. Louis, September 1944). In an editorial in *Fortune* magazine of November 1944, p. 101, it is said, 'Social security and the use of a fiscal policy aimed to prevent the waste of boom and depression are fortunately no longer minority notions. They are English-speaking common sense.'

able resources. The second factor is an equally deep-rooted aversion to direct government regulation of economic activities. Fiscal policy appears to be the ideal instrument of government. It promises to influence private economic activities by a stabilization of aggregate markets with a minimum of direct government control of individual industries.

In this respect fiscal policy has an appeal similar to that of the neoclassical idea of use of central bank policy to steer a free competitive economy. The discount policy of the central bank was regarded as an effective instrument of over-all control at a time when regulation of the rhythm of business expansion was the main problem of economic policy. This concept of economic policy was in accord with the general economic conditions prevailing in the decade before and the decade after World War I. Variation in the discount rate was thought to work like applying and releasing the brakes of a vehicle moving downhill. It was no problem to make the vehicle move; the problem was to regulate its speed. When the vehicle has to climb uphill, however, the brakes can no longer regulate the movement; speed must then be regulated by feeding the engine with the proper amount and mixture of fuel. Markets are the fuel that makes the engines of business run. An assurance of markets becomes essential when business expansion is threatened by lack of markets. Thus it is certainly not an accident that the concept of fiscal policy was developed on the basis of the experience of the Great Depression.

Is the current acceptance of fiscal policy as a tool for postwar reconstruction then perhaps another example of 'cultural lag'? Is a tool derived from the unique experience of the 'thirties being recommended for a basically different postwar situation? What evidence do we have that the postwar world will be characterized by a lack of markets? The belief that there might be not only a temporary lack of markets but also continuing unemployment is by past standards truly unorthodox. It is a negation of the basic traditional notion of capitalistic expansion.

These patterns of classical economic dynamics are questioned among other factors on the ground that business expansion is largely guided by *existing* markets rather than by the confident anticipation that expansion will itself create *new* markets. Under such conditions, a decline in wage rates will not induce additional investments by improving profit expectation; it will deter investments because of the depressing effect of wage reductions on the markets for consumers' goods. Unless business actually expands more than is justified by *present* markets and unless business anticipates *future* markets, there is little chance that all savings will be absorbed by business investments at a high level of national income.

The essence of the so-called 'mature' economy is not 'saturation' of demand, or technological 'stagnation,' or decline in population increase, but the fact that the patterns of development differ in the earlier stages of industrialization from the patterns of growth in the later stages of industrial and institutional development.[2] If this interpretation is valid, then the Great Depression of the 'thirties was not merely another depression. It revealed a change in the structure of our economic institutions. Then it must be expected that the same fundamental problems will occur again sooner or later. The problem is one of adjusting our economic institutions, including government policies, to the requisites of balanced economic expansion at our stage of industrial development. Economic reconstruction is thus interpreted here to include adjustment to present-day patterns of economic dynamics. The general objectives of economic reconstruction, understood in that broad way, might be formulated as follows:

(1) Liquidation of certain distortions and maladjustments which the postwar period will inherit from the war period. Examples are mal-distribution of labor in relation to peacetime

[2] By pointing out one factor which I believe is of importance for the discussion of fiscal policy in a 'mature' economy, I do not deny that other factors—particularly changes in the *character* of technological developments—are of equal or even greater importance.

location of industry (involving a migration either of labor or of peacetime industries, or both); concentration (from special war advantages of large corporations); lag in technical equipment in certain farm regions and non-war industries; disproportionate development of certain wartime price and wage rates.

(2) Assurance that the sum total of the demand of consumers, business, and government will equal the potential production of goods and services at a level of full employment.

(3) A composition of total production, particularly a relationship between business expansion and consumption, which will be in such balance as to facilitate *sustained* expansion with a minimum of fluctuation.

(4) A composition and distribution of work and product that will give a maximum of social benefit compatible with that inequality in the distribution of incomes necessary to give adequate production incentives. We are interested not only in a high-speed, full-employment economy but also in an economy that serves the people and provides them with the goods and services most needed. This objective includes a proper proportion of years devoted by each individual to schooling, training, household work, gainful employment, retirement, and of work and leisure.

These four objectives are not all of the same immediate importance. A full-employment demand can probably not be assured unless certain wartime distortions are eliminated at the same time. The second objective, however, is of primary immediate importance. In pursuing it, the third and fourth objectives should be kept in mind, although they are guideposts rather than directly attainable goals.

What is the role that fiscal policies can play in the achievement of these objectives of economic reconstruction?

FISCAL POLICY IN THE PERIOD OF PARTIAL RECONVERSION

War curtailments have resulted in a considerable amount of deferred demand. Some part of war restrictions results simply in a loss of individual satisfaction which cannot or will not be deferred. The steak we did not eat during the war we shall never eat. There is, however, on the other end of the scale a category of deferred demand that is very likely to be made up. Certain household necessities, repairs of buildings and business equipment, certain public works, and restocking business inventories for trade in peacetime goods belong in this category. In between these extremes is that deferred demand which will become active demand if jobs appear pretty safe but which may be further, and perhaps indefinitely, deferred under conditions of postwar insecurity.

When victory in Europe makes possible partial resumption of production of civilian durable goods, while war production is still continued on a considerable scale, it is likely that demand will run high. Even if a cut in overtime should reduce current earnings, it can be expected that additional demand may be financed by accumulated wartime savings and that foreign demand will be high, offsetting a part of the decline in purchases from current domestic income. In that period markets for nondurable goods and services may decline while markets for durable goods may be under inflationary pressure.

Simultaneous inflationary and deflationary developments might well characterize that period of transition. Fiscal policy can make only a limited contribution at that time. Tax rates can be reduced to a considerable extent only when goods become plentiful again, presumably not before final victory. The possibility of tax reductions will be particularly delayed if some upward adjustment in wage rates should take place in this interim period. Proper timing of removal of direct controls and appropriate industrial reconversion policies will be of greater importance than variations in fiscal policies in the transition period.

FISCAL POLICIES IN THE POSTWAR PERIOD

Possible patterns of a peacetime full-employment economy

It is difficult to say how long the extraordinary demand for consumers' and producers' goods will sustain a high level of employment when war production is curtailed and finally reduced to a peacetime level.

It might be useful to demonstrate the order of magnitude of the problem. Under conditions of full peacetime employment in 1950, the gross national product should be not much less than the wartime gross national product in 1944.[3] Full peacetime employment requires that demand for non-war goods and services must increase by about the same amount by which war production and war services are reduced.

Such an increase in demand may occur in a variety of ways, depending on the proportionate share of consumers', business, and non-war government activities. Economists have developed possible patterns of a full-employment postwar economy and these aid greatly in helping us visualize the magnitude and character of the job to be accomplished.[4]

The National Planning Association has published a number of models of full-employment budgets for the nation.[5] These projections are expressed in dollars of the 1941 price level. I am selecting here only three of the seven National Planning Association models. These three models all show the same full-employment total gross national product. They differ, however, in the way in which the full-employment level is sustained.

The full-employment level of gross national product is achieved in model 1 by extraordinarily high expenditures of consumers; in model 2 by extraordinarily high business investments; in model 3 by heavy government spending. These various models can be

[3] This conclusion is based on an estimate of the size of the peacetime labor force in 1950 and the average output per man-hour at that time. It is assumed that the shift of workers from war industries implies in general a shift from higher to lower dollar output per man-hour. It is assumed further that productivity in each industry will continue its prewar increase and that wartime innovations in war production will be applied gradually in peacetime industries.

[4] See, among others, Department of Commerce, *Markets after the War;* Grover Ensley, 'A Budget for the Nation,' *Social Research*, x, September 1943; an address by H. C. Sonne, 'A Preview of National Budgets for Full Employment, "Model T," ' 8 June 1944.

[1954 Fn.] See 1954 Appendix, p. 169ff.

[5] Sonne, ibid.

TABLE I. THREE NATIONAL PLANNING ASSOCIATION MODELS *
OF THE NATION'S FULL-EMPLOYMENT BUDGET IN 1950,
COMPARED WITH 1941 AND 1944

(in billions of 1941 dollars)

Expenditures of	Model 1	Model 2	Model 3	1941	1944 **
Consumers	**$120**	$112	$99	$75	$76
Business (gross investment)	21	**29**	14	19	2
Government	29	29	**57**	26	93
Total gross national product	$170	$170	$170	$120	$171

* The National Planning Association publication gives considerable details
of the incomes and expenditures for each of these models. **Bold face** figures
indicate items in which an extraordinary increase is assumed.
** First half, annual rates, not seasonally adjusted.

of great help in an analysis of the various ways in which a
high-level peacetime economy can be sustained. They demonstrate that consumers' expenditures, or business investments, or
government outlays, or a combination of the three, must be
raised to an extraordinary (extraordinary, as compared with prewar patterns) level. How can fiscal policy affect consumers' expenditures, or business investments, or government outlays?

These projections present consistent patterns of a full-employment economy. In each case, the probable magnitude of two of
the main components is estimated on the basis of past experience, and then it is asked: How large must the third component
be in order to fill the 'gap'? A realistic target should probably
aim at a combination of the three with shifting emphasis in the
component parts.[6]

There is considerable doubt that consumption—given the expected distribution of income—would increase by about 45 billion dollars above present levels, even if a restocking boom
should lift total production and income to the full-employment
level in the transition period. This is true even if during that
period a part of consumers' savings is offset by some liquida-

[6] Balanced federal, state, and local budgets are assumed in the models
shown, and in models 1 and 2 they are assumed to be balanced at the minimum practical level of expenditures.

tion of the extraordinary wartime savings. An increase in consumers' demand to the level required to sustain a high-level income would necessitate specific efforts by government policy. Otherwise, a high level of income reached, say, through extraordinarily high investments during a postwar restocking boom would be bound to drop. If, however, an increase in demand is expected not only to *support* a high-level income but to help bring it about—in other words, if a high-level demand should be necessary to induce large investments and thereby cause the increase in incomes—the policy task becomes still greater.[7]

If balanced government budgets on minimum levels and a level of consumers' demand in accord with past experience are assumed, business investments must serve as the pivotal component to assure that a full-employment income can be sustained. The models indicate that in this case business investments must amount to about $29 billion (1941 prices).

It is very difficult to estimate what business investments are likely to occur after the restocking activities of the transition period have spent themselves. Although the required business investments are about 29 billion dollars (1941 prices) according to the models, the highest amounts realized in the period between the wars were 19 billion in the year 1920, and 18 billion in 1929. These were 22 and 18 per cent of the gross national product of these years. Gross investment was 17 per cent of gross national income in the decade 1920-29, 10 per cent in the decade 1930-39.[8]

For a gross national product of 170 billion dollars, the ratio of the 'twenties would suggest business investments of about 29 billion. This, however, is questionable in several respects. First,

[7] I emphasize this point of dynamics because the models indicate only the magnitudes needed to sustain a certain level of income and employment. They are 'static' models. What we need, in addition, are dynamic models that outline the ways in which we can make the transition from a low- to a high-level economy or can sustain a high level if one or more components (e.g. business investments) change.

[8] Derived from tables in the Appendix of the National Planning Association publication quoted above.

158

there are in the category of business investments component parts such as residential construction and net exports (or net capital investments abroad) which may move independently and differently from the gross national product. Second, in a period of heavy fluctuations the ratio of investment in plant and equipment to gross national product may be different from a level that can be sustained over a longer period of time.[9] Third, granted for argument's sake that there will be investments of 29 billion dollars *if* we have a full-employment income, it still would not follow that that level of investments will precede the high level of income so that these high investments will aid us in reaching a full-employment income. This leads us back to the statement made in the introductory section that business investments may fail in *anticipating* the full-employment level of markets.

An analysis of the various full-employment models in the light of past experience, with respect to the propensity to consume and the propensity to save and invest, indicates that a sizable amount must be added to consumption, investments, or government outlays, above what they would be without any special policy, in order to sustain a high-level income and employment. There can be much argument about the size of full-employment income and employment and about the appropriate conclusions from past experience concerning consumption and investments, but I do believe that the general order of magnitude cannot be very different unless a drastic change in behavior of business or consumers is expected.

Full-Employment Policies in General

Full-employment policies can be classified on the basis of these considerations as follows:

[9] A historical relationship for business investment, particularly plant and equipment, should be computed by possibly including, among other determining factors: (1) level of disposable income, (2) change in disposable income as compared with preceding year, and (3) the capital value (depreciable assets) of industry. The determining influence of investments on national income, however, appears to have been so strong that the statistical measurement of the influence of income on investments is hazardous.

1. Policies affecting the size of the full-employment income by influencing, for example:
    a. Hours of work.
    b. School age.
    c. Retirement age.
    d. Productivity of labor.
    e. Social hygiene measures.

2. Policies affecting consumers' demand by influencing, for example:
    a. Minimum wages.
    b. Propensity to save.
    c. Social-security measures.
    d. Tax policies, affecting size and distribution of disposable income.

3. Policies affecting business investments by influencing, for example:
    a. Replacement of worn-out or obsolete machinery in industry and agriculture.
    b. Stimulation of low-cost housing.
    c. Promotion of foreign investments and exports.
    d. Promotion of technological research.
    e. Development of power resources.
    f. Promotion of competitive investments.
    g. Tax policies designed to stimulate investments.
    h. Government underwriting of business investments (particularly for small business and investments not financed by private sources because of the risk involved).

The job of sustaining a full-employment economy is of such magnitude that it cannot be expected to be accomplished by any single device, certainly not by fiscal policy alone. On the other hand, it cannot be assumed that employment can be stabilized on a high level in a free-enterprise economy without the use of fiscal policies. It is difficult to sketch a blueprint of a future full-employment program in detail. It appears more important that the various types of policy be appraised regarding their potential contribution to a consistent and comprehensive full-employ-ment policy program.

REDUCTION IN WARTIME TAX RATES

In Models 1 and 2 above, it is assumed that the federal, state, and local tax systems of the postwar period will permit balanc-ing all budgets at the minimum practical level of expenditures and a high level of incomes. This tax objective requires tax rates well above peacetime rates but substantially below wartime rates. Let us assume, for instance, that this tax target permits a re-duction of tax rates equivalent to a yield of 10 billion dollars on the present tax basis. In deciding what kinds of taxes should be reduced, a number of factors will be considered, such as equity and costs of administration. From a fiscal aspect, that combina-tion of postwar tax reduction is best which will give the greatest increase [10] in the national product and employment.

Tax reductions (leaving other factors unchanged) affect income and employment through their effects on business investments and consumers' purchasing power. Pay-roll taxes, excise taxes, and the individual income tax are the taxes which—in that se-quence—affect purchasing power most directly. Wartime taxes on corporate profits are much more drastic than those on individ-ual incomes. Therefore, if only a limited reduction in taxes from the wartime level is possible, the reduction should aim first at removing wartime impediments to investment. If we could re-duce taxes only by the equivalent of, say, 2.5 billion dollars, the most desirable reduction would probably be a reduction in taxes on corporate profits. Wartime rates not only impair the incen-tives to economical management but also tend to restrict, and were designed to restrict, non-war investments. When corporate taxes are reduced, however, to the point where investment in-centives are restored, then each further reduction in rates will result only in a smaller increase in gross national product and

---

[10] The increase is measured by comparison with the gross national product as it would be under continuing wartime tax rates. It is possible, for instance, that this 'increase' in reality may be a smaller decrease in gross national prod-uct than would occur without the tax revision.

employment. If a further reduction becomes possible, excise taxes and individual income taxes should be reduced too.

In the accompanying chart, an attempt is made to illustrate the comparative effect of two groups of taxes: taxes on corporate profits and taxes on individual incomes.[11] The chart is so constructed that it shows what I believe are reasonable assumptions about the effect of the reduction of wartime tax rates. A re-

Chart I. Comparative Effect of Two Groups of Taxes

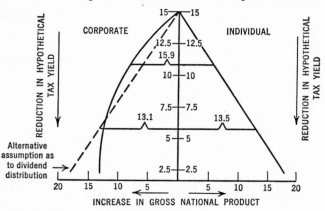

duction in taxes on corporate profits equivalent, for instance, to a yield of 10 billion dollars results in an increase in the gross national product of 13.1 billion, according to the major assumption [12] of the chart. A corresponding reduction in the standard rate of the individual income tax shows an increase of 13.5 billion dollars in the gross national product. If, however, the 10-billion-dollar reduction is divided equally between corporate and individual taxes, the resulting increase in gross national product, shown on the chart, is 15.9 billion.

[11] Richard Goode has provided the estimates on which the chart is based.
[12] The estimates vary, of course, according to specific assumptions with respect to the specific provisions of the tax reduction. The effect also differs in the case of large and small corporations. Many other factors should be taken into consideration which cannot be discussed here.

Once taxes have been reduced from their wartime level, each further reduction has a diminishing effect on investments and consumers' demand.[13] Tax reductions from lower levels result to an increasing extent in an increase in savings rather than in an increase in active demand.

The income- and employment-creating effect of tax reduction could be greatly increased if it were possible to discriminate between profits or incomes used for actual purchases or investments, and profits or incomes left idle. Also a liberal allowance for carry-over of losses may be more effective in stimulating investments than a small reduction in rates—once the rates are reduced from the prohibitive wartime level. Expenditures financed by a tax on idle funds [14] affect income and employment about the same as expenditures financed by bank borrowing, the former not resulting in an increase in the national debt.

Tax reductions or tax abatements will be effective as incentives for investment only if there are prospects for sufficient markets. Even with satisfactory market prospects, however, there may be certain factors hindering investment. Some of these impediments may well be offset by tax incentives. This whole question requires further exploration.

If reduction of federal taxes were the only means available for increasing consumers' demand, it might be concluded that most federal taxes should be at least temporarily discontinued.

The most important among the purposes of taxation, in my judgment, is to allocate relative contributions to the costs of government. This is not incompatible with the requirement to take into account economic considerations in revision of the tax system. Also the feasibility of varying certain tax rates within the limits of the basic tax structure should be explored and carefully weighed against the disadvantages resulting from tax-rate changes.

[13] The statement in the text refers to tax reductions in general. One can think, of course, of a specific sequence in tax reduction in which later reductions would have a greater economic effect than previous reductions.

[14] For the possibility of devising such a tax, see Chapter 4.

Reliance on tax reductions or tax bonuses as the major or sole device for regulating demand, as Lerner suggests, would violate all the other purposes of taxation. Such a policy would distribute the primary addition to disposable purchasing power in accord with what happens to be the distribution of the tax burden. Furthermore, it would give windfall gains not justified by economic effects to those individual or corporate taxpayers who use the tax reduction for an increase in savings rather than for an increase in actual consumption or direct investment.

It seems a fair conclusion that tax policy can help increase consumers' demand and business investments above wartime levels, but it can make only a moderate contribution toward bringing consumption and investment to the levels required for sustained full-employment.[15]

INCREASE IN GOVERNMENT EXPENDITURES
(FOR OTHER THAN WAR PURPOSES)

The high standard of living that is possible with present-day productivity also includes a high standard of government services. A high standard of government services in turn makes the accomplishment of a continuously high level of employment and incomes more feasible. A high standard of government services means enlarged government budgets (i.e. larger than the minimum figures of the models), but it does not mean waste of public money or make-work expenditures. Enlarged government functions must be discharged with even greater economy than expenditures on a smaller scale. The same instinct that revolts against spending money in an uneconomical fashion also revolts against letting national resources remain idle when there are such urgent needs to be served.

Various types of expenditure programs differ in their fiscal effectiveness just as various types of tax reductions have a different effect on income and employment.

There are, first, social-security programs with an automatically

---

[15] This discussion is not intended to deal adequately with all desirable revisions in the tax system.

anti-cyclical effect. They provide a cushion which mitigates the spiraling effect of a reduction in employment and incomes.

Second, there are expenditures with a high leverage effect. The railroad grants of the last century are an outstanding example. These grants made possible and stimulated investments of large private funds in railroads and railroad-equipment industries and opened up the development of entirely new industries and regions. Today there are still opportunities for developmental programs with a considerable leverage effect, such as programs for river development, urban rehabilitation and housing, and air-transport facilities. Regional programs are among the most effective means of stimulating private business investments. It is also possible that government programs may have a negative leverage effect, for example, those that deter business investments. In many fields desirable investments can be stimulated by government underwriting and guarantee. In such cases no directly corresponding budget expenditure is implied. It is quite possible that there will be in the future a growing amount of such quasi-private or quasi-public investments. We are only at the beginning in developing an adequate machinery for this type of government-business co-operation.

Besides the leverage effect, there is, of course, the effect of government expenditures on consumers' demand, and the effect on investments working indirectly through the increase in consumers' demand. The effect of government expenditures on consumers' demand during the 'thirties occurred to the extent expected, in accordance with economic theory.

There is more doubt about the indirect effects on investments during that period. One important factor may have been the uncertainty that existed about the continuation of a determined recovery policy. The fact that the need for a full-employment policy is so generally recognized now is an important condition for making the objective more easily attainable. I feel, however, that we should not rely too much on policy declarations alone. Business will have confidence in sustained demand only when it sees that policy declarations are implemented by provisions for an adequate legislative and administrative machinery.

Deficit Spending and Economic Reconstruction

It is very unfortunate that an active fiscal policy is frequently identified in the public mind with simple 'deficit spending.' The concept, deficit spending, is misleading because it suggests that it is the deficit—or the surplus—which is the essence of the income-creating or income-absorbing effect of fiscal policy. That is an unwarranted oversimplification. As far as the size of the deficit is concerned, it makes no difference whether taxes are reduced or expenditures increased. As to the effect on actual demand and employment, there is a considerable difference, however, between a tax reduction of $1 billion and an increase in expenditures of the same amount. With respect to tax reductions or tax increases, the effect depends on the type of taxes; and the same holds true in regard to various types of expenditures. There is the possibility of income-creating expenditures financed by taxation, provided the right kind of expenditures and the right kind of taxes are selected.

An increase in government expenditures contributes most to aggregate demand, of course, if it is financed by methods of taxation or borrowing that curtail consumers' demand and business investments by only a minimum. Considering the limits of progressive taxation and of taxing idle funds, it is probably true that an effective fiscal policy does imply in practice that a portion of government outlays must be financed by borrowing at times when a contracting tendency prevails in the economy. Surpluses and debt redemption can be expected in periods of excessive demand. The deficit or the surplus, however, is not the essence of an effective fiscal policy.

The models demonstrate that the nation's budget is in balance only when an excess of private incomes over expenditures is offset by an excess of expenditures over revenue in the government sector, or when an excess of outlays over income in the private sector is offset by an excess of revenue in the government sector. The presentation of the models in the form developed by Grover Ensley and the National Planning Association demonstrates this relationship very clearly. The presentation above gave only the expenditure side of the nation's budgets. As an example, two other of the National Planning Association's models are given in more detail in order to demonstrate the income-expenditure relationship in case *A* of a federal surplus, *B* of a federal deficit.

This presentation should not detract from the fact that fiscal operations do affect not only these government surpluses and deficits but also consumers' spending and savings and business investments and accumulation of business funds. Fiscal policy truly affects each component part of the nation's budget.

TABLE II. THE NATION'S BUDGET IN 1950 *
(in billions of 1941 dollars)

	A		B	
Consumers:				
Disposable incomes	$120		$129	
Expenditures	106		113	
Net savings		$+14		$+16
Business:				
Accrual of funds (undistributed profits and depreciation and other reserves)	13		10	
Gross investments (including residential construction and net exports)	32		14	
Use of additional funds (equity capital or borrowing)		−19		−4
State and local government:				
Income	11		10	
Expenditures	10		10	
Surplus		+1		0
Federal government:				
Income	26		21	
Expenditures	22		33	
Surplus or deficit		+4		−12
Total:				
Funds disposable for expenditures	$170		$170	
Expenditures	170		170	
Surplus or deficit		0		0

* *Cf.* Sonne, op. cit.

167

Fiscal policy does imply an influence on consumers' demand, but it requires more than simply turning on and off a faucet to regulate the flow of purchasing power by deficit spending. It is true that each disturbance in economic relations resulting in contraction of production and incomes *can* be offset by creating additional purchasing power. An economic disturbance is not eliminated, however, by overcompensating its contracting effect. Economic and fiscal measures as part of a policy of economic reconstruction must aim at creating conditions for *sustained* and *balanced* expansion.

A policy of sustained and balanced expansion may require changing the emphasis on various aspects of a full-employment policy. Such a policy can be outlined only on the basis of a detailed analysis of expected economic development over a number of years. Here I can only allude to the possible changes in emphasis that may be required during the postwar decade.

In the period of transition from a war to a peace economy, it will probably be of paramount importance first to facilitate business investments which were delayed during the war and which will be necessary for a high-level peacetime economy, in addition to those outlays abroad which may be necessary in the interest of international reconstruction. At the same time, it will be necessary to strengthen the income cushions which protect the system against the shock of contraction in case the restocking boom should come to an abrupt end.

As an objective of a longer-run policy, all measures, including fiscal policies, will be essential that assure a permanently high-level consumers' demand and an increase in the average time an individual spends in school and training or retirement. A shortening of working hours also belongs in this category.

All these efforts may fall short of the objective, either because they are not sufficiently effective or because they are subject to cyclical variation. Variation in expenditure and tax policies appears to be the most appropriate policy to deal with such situations. Fiscal policies are involved in each of these phases of a policy of economic reconstruction, but the fiscal policies must, with a variety of other measures, be integrated into dynamic patterns of economic policy.

INSTITUTIONAL ARRANGEMENTS

This outline of a dynamic economic policy may be regarded as aiming at an unattainable ideal. It might be questioned whether our government institutions and our knowledge of economic facts are adequate for the task. This is certainly a valid question. But such an admission should not discourage a movement in the direction of a necessary policy. We learn to swim only in the water. We shall develop an improved machinery for a comprehensive and consistent policy only by embarking on such a policy.

Projections may be needed not only of the broad outlines of the nation's budget but also of the demand for specific categories of consumers' and producers' goods to be expected on an anticipated level of national income. A projection of future current demand in turn should make possible estimates of the needed increase in capital equipment. Statistical projections of this character will be useful as a guide for government policies (for instance, with respect to stimulation and underwriting of business investments). They will also help in raising the sights of business. If business determines its investment policies in the light of expected, and not just existing, markets, the task of government policies to assure full employment will become more manageable.

[1954 APPENDIX]

The models used in this chapter were taken from the National Planning Association publication, 'A Preview of National Budgets for Full Employment, "Model T," ' June 1944. A number of revisions and refinements were subsequently made in the models, and the final versions were published in 1945 in the NPA study, *National Budgets for Full Employment*. One model presented purported to represent the distribution of production most likely to materialize if 1950 should be a year of full employment.

169

In the NPA study, *The American Economy in 1960,* 1952, the old projection for 1950 was re-examined. With respect to both size and distribution of gross national product, the NPA projection was found to be remarkably close to the pattern that actually emerged in 1950. This was true when a comparison was made of the percentage distributions of the shares purchased by the major sectors, and also when the shares were expressed in constant dollars.

TABLE III. COMPARISON OF NPA PROJECTED DISTRIBUTION AND ACTUAL DISTRIBUTION OF 1950 GNP

Purchaser	Actual		NPA Projection	
	1950 Dollars	*Per cent*	*1941 Dollars*	*Per cent*
Consumers	194.3	68.4	116.3	68.4
Business	48.0	16.9	28.3	16.6
Government	41.9	14.7	25.4	14.9
Total GNP	284.2	100.0	170.0	100.0

	Actual		NPA Projection
	1950 Dollars	*1941 Dollars* *	*1941 Dollars*
Consumers	194.3	116.5	116.3
Business	48.0	28.9	28.3
Government	41.9	24.1	25.4
Total GNP	284.2	169.5	170.0

* Consumer and government purchases were deflated separately by Commerce Department deflators for these series, and their total subtracted from deflated projected GNP to arrive at business expenditures as a residual. Business expenditures, as used here, cannot be deflated directly because no account is taken in the published deflator index of change in business inventories or of net foreign investment.

The pin-point accuracy of the NPA projection is partly fortuitous. In the first place, 1950 was not a 'normal' full-employment year; the latter part of the year was affected by the outbreak of hostilities in Korea. Secondly, the projected and the actual 1950 figures are not strictly comparable because of the conceptual revisions made in the GNP series in 1947, such as the exclusion of government interest payments and the inclusion of imputed net rent on owner-occupied houses. Thirdly, since the projected 1950 GNP was the result of a rather refined estimating process, it is possible that a correct total might conceal some incorrect but offsetting components. Nevertheless, disregarding the spurious exactness of the projection, it still remains that the projected increase in potential production over a number of years was very close to the actual increase, and that the projected distribution represented a fair approximation to a realistic pattern of resource allocation. To that extent, this experience gives some confidence in the method.

9

Technical Requirements
for an Effective Fiscal Policy

(1945) *

I

Maintaining high-level production and employment is widely recognized today as a desirable objective of government policy. Those who oppose the government's accepting express responsibility for the achievement of this objective insist that government in a free-enterprise economy is not equipped to live up to such a responsibility. Criticism comes from two sides. Protagonists of a *laissez-faire* economy fear that a government pledged to assure full employment will be driven into more and more planning and regimentation. Protagonists of a planned economy, on the other hand, insist that any attempt to solve the problem of full employment within the framework of free enterprise will

* 'Maintaining High-Level Production and Employment: Technical Requirements,' *The American Political Science Review*, XXXIX, December 1945, pp. 1126-37.

be futile. They fear that such an effort will only delay the transition to a planned economy, which they believe is the only final solution of our economic and social problems.[1] Both groups of critics maintain that the technical requirements of a policy designed to maintain full employment are incompatible with a free-enterprise economy.

What, then, are the technical requirements of a policy of full employment? Is the government equipped, or can it be equipped, to do the job without paying the price of adopting a regimented economy? Perhaps those who speak of full employment in a free-enterprise economy are driven into the same dilemma in which the oldster found himself when telling his grandchild about the alligator chasing the frog. The frog jumped from the log into the river, swam through the river, hopped on land—the alligator coming closer and closer. When the alligator finally cornered the frog under a tree and opened his mouth to swallow him, things were getting desperate for both frog and storyteller. The old man knew only one solution: 'The frog looked up and saw the tree and just as the 'gator's jaws were closing down, the frog flew up into the tree.' 'But Grandpa,' said the little boy, 'frogs can't fly.' ''Deed they cain't, Son, 'deed they cain't,' was the answer, 'but this frog flew . . . he had to.'

Economic insecurity threatens our national and individual existence. What is the solution? Must we change from a jumping, swimming, and hopping frog into a flying frog? Must we radically change our institutional equipment, our ways of work and living? Or can we influence the general level of economic activities without attempting to control all of them in detail? Can we, in other words, insure job opportunities without telling everyone what to produce and what to consume? No exhaustive answer to these questions can be given in a short paper. But before even trying to answer them we should investigate the requirements of a policy of full employment in a free-enterprise system.

---

[1] [1954 Fn.] For a recent example of this type of criticism, see Paul A. Baran, 'National Economic Planning,' in *A Survey of Contemporary Economics,* vol. II, ed. by Bernard F. Haley, 1952.

II

There has, of course, never been a free-enterprise system without important governmental activities supporting, supplementing, and limiting private economic activities. We observe in reality a multitude of intermediate stages between the hopping and the flying frog of our parable. Here we are not concerned with public policies that affect only specific interests, such as measures designed to protect labor, aid agriculture, subsidize shipping, or foster any particular industry. We are concerned only with policies that affect the general level of economic activities and thereby the general availability of job opportunities. All through the history of economics and economic policies governments have searched for that device of policy which could be used as a lever for influencing economic development as a whole.

In the time of mercantilism, it was thought that the circulation of money—and money meant coin minted of precious metals—was the critical element in economic expansion. More money in circulation meant more business; reducing money in circulation caused economic stagnation. Money was added by import of precious metal, which in turn required stimulating exports and discouraging imports of merchandise; this was called a 'favorable balance of trade,' while an 'unfavorable balance of trade' drained money off for payment of the import surplus. Thus, influencing foreign trade was regarded as the key to a government policy designed to promote economic expansion.

When it was recognized, however, that money could be added not only by the import of precious metals but also by the creation of bank credit, policy guidance of foreign trade lost its use as a lever for influencing economic activities as a whole. It was relegated largely to the status of a device for protecting specific industries and interests. Central bank policy now took the role of the prima donna in the theater of economic operations. Lowering the discount rate was viewed as a means to stimulate the use of bank credit and to encourage economic activities in general. Conversely, an increase in the discount rate was looked upon as an effective damper on such activities, particularly speculative ones. This was the economic policy devised by the so-called neo-classicists—a policy believed to be effective for influencing economic activities in general and yet compatible with an otherwise *laissez-faire* attitude. The neoclassical theory prevailed among economists during the first quarter of this century.

The Great Depression of the 'thirties shattered confidence in the effectiveness of central bank policy as a steering mechanism for a free-enterprise economy. Even though credit policy was not ineffective as a brake on speculation and remained in use for stimulating certain types of business investments, it could no longer be regarded as *the* strategic weapon with which a slack economy could be lifted to a level of full employment. The conclusion suggested itself that the government must come to grips with a more vital element of the economic mechanism. What could be assumed to be the most vital element in economic development?

Classical theory taught that low prices for the factors of production—particularly low wages and low interest—cause expectation of profit and induce businessmen to expand production and hire more workers. More production means increased disbursement of money in the form of payrolls, and hence additional purchasing power. Expanding business thus creates its own market—if only (a) the costs of factors of production are sufficiently low, and (b) credit is available to bridge over the time until markets have been expanded. But during the depression costs of factors of production were low, and plentiful credit was available, yet business did not expand.

Perhaps business does not dare to expand except when orders come in or markets can be anticipated with a high degree of certainty. If government wants to influence business activities without directly telling business what to do, it must increase the amount of active purchasing power in the hands of consumers. It can do that, for instance, by additional government expenditures for public works and other developmental projects which put idle resources to useful work, at the same time augmenting wages and purchasing power and creating markets for business. Or the government can reduce taxes, thus freeing purchasing power and helping to revive markets.

With the recognition of these interrelations, a new weapon was added to the economic arsenal of democracy: fiscal policy. Fiscal policy has been defined as government expenditures, revenues, borrowing, and debt management, considered with a view toward their impact on the flow of purchasing power. Fiscal policy does affect the general level of economic transactions and job opportunities without interfering with the basic principles of free enterprise, freedom in the choice of a job, and freedom in the choice of consumption. It can be used for deflating a boom and for stimulating a slack market. Thus, it appears that finally, on the basis of more refined economic theory and the depression experience, the long-sought lever of economic policy has been found.

III

The experience of the Great Depression not only furthered the development of fiscal theory but also served as a first testing ground for the effectiveness of fiscal policy. The statistical record of the depression years made it almost certain that an increase in government expenditures caused an increase in purchasing power and recovery in business activities. War experience has proved the point beyond doubt. Yet there remained the fact that the same amount of additional federal expenditures had a different effect on production and employment under various circumstances. Analysis of the record suggests that during certain periods the results of a job-creating fiscal policy of the federal government were partly offset by unfavorable effects of other policies, federal, state, and local. For instance, during the depression state and local governments adopted sales taxes which hindered a price decline and reduced consumer purchasing power. These governments were also often forced to reduce their

176

own outlays for public works and other purposes. By the financial exigencies of the depression, they were driven to pursue policies that directly counteracted the efforts of the federal government.

The policy of emergency expenditures induced an increase in consumer expenditures in accord with theoretical expectations. It brought forth, however, only a relatively small amount of additional business investments. Business apparently did not feel sufficiently assured that the government would continue the recovery policy of sustaining purchasing power—a strong argument in favor of clear statutory sanction of a governmental full-employment policy.[2] Nor was the tax policy of the federal government brought into accord with its other fiscal policies. In addition, some measures of wage policy, while fully justified on their own grounds, were not conducive to the recovery of production and increased employment. The price policy of the National Industrial Recovery Administration is another example of inconsistency. It is true that low costs of factors of production were not sufficient to engender profit expectations in view of shrinking markets. It is also true, however, that government-supported markets will induce economic expansion only if business has confidence in sustained profit expectations.

The war experience afforded another test of the effectiveness and limits of fiscal policies. Fiscal policy was included in President Roosevelt's program to combat inflation and insure economic stabilization. If fiscal policy alone had been chosen to do the job, we should have needed much more drastic tax or saving measures than were politically acceptable. Fiscal policy had to be supplemented by a great many other measures, such as price and wage and credit policies. Both the depression and the war taught us the lesson that fiscal policy is a very useful tool, but not a panacea. The task of maintaining high-level production and employment is too big to be accomplished by any single device. Fiscal policy can be effective only when reinforced by many other policies.

[2] [1954 Fn.] Written before the adoption of the Employment Act of 1946.

An example may illustrate the limits of fiscal policy as a governmental tool. Assume that monopolistic organizations exist in an economy, enabling certain businesses to realize extraordinary profits. Assume further that a large part of these profits is neither distributed as dividends nor used for expansion of industrial facilities, but accumulated in the form of deposits or invested in securities. An accumulation of 'idle' funds may introduce into the economy a deflationary trend and cause a slump in employment. In a situation like this, it is possible, of course, to offset the deflationary trend caused by monopolistic profit accumulation through additional government expenditures or tax reduction in order to assure continuing full employment. Such a policy would be possible but unwise, for it would not remove the basic cause of the deflationary trend. It would be wiser to introduce measures designed to prevent the monopolistic practices or to tax away a portion of profits not put to active use. Such measures may often require time to work out and fail to succeed fully in removing the cause of deflation. Fiscal policy, then, should be used as a prompt but temporary device, to be applied to those situations in which other measures fail to bring about the desired result. It is therefore not enough to identify deflationary trends and use compensatory fiscal measures. In addition, the underlying causes of such deflationary trends must be analyzed and all policies available in the 'tool chest' of government must be put to work on them.

These additional policies include foreign-trade policies, wage policies, price policies, subsidies, federal grants to state and local governments, education policies, and so forth. All of them are used for specific purposes, often for purposes of particular vested interests. They are powerful tools of policy, but partly ineffective as far as the general level of employment is concerned, because frequently the effects of one type of policy counteract another. Perhaps high-level production and employment can best be secured not by any further addition to our tool chest of policies but by a procedure that permits the consistent and sustained use of all available policies in a co-ordinated program.

178

'The most powerful weapon in the economic arsenal of democracy is coordination of a great variety of policy devices.'[3]

The proposed Full Employment Act reflects the experiences of the depression and the war with respect to economic and fiscal policies. Its forerunner, the so-called Patton Bill,[4] placed all emphasis on a provision for increasing government outlays should private business fail to invest an amount sufficient to keep the economy going at full blast. No reference was made to any policy except government lending to business, and outright government spending if private enterprise should be unwilling to borrow for business expansion. Quite contrary to this version, the pending Senate bill (S. 380) lists a long catalogue of federal policies which should be considered in the President's program of action.[5] The emphasis of the present bill is placed (1) on a declaration of policy of full employment, and (2) on the establishment of a legislative and administrative procedure for formulating a co-ordinated program of policies designed to attain full employment. Government expenditure is treated as one instrument of policy to be used if all other policies combined prove inadequate to assure full employment in a specific period. Government expenditure is also regarded as being the policy device most adaptable to short-run fluctuations in business conditions and as being particularly useful because it is the most flexible element in the whole program.

The present bill provides only for the use of policies which are authorized by existing statutes or which Congress may authorize by future legislation. It proposes a legislative and administrative mechanism designed to achieve co-ordination and timely application of whatever policies Congress has adopted. Only the co-ordinated and well-timed use of these policies can accomplish the job. Confidence in the government's determina-

[3] Budget Director Harold D. Smith, in his testimony on the Full Employment Bill before the Subcommittee of the Senate Committee on Banking and Currency, *Hearings*, 79th Congress, 1st Session, 30 August 1945.

[4] See James G. Patton, 'The Federal Government's Role in the Postwar Economy,' in *The American Political Science Review*, XXXVIII, 1944, pp. 1127ff.

[5] [1954 Fn.] This catalogue of federal policies was eliminated in the final version of the Employment Act of 1946.

tion is the most essential prerequisite for the success of a policy of full employment because assurance of job opportunities, by the same token, means assurance of markets conducive to business expansion.

IV

Even the most perfect policy devices can be used effectively only when the program they are to serve is formulated on the basis of an accurate diagnosis of business conditions. One of the most interesting features of the Full Employment Bill before Congress is the provision for a 'production and employment budget' (national budget). In the version adopted by the Senate, the bill requires the President to transmit to Congress annually, with quarterly revisions, two kinds of estimates: (1) for the ensuing year or longer periods, estimates of the employment opportunities needed for full employment, the production of goods and services at full employment, and the volume of investment and expenditure needed for the purchase of such goods and services; and (2) estimates of 'current and foreseeable' trends in the number of employment opportunities, the production of goods and services, and the volume of investment and expenditures for the purchase of goods and services, not taking into account the effects of the general program of policies that is to be recommended in the same message.[6]

[6] It is not intended to review here all statistical requirements of the bill in detail. The discussion is limited to the essentials.

[1954 Fn.] The Employment Act of 1946 dropped the specific provision for a 'production and employment budget,' but it did require the President to include in the Economic Report estimates of (1) 'levels of employment, production, and purchasing power . . . needed to carry out the policy' of the Act, (2) 'current and foreseeable trends in the levels of employment, production, and purchasing power,' (3) 'a review of the effect of existing economic programs upon employment, production, and purchasing power,' and (4) 'a program for carrying out the policy . . . [of this Act] . . . together with such recommendations for legislation as [the President] may deem necessary or desirable.'

The estimates of employment, production, and purchasing power objectives, of current and foreseeable trends, and the appraisal of existing programs and the recommendations of new programs that may be needed require actually the same kind of projections which the original bill contemplated for inclusion in the Production and Employment Act.

In the event that the projected national income is estimated to be below the national income necessary for full employment in the ensuing period, the President is required to recommend a program of policies designed to lift the national income to the full-employment level. If the projected income exceeds the income necessary for full employment, an inflationary tendency is indicated and the President should recommend measures designed to curb the inflationary trend. This is a very neat, logical prescription for policy formulation. Are we at present technically equipped to supply these estimates with a reasonable degree of accuracy? What technical arrangements are necessary to secure such estimates?

V

The estimate of the labor force should not cause great difficulties on the basis of current statistics. The factual data are supplemented by surveys of employment intentions. There are special difficulties in the period of transition—when millions of workers pulled into the labor force during the war must decide whether to withdraw from it or to seek continuing employment, and when millions of veterans must make up their minds whether to turn to civilian employment or to avail themselves of the educational facilities offered them. Under peacetime conditions, the estimate of the labor force for the ensuing year will be less problematical.

The estimate of the national income required for full employment and production implies an estimate of the average productivity per worker. This may raise considerable difficulties if the estimate is intended to cover a period far into the future. For the ensuing year, a reasonable approximation should be much easier because productivity does not change very suddenly from year to year.[7] When there is considerable unemployment at the time the estimate is made, it cannot be assumed that the unemployed, if employed, would produce the same as the av-

---

[7] [1954 Fn.] Today I would modify this statement by saying that year to year changes in productivity are rather erratic, but that a projection over a number of years can be made with somewhat greater confidence.

erage of all workers. But this difficulty can also be overcome on the basis of reasonable assumptions about possible ways in which the unemployed might be re-employed.

More serious problems arise when a projection of national income and production and a quantitative appraisal of proposed policies are to be made. The past record of business forecasting is not too encouraging. More cases of dismal failure than of successful prediction can be cited. Strictly speaking, the pending Full Employment Act does not imply prediction of business conditions but projections—that is, hypothetical predictions based on the assumption that no new policies of full employment or economic stabilization are to be adopted by the federal government. Thus the bill avoids the need to guess what policies Congress will enact.[8] More important, however, is the fact that most business forecasts of the past, particularly of the 'twenties, were based on the so-called 'business barometers.' These 'business barometers,' in turn, rested on very shaky statistics and theories. Recent developments in the theory of economic dynamics and a spectacular improvement in statistical methods and sources have greatly increased the possibilities of economic projections. The growth of scientific sample surveys should be mentioned particularly.

This is not the place for a detailed description of the methods of economic projection which may be used under the Full Employment Act, and which, as a matter of fact, are already in use by many business and government economists. I shall only describe briefly the main principles on which the possibility of economic projections rests.[9] It is very important that actual

[8] The often mentioned inaccuracy of the forecasts of federal expenditures in the official budgets can largely be explained by the fact that these estimates usually did not take account of legislation subsequently adopted by Congress. Critics overlook the fact that they were hypothetical projections rather than predictions.

[9] In a British White Paper, on Analysis of the Sources of War Finance and Estimates of the National Income and Expenditure in the Years 1938 to 1944, Cmd. 6623, London, 1945, it is said: '. . . the problem of maintaining employment is very largely the problem of maintaining total expenditure, public and private, and in an economy where this is accepted as one of the prime aims of government policy it becomes peculiarly important to have not only

estimates of the so-called national budget should be available for the most recent past, if possible up to the time when the projection is to be made.[10] It is much easier to project economic trends by estimating changes from the most recent past than by estimating directly the absolute totals for a future period.

Changes from the base period may be divided into primary and secondary. Going down the line, item by item, the estimator asks himself what changes in economic transactions he has reason to expect. Assume, for purposes of illustration, that we are in a postwar restocking period, say in 1948, with conditions of high employment, and now have to make a projection for 1949. First, there are the expenditures of the federal government. They are expected to decline—disregarding in the projection all new programs that may be enacted on the basis of the President's recommendations—because certain demobilization expenditures will be discontinued.[11] Business investments have been running high, and the ratio of capital in plant and equipment to current sales indicates that a turning point in business investment may be near. The sample survey of contemplated investments in plant and equipment confirms that some of the investments, deferred during the war period, have now been completed, and that businessmen expect a decline in their new investment. Residential construction, however, is still increasing. Statistics of permits for residential construction show an upturn. A continuing increase in residential building is therefore expected. Also, the deferred demand for automobiles and for durable household

statistics adequate to measure that expenditure, but a method of bringing them together and classifying them which makes possible the necessary comparisons with the immediate past and with the present position in other countries' (p. 2).

[10] It is quite significant that the President's budget for the fiscal year 1946, submitted to Congress early in January 1945, included estimates of the nation's budget for the calendar year 1944, and that the 1946 budget review, issued by the budget director 2 August 1945, presented the nation's budget for the fiscal year ending 30 June 1945. The last quarter in each of these estimates has, of course, more the character of a forecast than of an estimate based on actual statistics. In the past, estimates of national income were available only several years after the end of the period.

[11] [1954 Fn.] I remind the reader that this hypothetical description of the business outlook for 1949 was written in 1945.

equipment has not yet been satisfied; the demand for television sets and other new devices is still going strong. All such impending changes are estimated with the help of available surveys and quantitatively appraised with the expert advice of the industries concerned. These are examples of the estimate of primary changes,[12] that is, of changes expected to take place under the assumption that *general* business conditions remain the same in the ensuing year. They are changes that result from the past rather than in response to presently occurring events.

When the expected primary changes have been added up, it is possible to compute their direct impact on the national income as a whole. Assume that the primary changes—expected increases and decreases—were estimated to result in a net reduction of ten billion dollars. Taking into account such factors as taxes and undistributed business profits, one can estimate the resulting change in incomes disposable for consumption and savings by individuals. From the change in disposable income, an estimated change in consumption can be calculated on the basis of past experience.[13] In a similar way, inventory accumulations, import requirements, and many other factors respond rather promptly to changes in general business conditions. These are examples of secondary [14] changes that must be taken into account before a final projection for the ensuing year can be made.

Projections therefore require (1) the most up-to-date actual data on national income and production and their component

[12] The primary changes are often called 'autonomous' changes. They are autonomous only with respect to the time period in which they occur; they are often determined by economic conditions of the past.

[13] Relationships obtained from past experience are not used mechanically. It is probable, for instance, that consumers may react differently to a reduction in income when they have considerable wartime savings than when they have fewer savings as a reserve to draw upon. For a realistic appraisal of this fact, we need more knowledge of the distribution of wartime savings than we now have.

[14] The secondary changes include the impact of increased or decreased primary changes on consumption—the so-called 'multiplier' effect; the impact of changes in markets on business investments—the so-called 'acceleration' effect; and other 'induced' transactions such as changes in inventories in response to changes in business conditions.

parts; (2) an appraisal of imminent trends, especially in government expenditures, business investments, and consumer attitudes; (3) a knowledge of the responses of business and consumers to changes in economic conditions on the basis of the record of the past; and (4), most of all, the exercise of good common sense in combining all the pieces of information and expert advice into a consistent pattern. Great improvements have been made in statistical sources and methods of investigation. Yet we are at the beginning rather than at the end of this development. Particularly, the surveys of business and consumer attitudes and intentions are still in the experimental stage. The determining factors of business investment—the role of market analysis and price-cost relations—have not yet been fully explored. More recent data on consumer expenditures and savings by income brackets are also needed.

When it comes to appraising the quantitative effects of recommended policies, still other statistical problems will arise. A technical tool for the appraisal of various policy recommendations is the economic 'model.' The model is even more hypothetical than the projection.[15] The projection is based on the assumption that the government does not adopt any new policy recommendations; the model is based on the assumption that policies necessary to achieve full employment are adopted. As there are always several ways for accomplishing this policy end, several models can be constructed; comparison of these various models serves the study of alternative policy programs.[16] With the aid of alternative models, feasibility and costs of various policies or combinations of policies may be analyzed. Projections and models of national budgets must supplement each other as tools for policy determination. Projections help to determine the

---

[15] [1954 Fn.] I would now prefer to call these estimates hypothetical forecasts and designate as projections both hypothetical forecasts and models.

[16] For an example of model construction, see *National Budgets for Full Employment*, National Planning Association, Washington, 1945.

[1954 Fn.] Now see the more recent study, Gerhard Colm with the assistance of Marilyn Young, *The American Economy in 1960—Economic Progress in a World of Tension*, National Planning Association, Staff Report, Planning Pamphlet No. 81, December 1952.

need for government action; alternative models help in appraising proposed policies that will meet this need.

VI

Perfection of the art of projecting economic conditions and of appraising proposed policies in quantitative form to the extent visualized by the authors of the Full Employment Act would be a great step toward providing a scientific basis for policy formulation. Of course, the main objectives of the bill can be pursued even before statistical sources have been sufficiently improved. If a downturn in employment becomes noticeable, for instance, measures could be proposed that would tend to offset a decline, though the magnitude of the decline and the effects of the counter-measures cannot yet be determined in exact quantitative terms. Even after our statistical sources and methods have been extensively refined, however, policy formulation will still be subject to political controversy and will always remain so.

Assume that at a certain time, given the generally accepted objective of full employment, the figures prove that purchasing power should be increased or curbed, as the case may be. There will then still be a variety of ways in which this could be done. Pressure groups and local interests would still fight for the increase or curtailment of purchasing power by a method most beneficial to the people they represent. Not only would the proponent of a special measure have to defend his recommendation on its own merits but he would also have to consider how it affected production and employment of the nation as a whole. The procedure incorporated into the Full Employment Act would not surrender political decisions to the economists and statisticians. The bill, however, would provide a more orderly way of appraising political controversies in the light of the general welfare. All the data needed for the decision of controversial issues would have to be submitted for public criticism and debate.

The procedure under the bill is similar in character to the appropriation procedure set up under the Budget and Accounting Act of 1921. That act did not determine the amount of appropriations for aid to agriculture or for salaries of federal employees, for instance. It only prescribed that whatever amounts the President should propose to spend under congressional authorization should be included in the budget estimates, so that Congress might fully consider the financial implications of its actions. High-level production and employment will certainly not be the only objective of government policy. It would be very desirable, however, if each policy proposal—such as a change in the minimum wage rates, or in tax legislation, or in the tariff, or in agricultural subsidies—should also have to be analyzed in terms of its impact on the so-called national budget. All policies would therefore be considered in terms of both their intrinsic merits and their social costs.

The Budget and Accounting Act intended to establish a system of financial accounting; the approach to be used in the nation's budget for the appraisal of policy recommendations would establish a system of social accounting. Far from undermining free institutions, such a development would add to the effectiveness of democratic discussion and democratic determination of economic policies.

10

Fiscal Policy and the Federal Budget

(1953) *

Fiscal Policy: The Evolution of an Idea

The Great Depression dramatized the dilemma in which Western capitalism had found itself in recent decades. The free-enterprise system had unleashed tremendous productive forces which carried the technical revolution from one field of production to another and from one region of the world to another. The standard of living in the industrial regions of the world showed great gains. It brought into sight an age of plenty.

On the other hand, there was a growing threat of instability. The expectation that the economic system of free enterprise and free markets would bring about steady and full utilization of all resources gave way to a growing fear that instability and

* Abstracted from 'Fiscal Policy and the Federal Budget,' in *Income Stabilization for a Developing Democracy—A Study of the Politics and Economics of High Employment Without Inflation,* ed. by Max F. Millikan, New Haven, Yale University Press, 1953, chap. v, pp. 213-59.

periodic depressions are the price that must be paid for freedom and progress.

The earlier hopes that the government could steer an otherwise free economy solely through the device of a deliberate central-bank policy were shaken by the experiences during the boom of the 'twenties and the depression of the 'thirties. Many people began to wonder whether liberal institutions and rapid and sustained economic progress were compatible with each other, or whether sacrifices with respect to one were necessary in order to gain the other.

In this situation what has come to be known as fiscal policy was proposed as a means to overcome depressions. It was greeted with enthusiasm, for it promised to combine steady economic and social progress with the maintenance of basic economic liberties. It appeared as the true middle-of-the-road policy that avoided the fatal mistakes of a do-nothing policy without choosing the equally fatal policy of economic regimentation.

This is not the place to describe how this idea of fiscal policy grew out of modern theory and recent experience,[1] but a brief explanation may be in order. In its simplest form fiscal policy is conceived as a means to counteract the economic instability that is caused at times by active purchasing power exceeding the supply of goods at existing prices or at other times by the sum total of demand falling short of potential supply. If inflationary tendencies prevail, the government increases taxes or curtails expenditures, thus reducing purchasing power. In periods of deflation and underemployment, the government decreases taxes and increases expenditures, thereby adding to active purchasing power and effective demand. If the government succeeds in influencing the total stream of purchasing power and active

[1] There is extensive literature on this topic, particularly with respect to the relationship between Keynes's theory of employment and Hansen's theory of fiscal policy. See, for instance, *The New Economics: Keynes' Influence on Theory and Public Policy,* ed. by Seymour E. Harris, New York, Knopf, 1947; and *Income, Employment, and Public Policy,* essays in honor of Alvin H. Hansen by Lloyd A. Metzler, and others, New York, Norton, 1948. Arthur Smithies has treated the subject of this chapter in 'Federal Budgeting and Fiscal Policy,' in *A Survey of Contemporary Economics,* ed. by Howard S. Ellis, Philadelphia, Blakiston, 1948.

demand, production will be forthcoming in the right amount and composition and no other government regulation is needed to stabilize the economy and promote economic growth.

Fiscal policy seemed to be the ideal tool which could repair the basic defect in a *laissez-faire* economy without any specific interference with the free decisions by management of what and how to produce, by labor of where to work, and by consumers of what to do with their money. No new government powers would be needed except an adaptation of conventional government activities, namely, collecting revenue, spending money, and managing the debt.

Like all great ideas, the concept of fiscal policy was characterized by its simplicity. Little of that simplicity is left in present-day discussions about the actual role that fiscal policy may play in an endeavor toward stabilization of income and employment.[2]

A MODIFIED CONCEPT OF FISCAL POLICY

From fifteen years of experience with fiscal policy, the following conclusions can be drawn:

(1) Fiscal policy, a combination of deliberate changes in expenditure programs, revenue and tax programs, and debt management policies, is well suited to aid in counteracting general inflationary or general deflationary tendencies.

(2) The fiscal policy of the federal government must take into account, and must be co-ordinated with, the fiscal policies of state and local governments.

(3) Fiscal and non-fiscal policies must be co-ordinated so that they complement each other and do not act at cross purposes.

(4) Inflationary and deflationary tendencies may result from economic maladjustments in the price-wage-profit or investment-consumption relationship. A policy that is suitable to combat an inflationary or a deflationary movement may not remove the mal-

---

[2] The recent report on *National and International Measures for Full Employment,* submitted by a group of experts appointed by the Secretary-General of the United Nations (December 1949), presents a very clear though oversimplified exposition of these problems. See also the discussion of this report in the proceedings of the Eleventh Session of the Social and Economic Council of the United Nations in Geneva, July 1950.

adjustments that cause these movements. It is desirable to use fiscal and other policies to iron out the maladjustments before they lead to inflationary or deflationary movements.

(5) If maladjustments have not been prevented in time and lead to inflationary or deflationary movements, then fiscal policies should be used at least as a temporary stabilizing device until more basic adjustment policies have been worked out. Fiscal policies are not adequate devices for combating the inflationary bias that may occur under a full-employment policy.

(6) The effectiveness of fiscal policy is increased when the community understands its working and has confidence in, and therefore anticipates, its results.

(7) Fiscal policy must be related to the long-range requirements of allocation of resources to improvement in the standard of living, to expansion of the productive plant of the nation, to adequate defense needs, and to helping economic development abroad. Emphasis on each of these objectives varies, depending on the foremost needs of each period in the life of the nation.

There is no doubt that the task of fiscal policy, as indicated in these conclusions, is much more complex than is suggested by the simple formula proposed in 'functional finance.' Recognition of this complexity does not imply, however, that fiscal policy is unimportant. While sustained and steady growth of income and employment and a rational allocation of resources cannot be achieved through fiscal policy alone, it is equally true that these objectives can best be achieved with the aid of fiscal policy in a political and economic system that tries to give widest scope to individual responsibility and initiative and to minimize direct regulatory action of the government. The contribution that fiscal policy can make toward these objectives cannot be finally appraised before the budgetary procedures through which fiscal policy must be realized are examined.

IMPLEMENTING FISCAL POLICY THROUGH THE BUDGETARY PROCESS

The idea of fiscal policy has a short-run and long-run aspect. In the short run it is the adaptation of government expenditure, revenue, and debt policies to the task of offsetting fluctuations in private activities. In the long-run aspect it involves the use of the same policies for the purpose of promoting self-sustained growth of the economy, thereby reducing the instability that causes cyclical fluctuations. Fiscal policy as a cyclical compensating device and, even more, as a long-run stabilizing device must be supplemented by other means of economic policy. Fiscal policy must be realized largely through budgetary procedures, and budget policy must be related to the national economic objectives.

Budgetary procedures were developed mainly as a means of legislative control and administrative management, with little consideration for cyclical variations and other aspects of economics. Improved legislative and administrative budget controls have to some extent made the budget procedure a more suitable instrument of fiscal policy. In some respects, however, the idea of fiscal policy clashes with other objectives of government policy that enter into budget-making and with the traditional manner in which budgets are determined and executed.

Conflict of objectives: economic versus non-economic objectives

The size of the federal budget and major changes in it are controlled largely by what we may term non-economic programs of the government. All programs of the government have, of course, political, social, and economic aspects. The aspect of foreign policy is predominant, for instance, in programs for national security and foreign policy. These programs, though 'non-economic' in their origin and purpose, are obviously 'economic' in their impact, and the determination of their size is of course not exempt from economic consideration.

The international situation forced the government to step up defense and foreign-aid programs while private business was engaged in a postwar investment boom. But obviously expenditures for foreign policy could not be delayed until the postwar boom began to peter out or until defense and foreign-aid or veterans' programs could be fitted nicely into a compensatory fiscal policy. Obviously fiscal policy has to be adjusted to the necessity of these national objectives, rather than having these national programs determined in a way that fits into a policy of economic stabilization.

Of course, it would be wrong to say that non-economic government programs are or should be determined without any consideration of the economic situation. The determination of these programs must take account of the political urgency of these objectives on the one hand, and of the sacrifices that result from diverting resources from other uses on the other hand. This diversion can take the form of curtailing other government programs or of diverting resources from private use. Even before the aggression in Korea, the armed services believed that substantial increases in defense expenditures were desirable in the interest of national security. It was argued, however, that under conditions of virtually full employment a substantial increase in defense expenditures would have required a substantial curtailment of government expenditures not directly related to defense, or a substantial increase in taxes, and possibly the adoption of some direct price and wage controls and allocations to prevent more serious inflation.[3] While everybody agreed that no costs—in terms of money, curtailment of desirable peacetime programs, or inconveniences of control—were too high to meet an actual emergency, balancing defense requirements and other objectives of government policy were believed necessary to meet a period of possibly prolonged international tension. No judgment is passed here on the question of whether economic considerations actually resulted in a curtailment of defense expenditure proposals, which proved unfortunate in the light of subsequent events. In any case it is absurd to contend that the increase in defense expenditures was initiated in order to forestall an otherwise unavoidable depression. What economic considerations there were were all on the other side.

[3] See Edwin G. Nourse, 'Economic Implications of Military Preparedness,' an address before the National Military Establishment Joint Orientation Conference, 10 November 1948, reprinted as *Economics in the Public Service, Administrative Aspects of the Employment Cut,* New York, Harcourt, Brace, 1953, Appendix E.

The fact that economic considerations must enter the deliberation of such non-economic programs places a great responsibility on the economist. The view that regards economic considerations as predominant and subordinates essential national objectives to an ironclad rule of 'sound finance' is dangerous.[4] It would be equally wrong if non-economic programs were determined without consideration of their fiscal impact. The fact that non-economic programs may require a sustained effort over a considerable period of time, and depend more than ever on popular support, makes it imperative that in their determination the fiscal, economic, and social implications of such programs be fully considered.

Conflict of short-range versus long-range economic policies

A possible conflict of objectives exists not only with respect to economic versus non-economic objectives but also within the field of economic objectives itself. During the postwar years the federal government deferred many public works and social programs, although there was no question about their long-range desirability. The longer the postwar boom lasted and the longer the policy of deferment was continued, the more voices were heard questioning that policy. It has been pointed out that it would be absurd to defer, for instance, urgently needed school buildings while building materials are being used for commercial construction of lesser social urgency. Similarly, it would be absurd to defer construction of hydroelectric power facilities if a real power shortage is a bottleneck in the expanded output of aluminum.

---

[4] Against this view was directed President Roosevelt's statement in the Budget Message of January 1942, four weeks after Pearl Harbor: 'There need be no fiscal barrier to our war effort and victory.' Perhaps it may be useful not to forget that Hitler's initial success in Europe was greatly aided by a 'conservative' financial philosophy of the democratic countries of western Europe during the 'thirties. Adequate defense preparation was directly hampered in these countries by fear of budget deficits—during the depression. The Nazi's own war preparations were not taken seriously enough because the leading statesmen of the democratic countries were told by financial experts that the unsound methods of Nazi finance were bound to result in an early collapse.

194

As a matter of fact, during the period of postwar inflation public works of state and local governments and some of the most urgent federal projects were initiated in spite of the general policy of deferment. A strict fiscal policy of deferment of all public works in periods of full activity implies the belief that private activities in principle have priority over all government economic and social programs; in accord with that philosophy, government programs would be undertaken only when private activities were not using all available resources. It would be absurd to argue that the people must wait for a depression before they can obtain urgently needed services of public undertakings. Many economic and social programs of the government obviously do not belong in the category of deferrable demand. The decision about which public undertakings should be deferred in a period of great business activity must take into consideration the social and economic urgency of the various projects. The fact that not all public works can be regarded as deferrable *per se* limits the variability of government expenditures.

The urgency of needed public works and the desirability of postponing them were in especially serious conflict in the postwar years. Once the public works deferred during the war have been completed and the most urgent demands have been met, the conflict between short-range and long-range economic objectives will become somewhat less troublesome.

Besides the existence of high-priority public works and other local developmental programs which have been deferred, the standard of relative usefulness in itself is subject to change. It is obvious that at a time when idle resources are available, programs regarded as deferrable in a period of full employment become desirable. This principle appears sensible not only in the interest of economic stabilization but also from the point of view of reasonable financial management. Resources are expensive in terms of social accounting as well as in terms of actual prices when they must be bid away from private use. They are inexpensive in slack periods. Many public works, such as irrigation projects, are managed on a self-supporting basis. They are supposed to be financed, at least partly, by farmers through payments of fees for water use. Fees computed on the basis of construction at peak prices may be prohibitive; if computed at somewhat lower prices, they may be tolerable. Even though market prices and costs should not be the determining factor in public activities, they partly reflect the relation between benefits and economic costs and to that extent should be taken into consideration.

The contention that sound policy precludes a cyclical variation in expenditure programs, except for so-called 'built-in-flexibilities' to be discussed later, cannot be maintained on theoretical or practical grounds.[5] Even if expenditure programs were to be determined strictly by their social benefits in relation to economic costs, they would have to be varied because that relationship itself is not independent of the business situation.

In practical political terms the reconciliation between short-run and long-run objectives of economic and social policy does not appear impossible. In a dynamic society there will always be desirable new economic and social programs, or an expansion of existing programs, in the discussion stage. In prosperous times there should certainly be no absolute embargo against the adoption and expansion of economically and socially urgent government programs. Under conditions of full employment, the merits of additional programs must be such that they are clearly preferred to private programs with which they may compete for labor and material. They also require financing by additional taxes designed to work as an effective brake on private activity. Under depressed conditions, the tempo in the adoption of needed programs can be speeded up. Their relative costs are then lower, measured in terms of government cost accounting, tax burdens, and social accounting. It may be difficult to accomplish an ex-

[5] An uncompromising suggestion in this respect was made by Milton Friedman, 'A Monetary and Fiscal Framework for Economic Stability,' *American Economic Review*, 38, June 1948. The position of the Committee for Economic Development is less extreme but tends in the same direction; see *Taxes and the Budget, A Program for Prosperity in a Free Economy*, New York, November 1948, and *Monetary and Fiscal Policy for Greater Economic Stability*, New York, December 1948.

pansion and contraction in government expenditures, depending on the ups and downs in private activities. There is, however, such a large backlog of highly desirable improvement programs that it is feasible to plan for a faster pace in periods of slackening business conditions and to hold to a somewhat slower pace as long as business activity remains high. In the postwar years we had a tremendous backlog of work to be done in housing and urban redevelopment, in transportation, educational and health facilities, and the development and conservation of national resources. Only very inadequate progress has been made on these programs during the postwar inflation. The rearmament program again forced postponement of many desirable projects. They can be developed as soon as we have passed the peak of defense preparations, serving short-run requirements by pursuing long-run needs.[6]

Only if desirable and needed programs are prepared in advance and are ready for adoption will an administration be able to resist the demand for less desirable emergency programs in case of a depression. There is the danger that, in case of a depression, pressure for all kinds of payments will develop. It is true that for the immediate impact on demand a quick outpouring of money is more important than a careful selection of projects. For the long-run effect, however, it is very important that additions to expenditures be truly productive. If they add to productivity and thereby to the future tax base, they will be self-liquidating in the broadest sense of the term.

Conflict of short-range versus long-range tax policies

Every argument that limits the use of short-run variations in the rate of government expenditures becomes an argument for exploring the desirability of short-run variations in tax policy for purposes of economic stabilization. In this area too we run into a conflict of objectives.

Some statements made by A. P. Lerner and Beardsley Ruml have suggested that it is the main purpose of a national tax

[6] See the *Midyear Economic Report of the President,* July 1952, pp. 118f.

197

policy to regulate the flow of purchasing power. Taxes should be low enough to permit the purchase of everything that can be produced and high enough to prevent inflation.[7] If that were the sole or the main purpose of taxes, then our tax system and, even more, our tax ideals would have to be basically revised. Then the most effective taxes would be those that have the greatest direct bearing on consumption because their increase would absorb purchasing power much more effectively than any change in progressive taxes and their reduction would free purchasing power more effectively than any reduction in progressive taxes. There would really be no ground for maintaining progressive taxes in the tax system.

Obviously, tax policy, no less than expenditure policy, must consider other long-run economic and social objectives as well as price stabilization. A wartime experience may be mentioned to illustrate a possible conflict between these objectives. When an anti-inflationary fiscal program was under discussion during the war, a modified sales tax was suggested for consideration. The tax proposal was devised so that the buyer could obtain refunds in bonds or cash on a per capita minimum of taxable purchases. Such exemption was believed necessary for reasons of equity and in order to reduce the effect of the tax on wage demands, which if too great would have nullified much of its anti-inflationary impact. Nevertheless, the proposal was turned down because of the opinion that a sales tax once admitted to the family of respectable federal taxes would probably be retained even at a time when the specific fiscal argument was no longer applicable.

In expenditure and tax policy, those measures are best that reconcile the requirements of both short-run and long-run policy objectives.

Conflict in jurisdiction: federal versus state and local programs

One of the definite lessons to be derived from the experience of the Great Depression and the war and postwar period is that

[7] Both authors have recognized other specific purposes of taxation and the need for non-budgetary devices for stabilization.

[1954 Fn.] See Chapter 1, page 5.

an effective fiscal policy cannot be limited to the operations of the federal government alone.

State and local financial policies tend to aggravate rather than to counteract cyclical fluctuations. During the depression state and local governments were forced to curtail expenditures and to raise tax rates. One scheme after another was devised to aid state and local undertakings—with only partial success and much criticism. Without the various aid programs, curtailment of state and local services would have been much more drastic.

During the war ample revenues and the limitations on spending, because of physical restrictions, created budgetary surpluses and temptations to reduce tax rates. Tax reductions could be kept within limits because many governors and state legislatures responded to the appeal for voluntary state co-operation in the national anti-inflation program. After the war, when the appeal to co-operate in a national program of anti-inflationary fiscal policy was less effective, state and local bodies rapidly spent much of their wartime surpluses and contributed substantially to the inflationary pressure. The absence of federal-state-local co-ordinating machinery constitutes one of the most serious limitations on an effective national fiscal policy.

A possible step toward such co-ordination might consist in the establishment of flexible grants-in-aid. The federal government pays about $2.5 billion per year to state and local governments in the form of grants for a variety of purposes. That is about 6 per cent of the federal budget but almost 15 per cent of state and local receipts.

An element of flexibility could be introduced into the federal-state-local relationship if the federal government were to contribute a lower percentage of state-local outlays as grants for specific programs in booms and a higher percentage in depressions.[8] Although such flexibility provisions may not be feasible in the case of all programs, they do appear feasible in some

[8] See the Report of the Joint Committee on the Economic Report, March 1949, pp. 37-8. For a detailed discussion see James A. Maxwell, *Federal Grants and the Business Cycle*, New York, National Bureau of Economic Research, 1952.

and could at least contribute to the prevention of cyclically 'perverse' fluctuations in state-local spending. Beyond that, at least in the case of some programs, such provisions might induce counter-cyclical timing of expenditures even at the state and local level.

Flexible grants-in-aid for state and local public works might be a useful instrument for building up a 'shelf' of state and local public-works projects. The trouble with a shelf of public works is that as soon as worth-while projects are prepared in blueprints, local pressures become active urging their immediate execution, irrespective of the business situation. An incentive for a more reasonable policy could be created if the federal government would pay nothing or merely make a nominal contribution to such projects when undertaken in times of prosperity, but a larger percentage contribution when conditions are less favorable. Such flexible grants for public works might help develop the kind of national public-works policy embracing all levels of government.

Conflict in procedures: requirements of legislative control versus the need for flexibility of government expenditures

The budget procedure was developed as a means of legislative control of government operations. The legislative machinery with its committee setup and public hearings is not designed for quick action except in cases of obvious emergency. Appropriation and tax legislation must usually be initiated a considerable time before the expenditures are to be made or tax changes become effective. For stabilization purposes, on the other hand, it is necessary that fiscal policy be quickly adaptable to short-run changes in the economic situation.

From the point of view of fiscal policy, it would be most desirable if the executive branch were given the authority to change the rate of expenditures within given statutory limits in the same manner in which the Federal Reserve System, for instance, is authorized to change reserve requirements within certain limits. Such delegation of authority obviously must be reconciled with the purpose of legislative control. A workable democracy requires that both the legislature and the executive share in the responsibility for stabilization policy. Thus some reconciliation between the objectives of fiscal flexibility and of legislative control must be worked out.[9]

The so-called built-in flexibilities achieve this purpose to some extent. An example is the unemployment-insurance program which provides by law that disbursements must be made to those who have a rightful claim. Since these payments are made out of trust accounts, no problem of appropriation is involved as long as the funds are not exhausted. Payments rise and fall automatically with the rise and fall in unemployment. Built-in flexibility also exists, though with somewhat less automatism, where basic legislation requires periodic appropriations to implement it. If prices for farm products fall rapidly and remain low over a considerable period of time, authorizations or appropriations will be needed to permit payments under farm-price-support legislation. Congress is usually prompt in appropriating money that is necessary to meet clearly defined legislative commitments.

We have in our present government machinery many more built-in flexibilities than we had at the end of the 'twenties. Thus we have cushions today that we did not have at the beginning of the last depression.

Several students of fiscal policy who are concerned with the conflict between the requirements of legislative control and the need for flexibility see the solution of the problem in exclusive reliance on such built-in flexibility.[10] Built-in flexibility has a special appeal because it seems to accomplish the job of a com-

[9] See G. L. Bach, 'Monetary-Fiscal Policy Reconsidered,' *Journal of Political Economy*, 57, no. 5, October 1949, p. 387: 'But to assume congressional renunciation of direct control over the power to tax and the power to spend, except possibly for some delegation of authority over timing of prearranged programs, appears to have little relevance to reality. Formulation of a workable monetary-fiscal policy must recognize the stubborn fact of congressional prerogatives.'

[10] See Milton Friedman, op. cit.; Committee for Economic Development, *Taxes and the Budget*, op. cit.; G. L. Bach, op. cit. Built-in flexibility should be distinguished from the formula flexibility for tax rates that will be discussed below.

pensatory fiscal policy, without the need for special legislation or the delegation of authority to the executive. Advocates of this theory argue as follows: if business activity shrinks, tax yields diminish and certain spending programs are stepped up automatically. Thereby a government cash deficit is created. If the cash deficit is financed by bank borrowing, it may create an inflationary, or reflationary, force that tends to restore a high employment level. The opposite is true with respect to a budget surplus that is the automatic result of inflation. It leads to the possibility of debt redemption and credit contraction. Built-in flexibility should achieve stability if mere changes in the potential money supply are sufficient to regulate economic activities. Those who doubt the effectiveness of changes in potential money supply will assign to built-in flexibility only a somewhat more modest role. They will contend that a mere passive response of government operations to changes in the private economy will mitigate the change but cannot possibly reverse its direction. A deficit that *results* from a drop in income acts as a cushion but cannot turn the drop into a rise.[11]

Unemployment compensation restores only a fraction of the normal earnings of a worker. It reduces the income loss caused by unemployment. Farm-price support gives the farmer less than prosperous markets for farm products but reduces the impact on income of farm-surplus production. Built-in flexibilities in themselves, therefore, cannot be relied on exclusively to stop a deflationary spiral and restore full employment. They mitigate a drop in incomes but must be supplemented in case of need by legislative or administrative flexibility which will permit an affirmative variation of expenditure or tax programs.

A possible way of reconciling the goal of legislative control

[11] A deficit that follows from a drop in incomes and tax yield has been called a *maintenance* deficit, which is distinguished from a *stimulating* deficit. See Chapter 6. For a critical discussion of the Committee for Economic Development proposal, see Alvin Hansen, *Monetary Theory and Fiscal Policy*, New York, McGraw-Hill, 1949, pp. 175-83. See also 'Federal Expenditure and Revenue Policies,' Hearings before the Joint Committee on the Economic Report, 81st Congress, 1st Session, 23 September 1949, p. 9.

with that of executive discretion would be to distinguish three types of expenditures in the budget. One type would include current operations of the government for which appropriations would be made on a strictly annual basis.

A second type of expenditure would be for public works and economic development. Appropriations for these purposes would be made, let us say, on a five-year basis, with executive discretion to vary the speed of program execution in line with economic requirements. In order to preserve the desirable legislative controls, it could be provided that the program be subject to annual legislative consideration for the subsequent five years, and that each year the President report if actual obligations or expenditures in any one year fall considerably short of or considerably exceed the obligations or expenditures scheduled for that particular year under the five-year program.[12]

In a third type of expenditure, the quasi-commercial outlays of government corporations, a high degree of administrative discretion should be permitted. Agencies such as the Reconstruction Finance Corporation or the Tennessee Valley Authority should be authorized to adapt their activities promptly to changes in economic conditions. While these agencies should be free of too specific legislative direction, they should be geared into a national development and stabilization program. It has been the experience in many countries that the directors of government corporations often want to be 'masters in their own houses,' just as much if not more than do directors in private corporations. In other words the activities of government corporations must effectively be made subject to executive control without depriving 'business-type' operations of the government of the desirable

[12] See Harold D. Smith, *The Management of Your Government*, New York, McGraw-Hill, 1945, pp. 96ff. See also Gerhard Colm, 'Comment on Extraordinary Budgets,' *Social Research*, 5, May 1938, pp. 168ff. Of interest is the provision in the Housing Act of 1949, which authorizes a six-year program of 810,000 units of public low-cost housing, or 135,000 a year, but permits the President, after receiving advice from the Council of Economic Advisers, to vary the number of starts for any of the six years to between 50,000 and 200,000. Even though this provision had no practical consequence, it may well be regarded as a significant landmark in economic legislation.

flexibility. The Government Corporation Control Act of 1945 is a step in that direction.

We propose different rules for the appropriation procedure concerning these different types of expenditure programs. This, however, is not intended to suggest breaking down the budget into three separate parts.

Conflict in procedure: requirements of legislative control versus the need for flexibility in government revenues

Recently, proposals have been made to introduce formula flexibility into the tax system by providing for changes in tax rates when an index of production or unemployment, or any combination of indices, indicates that a substantial change in economic activities has taken place.[13]

While very good arguments in favor of formula flexibility have been advanced, there are probably more valid reasons against adoption of this plan under present circumstances. First of all, we know too little about what kind and amount of tax change would be called for when unemployment has reached a certain point. Much more trial-and-error experience with fiscal policy will be needed before we are ready to crystallize a definite scheme of flexibility in legislation.

Second, legislation must consider a variety of objectives and, depending on the particular circumstances, different tax measures may be needed in conditions that appear statistically similar. Formula flexibility may not be flexible enough.

Third, formula flexibility assumes that short-run changes in tax rates can be entirely separated from the changes that are in the long-range interest in an improved tax system. If a situation calls for tax reductions, the most desirable will be those that will help the immediate situation and at the same time be justified as long-run improvements in the tax system.

[13] See 'Federal Expenditure and Revenue Policies,' Hearings before the Joint Committee on the Economic Report, *Economic Report of the President,* 17-20 January 1950, and *National and International Measures for Full Employment,* United Nations Report, December 1949.

Finally, legislative prerogative with respect to tax legislation is even more sacrosanct than with respect to the power of the purse.

The case may be somewhat different with respect to social-insurance contributions. They are not regarded as part of the general revenue and are appropriated to special social-insurance funds. If the recent recommendations for an extended social-insurance system are adopted, payroll taxes will increase within a few years to an aggregate of about 10-12 per cent. A variation in this percentage could have a very significant economic effect. There may be fewer objections to an administrative flexibility in social-insurance contributions paid into trust accounts than in general taxes. Increases made in social-insurance contribution schedules by legislation in the past have been repeatedly 'frozen' by legislation on short notice, and Congress has recognized that possible future deficits in the funds must be met by appropriations from general Treasury funds. It is perhaps significant that the wartime coalition government in Great Britain also identified social-insurance contributions as the most suitable instrument of a flexible tax policy. Still, such variations in social-security rates can at best make a moderate contribution to a stabilization policy.

If a delegation of power to vary the rates of either taxes or social-insurance contributions, with or without a formula, does not appear acceptable, it is not entirely unrealistic to envisage simplified legislative procedures for enactment of specified changes within a short time. On request of the President, or on its own initiative, the Joint Committee on the Economic Report could, for instance, be authorized to recommend temporary changes in tax rates for purposes of an anti-cyclical policy. In this case a representative of the Joint Committee might testify before the Ways and Means and Senate Finance Committees and the hearings could be limited to a minimum. The legislation might provide that the changes would be for a specified limited period. If changes were intended to become permanent, the limiting clause would have to be eliminated by ordinary legislation, presumably after hearings that would be more detailed and extensive than those held under the simplified procedure.

I believe that neither built-in flexibility nor formula flexibility nor delegated flexibility can be the full answer to a cyclical tax policy. To a large extent we must depend on improvements in the normal procedures of tax legislation and on much closer cooperation of the executive and legislative branches in economic stabilization policy.

Conflict in procedure: mechanism of budget making versus the need for flexibility

One specific difficulty with a cyclical consideration of expenditure policy follows not so much from the conflict with legislative control as from the sheer mechanical requirements of budget making. On what assumptions with respect to economic developments should the budget request of the various agencies be prepared?

With the Call for Estimates, a policy letter formulated by the budget director is sent to the agency telling them by what assumptions they should be guided in preparing their requests for the ensuing year. These assumptions must be formulated more than two years before the end of the period for which the esti-· mates are prepared. The attempt to base the budgetary require;-ments on anything like a realistic economic forecast seems to be utterly impossible. First, we do not now have, and I doubt that we shall ever have, the ability to make a reasonable forecast covering a period two years hence.

Second, even if forecasts were more reliable than they are, it would be difficult to base the budget preparation on them. Budget preparations, for instance, for the fiscal year ending in June 1955 begin in the spring of 1953. Let us assume, for discussion's sake, that at that time experts expect that business conditions are likely to decline so that at least for part of the fiscal year 1955 depressed conditions should be assumed. Such a 'forecast' can only mean that the experts expect a business contraction under the assumption that current government policies continue and that no effective stabilization program of the government is initiated. Under the Employment Act the President would have to make recommendations to Congress to counteract a depression as soon as such a forecast could reliably be made. Assuming the government initiates such counteraction in time, the outlook for the fiscal year 1955 would appear quite different. The downward tendency may be halted or reversed, depending on the promptness and effectiveness of the program. In any case, basing the budget preparation on the assumption of a depression in the next fiscal year for purposes of the formulation of departmental requirements would really imply forecasting failure on the part of the President or the Congress to take effective measures to forestall or counteract an anticipated depression.

Therefore it appears preferable that the budget as a whole should always be prepared under the assumption of approximately full employment. This budget would show expenditures and revenues, disregarding the effects of a possible business recession. For programs that would be initiated or increased immediately if business should begin to slacken, a contingency appropriation should be requested so that a minor fluctuation does not make it necessary to ask for a deficiency appropriation. This contingency reserve should, however, be impounded, to be released only by specific presidential action. This would make it unnecessary to base the budgetary requirements on any specific forecast but would make available to the President funds which would be needed in case of a mild depression. In case of a severe depression, however, the President would have to submit to Congress a supplementary or deficiency request for funds for additional programs, along with other recommendations for economic and fiscal policies as they would be formulated under the Employment Act.

It is important for Congress and the public to recognize clearly the basis on which budgets are formulated. If a hypothetical full-employment basis is used, later revisions may not be due to erroneous estimates but to a discrepancy between assumed and actual events. The budget should be thought of less as a forecast than as a working plan designed as the basis for later adaptation to unfolding economic conditions.

Conflict in accounting

The conduct of fiscal policy requires different accounting guides from those needed for program formulation and program control.

Program formulation requires estimates of costs for a program as a whole. For deciding whether a program is worth undertaking, and especially for comparing various alternative programs that are under construction, true cost estimates are essential as are, to the extent that they can be made, appraisals of the benefits to be derived from the program. If, for instance, construction of a dam is under consideration, estimates of the costs and benefits of the whole project are more essential than an estimate of expenditures that would have to be made in the first year.

Program control requires statements that relate the legislative authorization to appropriations, obligations, and actual expenditures. These statements permit a review of the legality of a government activity, of the progress made in its execution, and of the unobligated appropriations and unliquidated obligations, which are factors to be considered in computing the need for new appropriations and for estimating future expenditures.

Financial planning requires estimates of cash expenditures and cash receipts that have an impact on cash balances of the Treasury, the need to borrow from the public, and the possibility of redeeming outstanding indebtedness.

The data developed for program formulation and program control must be adjusted before they can be used as guides for financial planning. While appropriations and obligations for expenditures and tax liabilities are very important for program formulation and program control, financial planning must be based on cash expenditures and cash receipts. Furthermore, accounting according to administrative organizations may very often lead to double counting. Money may be appropriated to trust accounts and reported as budget expenditures or as a reduction from gross receipts.[14] On the other hand, the trust accounts reflect disbursements of these accounts to recipients. The purpose of this administrative accounting is control and supervision. Adding up these administrative accounts does not necessarily give any meaningful totals. Meaningful totals are needed, however, for financial and fiscal planning.

For financial planning, therefore, statements are needed which (1) reflect only cash transactions; (2) include disbursements of all the various government accounts, including accounts of government corporations and trust funds; and (3) eliminate transfers from one government account to another. Such estimates have been called the *consolidated cash statement*. This statement presents meaningful totals.

The consolidated cash statement is not only an instrument for financial planning but also one for *fiscal policy*. Fiscal policy views the government budget as an aid in balancing the nation's economic budget. Fiscal-policy considerations, therefore, require new concepts and new classifications in government and national economic accounting. Statements for past, current, and future periods are needed to portray the relationship between the government accounts and the national income and expenditure accounts. We must know what money is being spent in a way that adds to the funds available to individuals, business, state, and local governments, or foreign countries, and what revenue is received through absorption of funds from the same groups.

Traditional budget accounting was developed as a tool for program control, program formulation, and financial planning. It cannot be said that the budget for the United States has been clearly devised to serve any one of these purposes. It includes cash and non-cash transactions, disbursements to the public, and internal transfers.

The various purposes of government accounting should be

---

[14] Most receipts from payroll taxes are directly appropriated to the social-insurance funds and appear in the budget as a deduction from gross receipts rather than as expenditures.

more clearly distinguished. We need cost data for program appraisal; we need data for purposes of budget control; we need data for financial planning and fiscal policy. No one set of figures can serve all these purposes. The consolidated cash budget and the nation's economic budget were designed for purposes of financial planning and for guidance of fiscal policy.

Fiscal policy requires the development not only of appropriate totals of budget transactions but also of suitable classifications. With respect to new classifications, the requirements of fiscal policy reinforce the need for a classification by character of expenditure. Such a classification distinguishes between expenditures for current operations and expenditures that are of an investment nature and hence represent benefits to be realized in future periods.[15] Furthermore, the fiscal analyst needs expenditures classified according to type of goods and services bought (object classification) and also a classification by type of recipients of the money paid out.[16]

The conflict between the conventional accounts and the accounts needed for fiscal policy can be reconciled, for the same basic data can be processed in different ways to supply various statements, each serving its own purpose.

The human conflict

Perhaps the greatest difficulty is the fact that the job of conventional budget determination and of fiscal policy requires dif-

[15] For an example of such a classification, see the *Budget of the United States Government for the Fiscal Year 1952*, pp. 969ff. For a corresponding discussion related to Great Britain, see J. R. Hicks, *The Problem of Budgetary Reform*, Oxford, Clarendon Press, 1948. Hicks deals especially with the problems of accounting for nationalized economic activities in Great Britain. They are of lesser importance in this country, but some corresponding problems exist with respect to, for instance, the Post Office Department, Tennessee Valley Authority, and other agencies with quasi-commercial activities. For a full discussion of the policy use of national economic accounting in various countries, see *Income and Wealth*, Series I, Erik Lundberg, ed., International Association for Research in Income and Wealth, Cambridge, England, Bowes & Bowes, 1951.

[16] As a sample of classification of expenditures by type of recipient, see Table A-8 in the *Midyear Economic Report of the President*, July 1952, pp. 134f.

ferent attitudes. The people whose job it is to screen budgetary requests and determine either budgetary recommendations or Congressional appropriations must be in a frame of mind quite different from that of those who can be most effective in the formulation and determination of fiscal policies. The legislator who has the job of examining budgetary requests usually assumes that the agencies are asking for too much. He knows by experience that a good executive who is devoted to his task wants to do the best possible job, and the best possible job requires money. The executive wants efficiency, too, but he usually wants efficiency not in order to reduce the amount of money needed but to do a better job with the same amount.

Thus the legislator feels called upon to counteract this natural drive toward expansion. Of course there is also the tendency for legislators to want more money appropriated for purposes in which their constituents are particularly interested. But the expenditures in which a legislator has a particular interest need not be the same as those for which the executive is making his request.

The same is largely true with respect to an efficient screening of budgetary requests on the executive side. True, the Budget Bureau is an important management arm of the President and wants to see that the President's program is implemented by budgetary allowances. The late Budget Director, Harold D. Smith, often emphasized that he no longer regarded it as the main function of the budget director to act as the 'watchdog of the Treasury,' but that he felt that the budget director is responsible for implementing the President's program in the most efficient and economical manner. Nevertheless, a comparison between agency requests and final budget recommendations shows that the Budget Bureau has continued to perform its watchdog functions effectively. Budget examiners by the very nature of their job must adopt a critical attitude toward budgetary requests and often regard the amount of dollars they are able to cut from a departmental request as a measurement of their effectiveness. There is certainly an urgent need for an effective performance of this screening job.

As long as the economy is in a state of inflationary pressures, the attitude of legislative or executive budget examiners coincides largely with the requirements of a restraining fiscal policy. In a period of threatening or actual business contraction, however, fiscal policy may require the stepping-up of government activities rather than curtailment. There is certainly the danger that in such a period the fiscal-policy view and the budget view may clash. To some extent such a clash did occur at the beginning of the 'thirties when Budget Director Douglas showed little enthusiasm in implementing the President's recovery program.

As a matter of fact, it would be utterly erroneous to have a less determined attitude toward budget requirements in a period of underemployment than in a period of high employment. We need stabilization policies, but the attitude toward budgetary screening should always be strict and conscientious. In the postwar years the Budget Bureau's policy letter accompanying the Call for Estimates has emphasized the need for tight budgeting in an inflationary period. It cannot be imagined that the Budget Bureau would or should ever send out a policy letter that did not ask for tight budgeting. Programs should always be executed with a minimum amount of money. What should be changed is the size and character of the *programs* and the speed of their execution rather than the attitude toward economy in budgeting.

The President's program should be determined after, first, long-range and, second, short-range economic and non-economic objectives and the total costs involved have been considered. The budgetary review should insure that these programs are formulated and executed with the greatest economy at all times. The Executive Office of the President must assist the President in both these functions, namely, formulating a program that takes account of economic requirements and also determining the most economical way of implementing this program. The Executive Office needs two types of people: those who have the attitude and imagination to be able to assist the President in program formulation and those who have the attitude and conscientiousness of the budget examiner.[17]

Whatever the best administrative relationship may be between these two groups within the Executive Office, it is clear that both attitudes must be blended if a national program is to be formulated that fulfills the necessary functions of supporting an expanding economy and assures that waste is eliminated and that the nation receives the greatest possible value from each dollar spent.

AN APPRAISAL OF THE SCOPE AND LIMITS OF FISCAL POLICY

We started this essay by describing fiscal policy as a steering mechanism which could keep the economy on an even keel merely by proper timing of changes in government expenditure, government taxes, and debt management. A review of the experience with fiscal policy during the depression, the war, and the postwar period was used to illustrate some of the complications and limitations of using fiscal policy as a device for economic stabilization. We distinguished between fiscal policy as a short-run compensating device designed to *offset* fluctuations in private business activities and fiscal and other economic policies as long-run adjusting devices designed to reduce the *causes* of economic instability.

We also emphasized the fact that a national program pursues a variety of objectives. The objectives of fiscal policy clash to some extent with other objectives and must be reconciled. Fiscal policy must be executed largely through the budgetary process, which again requires reconciliation of various purposes.

Yet it would be wrong to conclude from these complexities that fiscal policy as a stabilization device is only of minor usefulness. The purpose of this final section is to summarize the potential usefulness of fiscal policy and to re-emphasize what ar-

[17] Thomas Blaisdell, Jr., probably had the distinction between these two attitudes in mind when, in a speech before the American Society for Public Administration in Washington, D. C., 11 March 1949, he said: 'The Budget Bureau methods are those of the control of the purse strings. The methods of the Council of Economic Advisers must be those of leading strings.'

213

rangements in our legislative and administrative procedures may become necessary to enable full use of this instrument.

It is true that fiscal policy in its original and simplest conception is designed to combat inflation or deflation. This means that compensatory fiscal policy is more suited to combating the results than it is the causes of economic maladjustments. It would be preferable, at least under peacetime conditions, if these maladjustments themselves could be prevented before they cause large swings of inflation or deflation. What, then, are these maladjustments and to what extent can fiscal policy contribute toward straightening them out?

It has been pointed out that an economy sustained at high levels of activity may have an inflationary bias which works through the mutual effect of prices and wages. In order to reconcile a continuing high level of employment, approximate price stability, and free collective bargaining, it appears necessary to develop a long-range wage and price policy with participation of business and labor.[18] This solution requires further development in collective bargaining within the general framework of a national stabilization policy. The other alternative, namely, permitting inflation to develop and then counteracting it by an anti-inflationary fiscal policy, is obviously much less desirable.

In a similar way active purchasing power may be hampered at times by a business price policy of large profit margins and retained earnings above those justified by investment needs. In such a situation, the lack of active purchasing power can, of course, be offset by a reduction in taxes or an increase in government spending. But again it would be more desirable to reinforce competitive forces and to correct the price policy that is responsible for the deflationary trend.

With respect to economic maladjustments that may lead to periodic depressions, most business-cycle analysts emphasize the heavy swings from expansion to contraction by private business investment as one of the main contributing factors. Again there

[18] Colm and Young, op. cit.

214

are two possible courses of action. One attitude accepts these swings as the natural way in which the economy grows by leaps and bounds and attempts to mitigate the impact of these fluctuations on the economy as a whole by a compensatory government fiscal policy. The other attitude tries to promote conditions in which there is a chance that business management may modify and 'regularize' its policies of investment planning.[19]

In the long run, success in the latter endeavor is crucial for a permanently successful stabilization policy. We cannot be too sure, however, that this objective can be reached within a very short time. Business investment in the postwar period had to make up for past deficiencies and to bring productive capacity in line with a greatly increased level of income and demand. Depleted inventories also had to be replenished. Steady economic growth does require a continued high level of investment. The national-security program also requires emphasis on expansion in productive capacity, although on a selective basis. Yet we must be prepared for the possibility that a period of high business investment may be followed by a period in which business investments contribute *relatively* less to total demand. While it would be desirable in such a situation to adopt a policy that supports investment, and adds to consumer income and expenditures, we must also be prepared to engage in compensatory fiscal policy in case total demand should contract or fail to expand sufficiently.

In the light of existing price and income rigidities and historically determined income distributions, we cannot be sure that the forces of the market and decisions by business and labor alone will bring about needed adjustments. Therefore, it is necessary for the government to support such adjustments by

[19] The latter attitude was expressed in the *Second Annual Report to the President,* by the Council of Economic Advisers, December 1947, p. 18: 'If the swings from expansion to contraction of private business which we have had in the past were to continue, offsetting operations would be too big to be left to "compensatory" Government policies. Economic stabilization can be achieved within our private enterprise system only if management accepts the responsibility for a more stable practice in planning its investment and operative programs.'

policy measures when necessary. These might include price and wage policies, social-security policies, long-range government investment programs, and tax revisions. In other words, fiscal as well as non-fiscal measures may be necessary to support these needed adjustments in basic market relationships.

Even though in all these respects it would be most desirable to adopt policies that effectively combat maladjustments before they lead either to inflationary or deflationary developments, it is not likely that we shall always be wholly successful in such efforts. We must, therefore, be prepared to use remedial fiscal policies to the extent that we fail in our preventive policies.

It has been pointed out repeatedly that very important structural changes have taken place in the American economy during the last fifteen years. We have on our statute books programs with an automatic built-in anti-cyclical effect. Progressive tax laws result in anti-cyclical changes in tax revenue without any change in rates. Social-security programs and social-assistance programs result in anti-cyclical variation of disbursements without any new legislation. Farm-price-support programs act in the same direction. Federal deposit insurance, changes in margin requirements, and several other programs add to the stability of the economy.

The President's Economic Reports of July 1949 and January 1950 stated the fact that personal incomes and personal consumption have maintained a high level while industrial production dropped sharply in the first half of 1949. This has been rightly attributed in part to the effects of the various cushions that have been built into our economic system. An economy with a very large government sector is probably in itself more shock-resistant than an economy with a smaller government sector.

On the other hand, it must also be recognized that a 300- or 400-billion-dollar economy is in some respects more vulnerable than a 100- or 150-billion-dollar economy. Business investment, which has been running at an extraordinary absolute and relative amount, is a very volatile element in the economy; also many items of consumer expenditures are of a deferrable char-

216

acter and they become more important in an economy at higher levels. Therefore, it would be foolhardy if we did not prepare fiscal policies to be ready to counteract either inflationary or deflationary trends that may develop under peacetime conditions. General acceptance of the government's determination to iron out heavy fluctuations by fiscal policy becomes in itself a stabilizing factor, particularly of business investment, and may help to bring about adjustments that will minimize inflationary or deflationary fluctuations. The possible 'announcement' effect of a determined policy of stabilization on the behavior of individuals and business certainly deserves extensive study and attention.

A program of fiscal preparedness cannot rely on built-in flexibility alone. It must provide for positive action. Built-in flexibility must be supplemented by legislative and administrative flexibility. The less we can rely on the accuracy of economic forecasts, the more it becomes necessary to emphasize the need for institutional arrangements that permit prompt action.

One of the unavoidable defects of the recovery policies during the 'thirties was that they were regarded almost wholly as the responsibility of the executive and were at best tolerated by the legislature. The effectiveness of fiscal policies depends largely on the belief that they will be consistently pursued. This belief will be strengthened if the legislature and the executive share in the responsibility for their formulation. Close co-operation between the co-ordinating agencies in the executive and legislative side of government, namely, the Council of Economic Advisers and the Joint Committee on the Economic Report, is essential in this respect.

The main suggestions for increasing flexibility that are made in this essay relate to the formulation of a five-year program of developmental government investments, of flexible grants-in-aid, and of the provision for some contingency expenditures in the operating budget. It is felt that on the revenue side social-security contributions may be the most suitable tax for variation in accord with business conditions.

The need for flexibility relates to expenditures as well as tax programs. In a depression the more conservative advocates of fiscal policy will usually favor tax reduction (because they may feel that taxes have been too high anyway and they prefer to have individuals or business spend additional money rather than the government), while the more progressive advocates of fiscal policy will think first of government programs which they wish to see increased (because they may feel that these programs should have been adopted long ago and they may fear that taxes, once reduced, will limit desirable government programs in the long run).

No dogmatic statement can be made that variation either of expenditures or taxes is preferable. If there are certain taxes that are particularly undesirable in a given economic situation (e.g. taxes that form costs of production or highly regressive taxes), then their repeal may have the highest priority. When private construction is dropping, additional public construction may be next on the urgent list. Under a system of progressive taxes, general tax reduction probably adds less to active demand than an increase in government expenditures. If available expenditure programs are concentrated, for example, in construction, the sharp increase in these programs beyond a point determined by available resources will drive up costs rather than volume of construction. Before that point is reached, other spending programs or tax abatements, particularly in the lower brackets, become more effective. Thus a combination of expenditure and tax measures is most effective economically in the short run and may be most effective in furthering long-run objectives at the same time. The specific combination will always depend on economic conditions, administrative preparedness, and legislative and political feasibility of the various elements of the program. Corresponding considerations apply with respect to curtailment of spending programs and increases in taxes in case of inflationary developments.

Basic legislation should enable the executive, always with Congressional approval or veto power, to meet moderate fluctuations. If the situation becomes serious and emergency measures with respect to government programs or taxes should be called for, the executive should formulate and present a specific program for legislative consideration.

The Employment Act of 1946 has provided machinery on the executive side through the Council of Economic Advisers, and on the Congressional side through the Joint Committee on the Economic Report, which should facilitate the formulation of stabilization programs and the integration of fiscal and non-fiscal measures. Even more important, the Employment Act, the United Nations Charter, and other international commitments have recorded a solemn expression of determination by the government to do everything in its power for a stable economy. The implementation of this policy objective requires adjustments in our institutional arrangements and attitudes.

Some suggestions for needed institutional adjustments have been made in this essay. Some readers may believe that our proposals are too drastic. They should remember that an attempt to achieve economic stabilization is a new responsibility of the government that cannot be met without equipping it with the necessary tools. Other readers will find that our suggestions have been too cautious. They should remember that there is no point in proposing tools unless we are convinced there is the professional and administrative ability to handle them and the political determination to use them. Determination and ability to use new policies depend, at least partly, on the seriousness of the situation that must be mastered. No attempt has been made in this essay to forecast the strength of inflationary or deflationary conditions which may develop. We have emphasized the direction in which we ought to search for solutions rather than how far it will be necessary to go in that direction. The answer to that question, I believe, must be left to the future and will be determined largely by the democratic process of trial and error.

Part
-IV-

GOVERNMENT BUDGETS

AND NATIONAL INCOME

11

Public Finance in the National Income

(1950) *

THE CONCEPT OF NATIONAL INCOME

Public finance has taken over such a large proportion of all economic transactions that their appropriate treatment in national income and expenditure estimates has become crucial. This treatment of public finance transactions is especially important when the national incomes of countries in which the government plays a different role are compared. The same is true, of course, when the national income of one country is compared for periods during which the role of government has changed.

* 'Public Finance in the National Income,' article published in Spanish in the *Bulletin of the Central Bank of Venezuela,* no. 59-60, January and February 1950, pp. 17-26.

For a more detailed treatment, see Gerhard Colm, 'Studies in Income and Wealth,' vol. I, National Bureau of Economic Research, New York, 1937, pp. 175-248.

'Social product' and government activities

It was suggested by classical economics that, in computing national income, taxes should be regarded as a drain on the income disposable for purchase of goods or saving but that government services are 'unproductive.' It follows that government expenditures which reflect the government services were not regarded as part of the national product. Under this concept it appears that a country would necessarily become poorer if it should increase taxes to hire more teachers or to enlarge its army or to build more roads. In the case of services of teachers or construction of roads, this result would obviously be absurd. In the case of expenditures for defense there may be a question.

It is necessary to examine the concept of national income or expenditures in order to have a criterion of what should and what should not be included. I propose to define national income or national expenditures as the *measurable part of the social product*. Social product is the work done by and for a social group. Work is the human activity that is part of the social production process. Under various forms of economic organization, different methods have been developed by which a human activity becomes part of the social production process.

By way of metaphor we may think of a machine that puts a stamp on those human activities which are socially produced and desired. It happens that through the ages mankind has been using different kinds of such social machinery. And still today different kinds of machinery are used, not only in various countries but even within the same country. What then are the basic mechanisms that determine the size and character of the social product?

In the household (or tribal) economy it is the head of the household (or tribe) who by his command determines what is work and what is play.

In the economy of free enterprise it is the command of the 'market' that determines the activities that are work. Writing a letter to a friend and writing an article for a magazine are both 'social' activities; both may (or both may not) bring enjoyment to the writer and the reader, but only the writer of articles for a magazine responds to a market demand. His activity is work, the letter writer's activity is diversion. In the area of the enterprise economy, it is the market that stamps an activity as part of the social product.

Government services are determined by the authorities in accord with processes laid down by the constitution and activated through the manifold forces of society. If the legislative authorities decide to grant a budgetary appropriation for the performance of a service, then this activity has been stamped as part of the social product. This applies to a defense program as well as to a road-construction program or the extension of educational services. The exclusion of defense expenditures could be justified only if the purpose is not measurement of all work done by and for a social group (social product), but only of work that is done for the direct benefit of individuals and is reflected in their standard of living. Individual consumption is an important counterpart of national income or, to be more exact, an important part of national expenditures, but it cannot be used as the basic concept of measurement of the social product or the general welfare.

Even less justified would be an attempt to distinguish between economically or culturally desirable and undesirable activities. Irrespective of the statistician's own judgment, he must count an activity as socially desired, though not necessarily desirable. To repeat, what is socially desired is determined by one of the basic processes in our society that decides what work is to be done, by whom, and for whose benefit. It is a characteristic of our modern society that there are not one but several such basic processes in operation, namely, the household economy, the private-market economy, and the public-budget economy.[1] The social product embraces the work done in accord with the decisions of any of these basic social mechanisms.

[1] Philanthropic institutions and non-profit research activities could be added as a further category.

In deciding what government transactions should be added to private transactions in the computation of national income, the first question must be whether or not they reflect an activity that is part of the social product.

National income—the measurable part of the social product

Social product is a very broad concept—too broad for un-qualified practical application in national-income estimations. I propose to define national income or national expenditure as the 'measurable' part of the social product. An element of the social product should be excluded as not 'measurable' if in the use of the data its inclusion would introduce a larger statistical error than its omission.

The decision about what should be included then depends to some extent on the availability of quantitative and comparable data, that means first of all data in monetary terms. To some extent, also, it depends on the purpose for which the national-income estimates are to be used. Suppose the purpose is to compare the national income in the United States for the period of a few years. In this case an estimate of the work done by housewives in, say, doing their laundry or preparing meals would not be included. As long as the national incomes of periods or countries in which the role of housework is about the same are compared, no major error is made by omitting this element of the social product. A larger source of error would be introduced by including an item for which no good basis of estimation exists.

The question would be different if national-income estimates were needed for comparing a country in which these activities are largely performed by enterprises, with a country in which the same activities are largely performed within the household. In this case it may be found that even a very uncertain guess-estimate of these activities may give a less erroneous comparison than omitting this area of activity. The question of whether an activity is 'measurable' as defined here serves as a secondary criterion that will be used in the later discussion of government

226

expenditures in the national-income and national-expenditure estimates.

The flow of incomes and expenditures

Most of the transactions that are reflected in the national income consist of money receipts and money payments. The flow of incomes and expenditures of the government in relation to those in the market economy may be demonstrated by a set of diagrams. Chart 1 demonstrates in the most simplified form the flow of incomes and expenditures in the market economy.

Households dispose of most of their money for the purchase of consumer goods, some of it for saving. These outlays by consumers become gross receipts of business enterprises or means of financing investments. Business enterprises in turn are paying out wages, rents, royalties, and profits to wage earners, landlords, stockholders, inventors, and others. These payments by business then become income of the households, thus closing the circle. Some of the profits are not paid out but 'plowed back' into direct business investment. These transactions are regulated through the merchandise markets, the labor market, and the capital market.

This simplified scheme neglects all direct transactions among consumers (e.g. gifts) or among business enterprises (e.g. purchase and sale of raw materials). The charts on page 229 illustrate that there are several methods for measuring the flow of funds through the economy. The different measurements depend on which spot in the circle the measuring rod is applied to. The following procedures are possible:

(1) Sum up incomes received. In this case, however, to the direct income of households must be added the undistributed profits (saving) of business enterprises.

(2) Sum up all consumer expenditures for goods and services plus business investment.

(3) Sum up business receipts from all sources, excluding those from other business enterprises, plus business investment.

The first formula leads into the national-income approach; the second into the national-expenditure approach; the third to the production (or 'value added') approach. Which measurement is used depends on available statistics and on the breakdown in component parts that is desired. It will be mentioned later that a juxtaposition of national-income and national-expenditure estimates is used in the presentation of a 'national economic budget.'

Under the simplified conditions sketched in the diagram, all three measurements should have identical results.

In reality there are a number of complications which are not being dealt with here. They result from the fact that the diagram does not take account of international transactions, production in kind, and the distinction between current flows and maintenance of capital. Here only one complication is introduced, namely, government receipts and expenditures in their relationship to the flow of incomes and expenditures.

This relationship is illustrated by superimposing Charts ii and iii over Chart i.

GOVERNMENT RECEIPTS IN NATIONAL INCOME

Personal taxes do not offer a particular problem as long as it is assumed that the individual pays for some of the government services just as he pays for consumer goods or for buying 'security' through purchase of life insurance or other forms of saving. To the category of personal taxes belong personal income taxes, poll taxes, death taxes, taxes on intangible property, and taxes on real-estate property.

Government activities financed by borrowing from individuals also do not require any special consideration. The simplest case is that the government finances a deficit directly by consumer saving (see Chart ii). This again is similar to the individual saving in any other form.

The situation is more difficult in the case of excise, business, and corporate profits taxes. They are taken out of the flow of funds (Chart ii) before they become income. If such taxes are shifted forward to prices, nominal incomes are the same as they would be without the tax, but *real* incomes are reduced by the amount of the tax. Real incomes therefore would not reflect

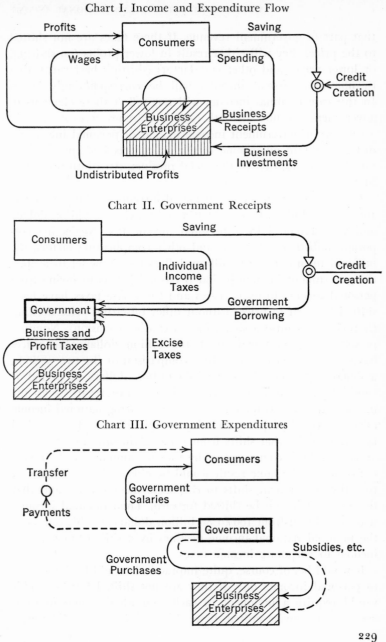

Chart I. Income and Expenditure Flow

Profits

Consumers

Saving

Wages

Spending

Business
Enterprises

Business
Receipts

Credit
Creation

Business
Investments

Undistributed Profits

Chart II. Government Receipts

Consumers

Saving

Individual
Income
Taxes

Credit
Creation

Government
Borrowing

Government

Business and
Profit Taxes

Excise
Taxes

Business
Enterprises

Chart III. Government Expenditures

Consumers

Transfer

Government
Salaries

Payments

Government

Subsidies, etc.

Government
Purchases

Business
Enterprises

that part of government revenue. If these taxes are not shifted to the price, they will either result in lower profits (no shifting) or lower wages and other cost factors (shifting backward), that is, nominal personal incomes will be correspondingly lower. In this case nominal incomes will not reflect these elements of government revenue. In both cases it becomes necessary to add a category of government income to that of personal income in order to obtain an income total that reflects both private and public activities, that is, the social product. An illustration may help to clarify the problem.

Let us assume the sum of personal incomes in the year A was 100 billion dollars. Government activities cost 20 billion dollars and were financed by a personal income tax. Neglecting corporate undistributed profits and other complicating factors, the national income was 100 billion dollars too. Now let us assume the government in time period B has shifted its financing from personal income to excise taxes and the excise taxes have been shifted forward to prices without other offsetting price declines (implying of course a simultaneous credit expansion). Nominal personal incomes remained at 100 billion dollars, but prices have increased 20 per cent. In a comparison of the two periods, a deflated personal income of 80 billion dollars in period B would be obtained. If these 80 billion are regarded as the national income (as the advocates of measuring national income at 'factor costs' propose), the absurd conclusion will be reached that the nation that shifts from personal income to excise taxation thereby becomes poorer by the full amount of the tax.

Essentially the same result would be obtained if it is assumed that the government shifts to corporate income taxes and that these taxes will not be shifted forward. Then nominal incomes will be reduced from 100 to 80 billion dollars. In this case even the nominal national income declines by a shift from personal income to corporate income taxes.

It would be, of course, quite impractical to add business taxes to personal incomes only if they are not shifted forward. This would require a judgment in each case whether and to what extent a tax can be shifted. If we think of changes or differences in national income in real terms, it does not make a difference whether these taxes are shifted or not. In both cases tax receipts from sources other than personal taxes must be added to personal incomes in order to obtain a national-income total that will be usable for a comparison in real terms. In other words: if national expenditures are measured as the sum of consumer expenditures plus business investment plus the costs of government activities, then the corresponding national income must be measured by the sum of personal incomes plus undistributed profits plus government taxes levied from business (including excise taxes).[2]

It is also possible, of course, to measure personal incomes after personal taxes and thus use 'disposable' income. This concept reflects the buying power rather than the earning power of individuals. National income then is equal to disposable personal income plus undistributed profits (after taxes) plus government revenue. This treatment has the great advantage that total government revenue can be used as one subtotal in the national-income computation.

This formula will still be the same if the financing of government activities by credit creation is considered. This may be surprising, for by credit creation 'money is pumped from the outside' into the economic system. Therefore the effect of credit creation must be examined in more detail. Two cases will be distinguished, namely, Case I in which large unused resources (unemployment and idle factories) are assumed in the economy; and Case II in which inadequate resources are available so that credit creation will result in an inflationary price rise and not in any increase in real output. The effect of government financing through credit creation on private incomes, undistributed profits, and the national income as a whole will be demonstrated by again using a simplified example. It is assumed that in period *A* a national income of 100 is divided between 90 personal in-

[2] The reader will remember that for simplicity's sake in this discussion international transactions, household production in kind, and other imputed incomes and expenditures are neglected.

comes and 10 undistributed profits. It is assumed that there is neither government activity nor government revenue during that period.

Period A

Personal income	90		
Expenditures		80	
Saving			10
Business undistributed profits	10		
Net investment		20	
Dissaving			−10
Government income	0		
Expenditures		0	
Balance			0
Total national income or expenditure	100	100	0

In period B government activity of 10 is introduced, financed entirely by credit creation and resulting in an increase in production in real terms. The increase is assumed to be three times government spending, adding 10 to the output of consumer goods, 10 to the output of producers goods, and 10 for government activities. All figures in period B are expressed in real terms, that is, they have been 'deflated' to take account of a possible price rise.

Period B, Case 1

Personal income	110		
Expenditures		90	
Saving			20
Business undistributed profits	20		
Net investment		30	
Dissaving			−10
Government income	0		
Expenditures		10	
Borrowing through credit creation			−10
Total national income or expenditure	130	130	0

Credit creation results in an increase in personal incomes and undistributed profits so that no allowance needs to be made for government income.

Now let it be assumed that credit creation results in inflation without any increase in real output. Then the price rise will force consumer expenditures down in order to free the resources that will now be absorbed by the new government activity. The price rise 'enforces' an amount of personal and business saving sufficient to offset government inflationary borrowing. The figures are again expressed in real terms.

Period *B*, Case II			
Personal income	85		
Expenditures		70	
Saving			15
Business undistributed profits	15		
Net investment		20	
Dissaving			−5
Government income	0		
Expenditures		10	
Borrowing through credit creation			−10
	—	—	—
Total national income or expenditure	100	100	0

This example demonstrates that borrowing through credit creation, as other government borrowing, does not require the addition of any item for government receipts to personal incomes and undistributed profits in the national-income computation. Thus the formula is not changed; national income is equal to disposable personal income plus undistributed profits (after taxes) plus government revenue (not counting government receipts from borrowing).

So far we have talked about the financing of government activities in general. Before the formula for national-income estimates can be regarded as final, it is necessary to examine what kind of government activities should be included as a part of the measurable social product.

GOVERNMENT EXPENDITURES IN NATIONAL EXPENDITURES

Transfer expenditures of the government

It follows from our definition of the social product that all government services determined by a decision of the appropriate authorities should be included in the social product. This, how-ever, does not mean that all government expenditures should be added to consumer expenditures and business investment. The so-called transfer expenditures of the government, for example, social-security benefits [3] or a veterans' bonus, add to the incomes of individuals and enable them to demand a share in the social product. They are, however, not payments for services that add directly to the social product in the same accounting period. To the extent that these payments are made in recognition of serv-ices, the services were rendered in an earlier period. Benefits and grants to individuals and subsidies to business or farms also belong in this category of transfer expenditures.

In the official national-income estimates of the U.S. Depart-ment of Commerce, interest on the public debt is also deducted from government expenditures because it is regarded as a transfer payment. To the extent that the debt was incurred for war finance, the debt service represents payments that do not reflect any current additions to the social product.

What then is the difference between interest on the war debt paid by government and interest on a private debt paid by business? In both cases expenditures for the original outlays—

[3] There might be some question of whether old-age pensions paid to workers should be regarded as transfer payments. It could be argued that they are payments for part of the worker's service rendered while he was employed. These services have been rendered in past periods and should have been fully accounted for in the past as a 'value' of his labor. But when an old-age pension system is established on a current basis, currently paid pen-sions may be regarded as equivalent to claims earned by the presently em-ployed workers. To that extent, it can be said that these pensions do reflect work currently done.

Old-age pensions paid by the employer without the employees' contribu-tion can be properly regarded as part of the wage or salary. It is different, however, for pensions that are financed out of taxes. This is a case in which some of the real costs of production are borne by the government. It will be explained in the next section that in principle government-cost services should not be included as an element in the social product because they are reflected in the final product that the consumer buys. For this reason I pro-pose to continue the practice of deducting old-age pensions from government expenditures to be included in the social product, irrespective of whether these social-security expenditures are interpreted as transfer payments or gov-ernment payments for the services of the worker.

234

for war services and war production on the one hand, for construction, for instance, of an industrial plant on the other—were counted as part of the social product in a past period. In the case of the industrial plant the use of the plant makes a continuing contribution to the social product. Interest paid on the capital invested in these plants reflects this contribution to the social product. Profits and wages do not fully reflect the contribution that capital goods make to the 'value' of the current output. Creditors, as well as managers, workers, and proprietors or stockholders, have a 'claim' against the yield derived from production. Only the total of payments, including interest, represents the monetary equivalent of the contribution of that output to the social product.

The creditors who lent money for war finance, however, have a claim that does not reflect a continuously productive capital asset. Unless we enter into very unrealistic hypotheses which impute a money value to the fruits of victory (and what would happen in case of defeat or stalemate?), there is no measurable element of the social product reflected by the interest on the war debt.

There can be a question, however, if we consider the service of a government debt that was incurred for financing capital expenditures, such as road construction or the development of power resources. In these cases the interest payments do reflect some part of the current services that are obtained from these public investments. With the largest portion of the federal debt in the United States derived from war finance, the error made by considering all federal debt service as a transfer expenditure is not very great. The situation is different with respect to the state and local debt service in the United States. These I would include in the national income because they largely reflect capital assets that make a continuing contribution to the national product. Therefore the treatment of interest on the public debt requires examination in each case.

Cost services of the government

There is one other question that has been widely discussed in the literature,[4] namely, the treatment of the so-called 'cost' expenditures of government. These are government expenditures for services that facilitate private production or expenditures by which the government shares in the cost of production of private enterprise.

The significance of this category of government expenditures may be illustrated in the following way: Let us assume that a business enterprise establishes a mining camp in the wilderness. It must build roads and harbor facilities at considerable cost. The price of the product will reflect the costs of the mining operation proper and of these quasi-public works.

Now let us assume that the government takes over the responsibility for public works, and a second mining camp which uses roads and harbor facilities built by the government is established. For simplicity's sake, let us further assume that these public works are financed by personal income taxes. The costs of production of this second enterprise will reflect only the mining operation proper and not the costs of these public works. Under competitive conditions the price will tend to drop. If national income of the two periods is compared, the real value of national income will show an increase—simply because an activity first performed by a private enterprise has been taken over by the government. Adding cost services of the government to private activities has about the same effect as adding to the value of the output of furniture the value of some part of the lumber that went into the furniture.

To the extent that these government cost services were financed by business taxes, it would be justifiable not to add the business taxes and government income to personal incomes. It was proposed above to add all taxes, other than personal taxes, to personal incomes. Then it follows that expenditures for cost serv-

[4] For the most recent discussion, see the debate by Simon Kuznets and J. R. Hicks 'On the Valuation of Social Income,' in *Economica,* London, England, February, May, and August 1948.

ices should be deducted not only from the expenditure side but also from the sum of private and government incomes. Therefore our previous formulations should be modified as follows:

National income is equal to the sum of personal disposable income plus undistributed profits (after taxes) plus government revenues minus transfer expenditures of the government minus expenditures for cost services of the government. This national income would be equal to national expenditures if defined as follows:

National expenditures would be equal to consumer expenditures plus business investments plus government expenditures minus transfer expenditures of the government minus expenditures for cost services of the government.

These formulations assume that, in the case of price changes resulting from changes in indirect taxes, real incomes rather than nominal incomes will be compared.

When the deduction of expenditures for cost services was first proposed in the debate in the United States and illustrated by tentative computations,[5] Kuznets objected that such classification would not be feasible. He recommended that all indirect taxes should be excluded and that it be assumed that they are paid by business in exchange for government services to business. This was Kuznets' assumption in justifying his exclusion of business and indirect taxes.[6] In the meantime Kuznets became convinced that it would no longer be realistic to assume that taxes paid by business tend to be equal to government services rendered to business, and he believes now that the error is smaller if an attempt is made to classify government expenditures in the manner I proposed in 1936.[7]

I have, however, in the meantime modified my own position to some extent. For the usual year-by-year comparison of national income I propose now to add all government expenditures (excluding transfer payments) to expenditures of individuals for consumer goods and of business for investment. I assume that

[5] See Gerhard Colm, *Studies in Income and Wealth,* vol. I, loc. cit.
[6] See Kuznets' article, quoted in footnote 4.
[7] Colm, op. cit. p. 237.

the cost services of the government do not change much from year to year and are also of the same general character in the major industrial countries. Then it would seem that the least error is made if all government activities except transfer payments are included in the national income, allowing thereby a small but relatively steady amount of double counting. This error is certainly smaller than neglecting business and excise taxes altogether and probably smaller than the error resulting from an attempt to classify government expenditures according to cost services and other activities. If, however, we are to compare periods or countries with significant differences in the provision of cost services by the government, or periods or countries in which the government directly shares in business expenses [8] to a large extent, I would still exclude expenditures for cost services from national-income and national-expenditure estimates.

THE NATIONAL INCOME TOTAL AND THE SYSTEM OF ECONOMIC ACCOUNTS

The concept of national income as the measurable part of the social product would be equal to what has been called the 'net national product,' that is, the 'gross national product' minus depreciation.[9] This concept does reflect all government activities (except transfer expenditures) in addition to all private activities. It is probably the best aggregate measurement of total economic activity. If comparisons are made between countries of a different economic structure or countries wherein the government plays a different role in economic relations, adjustments in the measurement must be made. There appears to be no theoretical justification in the use of the concept 'national income at factor costs,' which is our concept of national income

[8] Subsidies are excluded as transfer payments from government expenditures, as stated above. Some subsidies will be interpreted also as government expenditures for sharing in certain business expenses. They should, of course, not be deducted twice. It seems simpler to regard all subsidies as transfer payments and neglect them as cost services.

[9] See U.S. Department of Commerce, *National Income Supplement to Survey of Current Business,* July 1947.

minus certain excise and business taxes. The use of this concept reflects an inadequate recognition of the role of public finance in national income.[10]

As important as a measurement of the aggregate national income is the analysis of its composition. By combining national-income and national-expenditure estimates for the major component sectors of the economy, such as households, business enterprises, government, and international transactions, a system of national economic accounts, or national economic budgets has been developed. A table of this kind has been used in the United States in the President's Economic Reports.[11]

This table summarizes the composition of gross national income and gross national expenditures (gross national product). While the sum totals of gross national income and gross national expenditures must be equal, receipts and expenditures differ for each of the categories. Consumer disposable income exceeds consumer expenditures by the amount of net saving. Business expenditures (for gross investment) exceed receipts from undistributed profits and depreciation reserves (after taxes) by the amount of investments financed by borrowing, utilization of liquid reserves, or floating of new equity capital. The government account shows the budget surplus or deficit (measured in a manner similar to the so-called 'consolidated cash budget' [12]): the international

[10] See Ragnar Frisch, 'Attempt at Clarification of Certain National Income Concepts,' stencil memo, *University Institute of Economics,* Oslo, Norway, 8 October 1949. 'The concept currently designated as "national income at factor costs" corresponds to the magnitude which in the terminology of the present analysis would be called privately earned income. . . It is a *specific part* of total national income (at market price), namely the part which remains when we disregard the part of national income that is earned by government proper (by the collectivity). It is, in my opinion, misleading to term this concept "national income at factor cost" because this would suggest that it is the whole of national income, but measured in a unit different from the market price, while in reality it is only a part of national income, measured in the original unit, namely market price.'

[11] See *Midyear Economic Report of the President,* Washington, D. C., July 1949. See Appendix A of that and previous reports for technical explanation.

[12] The consolidated cash budget differs from the conventional budget in that it includes all government accounts (including trust funds), eliminates transactions between various government funds, and eliminates non-cash trans-

account shows the excess of receipts over foreign investments.

It follows from the basic equality between total income and total expenditures that the net saving in one sector of the economy must be equal to the net dissaving (or deficit) in other sectors. By combining income and expenditure estimates, the Nation's Economic Budget gives us not only a mutual check on the accuracy of the estimates but also affords an insight into the interrelationship between the various sectors of the economy. This approach is particularly useful for studying the relationship of government transactions to the transactions in the other sectors of the economy.

The national economic accounts are now used in many countries to give guidance for economic and fiscal policies. In countries with a high degree of government intervention, they are used for direct policy determination; in countries of predominantly free markets and a minimum of government regulation, as in the United States, they are used for general orientation by business and government. They have become a useful tool for a high-employment policy.

---

actions. There are some technical differences in the treatment of government income and expenditures in the national economic accounts and in the consolidated cash statements (besides the treatment of transfer payments). For details, see explanation in the U.S. Budget documents and the Economic Reports of the President of the United States.

[1954 Fn.] There are conceptual differences between the consolidated cash budget and the government account, the most important of which are that (1) the economic accounts are largely on an accrual basis, and (2) the economic accounts exclude purchase and sales of existing and financial assets which are included in the consolidated cash budgets. If the consolidated cash figures are used as a point of departure in the government sector of the national economic account, a number of adjustments must be made. For a detailed discussion of these problems, see two papers presented at the Conference on Income and Wealth of the National Bureau of Economic Research, October 1954: Gerhard Colm, *The Government Sector in National Economic Accounts: A Reexamination of a Few Controversial Issues,* and Marilyn Young, *The Government Sector in National Economic Accounts: Three Federal Budgets: A Reconciliation,* National Bureau of Economic Research, New York, in press.

12

National Economic Budgets

(1951) *

In this article I propose (1) to trace the steps that have led from national-income estimates and government-budget procedures to national economic budgets; (2) to discuss the nature of national economic budgets in a free-enterprise economy; and (3) to consider the role that national economic budgets play or may play in the formulation of private and public, national and international policies.

THE PEDIGREE OF NATIONAL ECONOMIC BUDGETING

National-income estimates and national economic accounts

National economic budgeting is the offspring of two lines of ancestors, of national-income estimations and of government-budget procedures.[1] The following diagram suggests a genealogy of national economic budgets.

* 'National Economic Budgets,' article published in Spanish in the *Bulletin of the Central Bank of Venezuela,* May-June 1951, pp. 13-20.
[1] See Chapter 11.

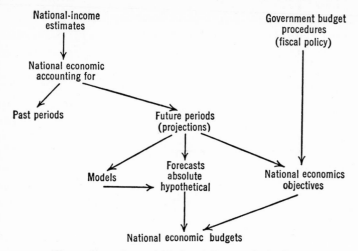

Fig. 1. Genealogy of National Economic Budgets

National economic budgets belong to the broader field of statistical estimations which have recently been called social accounting or, better, national economic accounting. In the estimation of national income, from which national accounting has developed, the emphasis is on finding one yardstick for measuring the aggregate of all economic activities within a country. National economic accounts, on the other hand, emphasize the interrelation between changes in the aggregate and changes in the major component parts of the economy such as households, enterprises, government, and the relationship to foreign countries. All economic transactions are reflected both in the expenditures and in the receipts of a household, enterprise, government, or foreign countries.[2] Receipts and expenditures for each economic group may differ. An excess of receipts over expenditures for households, for instance, indicates positive personal saving. An excess of payments over receipts in the government sector indicates a government cash surplus. An excess of

[2] For simplicity's sake I neglect the non-profit organizations such as churches or philanthropic foundations, etc., which are neither households, nor enterprises, nor government units.

242

business investment over receipts (undistributed profits, depreciation, and other reserve accrual) means an absorption of non-business saving for business investment. For the economy as a whole, the aggregates of gross national receipts and gross national expenditures are usually so defined that they are equal.[3] Then saving in one sector will be equal to the absorption of saving in other sectors of the economy. Differences between the estimates of gross national receipts and gross national expenditures reflect statistical discrepancies. As a matter of fact, the double-entry system in national accounting permits a check on the reasonableness of independent estimates of various component parts. While estimates of national-income totals still serve a variety of important purposes, national economic accounts have been found more informative as a tool of analysis and as an aid in policy formulation.

With respect to the period covered by national economic accounts, in our diagram we distinguish estimates for the past from estimates related to the future, or projections. Estimates for the past are based on a great variety of statistics of income, production, sales, and so on. Of course no country has statistics covering all economic transactions that enter the national accounts. The gap must always be filled by estimates or often by guesses. Nevertheless, for the past most countries have statistics that can be used as a solid foundation on which the lofty edifice of national economic accounts may be erected. Estimates of the past are important because they give us the most reliable picture of economic magnitudes and relationships and can be used as a basis for more current estimates or for estimates related to the future.

Estimates related to the most recent period are technically

[3] This is certainly true for the sum total of 'world' income and expenditure or for the isolated economy. For national economies a difference between gross national receipts and expenditures may result from 'unilateral' payments to or receipts from foreign countries. Even in such a case, however, a bookkeeping entry is often used so that the accounts balance even if there are unilateral payments or unilateral receipts from country to country.

more in the nature of forecasts than of statistics. Such estimates may refer to a year just ended or to a shorter period, for instance a quarter of a year, usually expressed as an annual rate adjusted for seasonal fluctuations. For such a recent period, statistics are not yet available; they are based on extrapolations of past statistics, modified in the light of what facts are known. Such current estimates are used as a point of departure for projections into the future.

Models

In the diagram, we distinguish three different types of projections of national accounts. There are, first, national account *models*. Models are tools for demonstrating and appraising in quantitative terms the results of theoretical analysis. They are not necessarily related to a specifically defined future period; but in order to be realistic they must take into account such variables as the growth of population, or technological advances. If we want to analyze the effects of, say, an increase in taxes on economic developments, we project the pertinent accounts under two assumptions, (1) an increase in tax rates, and (2) no increase in tax rates.[4] This may help us to demonstrate the effect that the increase in tax rates would have on consumer income and expenditures, on business receipts and investment, and so on. National economic models themselves obviously cannot solve a theoretical problem of tax incidence. The analyst who uses the model determines the answer. The model gives him, however, the possibility of quantifying various, often counteracting, effects, and of determining the net result of a variety of repercussions that may result from one particular phenomenon such as an increase in tax rates. The use of national economic models makes it possible to analyze the effects of an increase in tax rates in terms of an economy that is in the process of development. The effect of a tax increase differs, for instance, in the case of

[4] For an example of the use of alternative models, see National Planning Association, *National Budgets for Full Employment*, Pamphlets No. 43 and 44, Washington, D. C., April 1945, and Colm and Young, op. cit.

steadily rising productivity and in the case of a strictly static situation. The need for a dynamic analysis is particularly obvious in a situation in which a program, such as a defense program, creates at the same time a rise in incomes and the need to increase taxes. Analyzing only the effect of additional taxes on incomes without considering the simultaneous effect of increasing expenditures on incomes would give erroneous results.[5]

Forecasts

A second type of projections are *forecasts* of national economic accounts. These may be of an absolute or hypothetical character. Absolute forecasts must include forecasts of what governments are likely to do, changes in behavior, and other non-economic facts. Hypothetical forecasts may take the following form: assume the government continues present policies—then income and expenditures of households, business, government, and so on may be expected to develop in such and such a manner. The businessman who seeks guidance for his decisions is interested in absolute forecasts. He cannot act on any 'if' basis. Absolute forecasts must depend, however, on so much subjective appraisal of a great many economic and non-economic facts that they are subject to considerable uncertainty.

An example may illustrate the complexity of the problem. Assume that the economic impact of defense programs of (1) a relatively small size and (2) a very substantial size are being analyzed. In case (1) a mild inflationary pressure was predicted; in case (2) a substantial inflationary pressure was forecast. If the question were asked what price increases would result from the inflationary pressure in both cases, the answer might well be that in the case of the smaller program and lesser inflationary

[5] Economic analysis often leads to incorrect conclusions when a change in only one variable element is considered but all other elements are assumed to remain unchanged. While such a 'ceteris paribus' assumption may have a legitimate place as one step in a comprehensive analysis, analysts often jump to a conclusion before considering the changes that are occurring. Projections of national economic accounts force the analysts to consider the effect of the one variable element under investigation on the other economic elements, which are all in process of change.

pressure, the increase in prices would likely be greater than in the case of the larger program and the greater inflationary pressure. In the case of the larger program, the government would be more likely to adopt a comprehensive stabilization program which would bring the price rise to an early halt. Making such predictions would involve judging the reaction of business and labor, the general public, and legislators, and the effectiveness of administrative controls of various kinds.[6]

For purposes of policy formulation, hypothetical forecasts are of greater usefulness than absolute forecasts. In a hypothetical forecast it is possible to assume rather than predict the responses of individuals or legislative and other groups to economic events. Often it may be useful to compute several projections using alternative assumptions. The selection of such assumptions must be guided, of course, by a judgment of their probability. This does not necessarily mean that projections for policy guidance should always be based on the most probable assumptions. In a period of international tension, for instance, certain policy decisions should consider the possibility of war, even though war may not be a most probable occurrence. The strategic selection of assumptions must consider not only the most probable but also the safest assumptions. In all cases it is essential that the analyst formulate explicitly what assumptions he has made.

[6] The phenomenon of the example given in the text is comparable to a 'feed-back' arrangement in physics. Assume that in a room we have a thermostat which controls a heating furnace. Opening a window and letting in some cool air may lower the room temperature below the critical point, causing the furnace to operate and to heat up the room. This gives us the paradoxical result that letting cool air enter is a means of increasing the temperature in the room. This phenomenon is comparable to the illustration in the text in which a greater inflationary pressure results in a lesser price rise than a more moderate inflationary pressure. The only difference is that the responses of individuals and groups are less predictable than the behavior of a thermostat. Nevertheless, it is useful to consider in economic projections the possible 'feed-back' effect of, or responses to, economic events or expected economic events. Such conditions demonstrate why satisfactory projections cannot be obtained simply by mechanical extrapolations of past trends.

National economic objectives

While the models state 'what might happen,' and the forecasts 'what is likely to happen,' national economic objectives or goals state 'what should happen.'

National economic budgets contain elements of each of these types of projection. Their main feature is that they reflect objectives and state policy goals.[7] But only a few key figures reflect objectives. The other figures are built around these key figures in such a manner that they depict plausible relations between the parts and the whole, and among the various parts. Plausible estimates for those figures are in the nature of hypothetical forecasts. As there may be more than one set of plausible relationships for a future period, the nation's economic budget may well be presented in the form of ranges or alternatives. The concept of the nation's economic budget thus includes hypothetical forecasts as well as statements of objectives or goals.

Statements of objectives or goals [8] have been developed by applying procedures of government budgeting or programing to the broader field of the economy as a whole. The idea that government action affects the economy as a whole is, of course, not new. But only recently have procedures been developed for stating the effect of government programs on the economy in quantitative terms.

Particularly during the Great Depression the idea developed that government budget operations (fiscal policy) could be used as an instrument for the promotion of recovery. During and after World War II, emphasis shifted to the use of fiscal policy

[7] The tables in the *Economic Reports of the President* of the United States, which have been named the Nation's Economic Budget, are really national economic accounts related to a period of the past. They do not reflect objectives or goals. The use of the term 'budget' may, however, be justified by the fact that past and current estimates serve as a springboard for discussing objectives and policies for the future.

[1954 Fn.] These tables were called National Economic Accounts beginning with the July 1952 Economic Report of the President. In the January 1954 Economic Report of President Eisenhower, no use was made of projections of national economic accounts except in an appendix table.

[8] Strictly speaking, an objective is a qualitative term. An objective, expressed in quantitative terms, is usually called a goal or a target.

as an instrument of anti-inflationary stabilization policy. In both situations government budgets had to be analyzed in relation to a national economic objective—restoration of full employment in the one case, economic stabilization in the other. In both cases the objective did not imply that the government should plan or regulate all private economic transactions. It meant that government expenditures, receipts, and debt-management programs should be so conducted that they would create conditions favorable to the achievement of the general economic objectives.

The present national defense program in the United States presents another illustration of government programs that extend beyond the sphere of direct government operations. The national defense program consists in a build-up of the military establishment, in aid to friendly nations, and also in an expansion of productive capacity in essential industries. The latter is largely financed by private sources but is promoted when necessary by government guarantees or special tax privileges. This part of the program is reflected not fully in transactions in the government sector, but partly in the business sector of the nation's economic budget. The recovery policy in times of depression, the stabilization policy in times of inflation, the defense policy in times of international crises are important examples illustrating that objectives of government policy may no longer be stated exclusively in terms of the government budget but must be related also to the other major categories of the national economy.

During the 'thirties, national-income estimates and government-budget data were combined in the measurement of the so-called 'government net contribution.' This was an attempt to measure the income-creating or income-reducing effect of government fiscal operations. Government-budget data were related only to national income as a whole, on the theory that changes in government fiscal operations were the main instrument for influencing the economy as a whole. The experience of the last two decades has taught that this approach was too narrow. During the depression of the 'thirties, deficit spending alone could not restore prosperity, because the willingness of business to invest was lacking. Conversely, in the United States we recently had heavy inflationary pressures in spite of government surpluses, because business engaged in large-scale inventory accumulation and expansion of plant and equipment. Only if sources of private as well as public credit creation and credit absorption are analyzed is it possible to appraise adequately the role of government policies in the expansion or contraction of the economy. This requires not only a presentation of government-budget data and national-income estimates, but, in addition, data that depict changes in consumer income, expenditure, and saving, in business receipts and investment, and in international transactions. National economic accounts can be used to visualize the crucial economic facts and relations projected in the perspective of broad policy objectives.

National Economic Budgets in Free-Enterprise Economies

The suggestion that national economic objectives should be stated in quantitative terms would have appeared wholly incompatible with the basic idea of a free-enterprise economy some decades ago. There are, indeed, some who believe that the idea of a nation's economic budget may be suitable for a wholly regulated economy but not for a free-enterprise economy.

This notion would indeed be correct if the nation's economic budget expressed, in the whole and in all details, economic objectives or goals. Actually, as stated above, the nation's economic budget is a statement of goals, a hypothetical forecast, and a tool of quantitative theoretical analysis. This combination distinguishes the nation's economic budget from an operational plan for the regulation of an economy. If the nation's economic budget is to be called a plan, the distinction must be made between a plan for economic policies (public and private) and a plan for government operation of the whole economy. The Russian five-year plan, for instance, is a blueprint that determines in advance every detail of production and consumption.

It has the character of a decree, for each and every part. It is a plan to be enforced by government control of management and labor. There is nothing hypothetical in it.

How much of a nation's economic budget reflects definite policy objectives, how much is merely estimates, and to what extent the statement is hypothetical depends on the relative extent of government and private responsibilities. The mixture of statements of goals and of estimates reflects the relative extent of responsibility of public policy in a given economy and a given period.

Some of the European countries found national-economic-budget projections useful policy guides for import controls, allocations, and investment controls during the postwar period of reconstruction. Such controls require very definite decisions about priorities among various industries. These countries needed statements bordering on operational plans.

In countries without extensive controls, the relative importance of setting goals diminishes and that of estimating increases. In such countries there are no specific goals for production or expansion in individual industries. It is assumed that business will respond to changes in demand. Yet the governments in most countries, by national legislation or international agreement, are committed to a full employment policy. Thereby the level of total employment and production becomes a matter of government concern. The President of the United States, for example, states in the Economic Report each year what goals for employment and total production for the ensuing year would be consistent with full employment, and what measures may be needed to promote attainment of the goals. In formulating these goals, the increase in the labor force, possible changes in the hours of work, and reasonable changes in labor productivity are taken into consideration. There are also other national objectives that can be expressed in quantitative goals. The United States is committed, for instance, to a policy of preventing farm incomes from dropping in relation to urban incomes. Also raising the standards of housing, education, health, or eliminating substandard wage rates are regarded as objectives of national policy.

Objectives of national policy must still be translated into specific goals to be attained within a given period of time, and there is room for much debate about what are to be regarded as attainable goals even among those who agree on the national objectives. The debate on the general objectives can best be brought down from generalities to earth if specific targets for a specific period are set for such activities as residential construction, education, medical aid, nutrition, minimum wages, farm incomes, et cetera. Yet under normal peacetime conditions, only a relatively few such items in the nation's economic budget represent definite goals as compared with all those transactions with no direct relevance to policy objectives. Whether consumers spend their disposable income on household equipment or apparel is not a concern of public policy. It is assumed that business managers in peacetime know best in which lines expansion is most promising or what the level of inventories should be. Most of the figures for consumer expenditures and business investment included in economic projections can only be guesses of a hypothetical character. They are derived by estimating, on the basis of past experience and special surveys, what consumers are likely to spend and what business is likely to invest if incomes are on a level consistent with the full-employment objective. Nevertheless, the result of these hypothetical forecasts of consumer and business behavior is subject to a further test, namely, whether or not consumption and investment are in a relationship to each other which appears to be sustainable, that is, a relationship which could be continued over time without creating major economic disturbances.

Economics is not capable of determining with any degree of accuracy an ideal relationship between consumption and investment. And even if we knew what that relationship was, the policy instruments in a free enterprise economy (such as tax and credit policy) are not so fine that consumption and investment could always be kept at such an ideal relationship. To some extent we must rely on adjustment through the market mechanism to bring about corrections in these relationships. If, however, the figures should indicate a glaring discrepancy between the prospective development of consumer spending and business investment, the conclusion may be drawn that prosperity is not on a solid basis and that remedial policy measures may need to be considered. Similar problems may arise with respect to other crucial relationships, for instance between the level of consumption and exports. What is a crucial relationship obviously depends on the economic structure of a country. It would be different, for example, in the case of a raw-material-producing export country and a highly industrialized country.

The relation between items determined by policy and those subject to hypothetical estimates changes, of course, when a country enters a re-armament effort and imposes on itself a variety of direct controls. In the United States there is at present a direct policy concern with respect to the production of metal-using durable goods or the adequacy of investment in essential industries. The range of transactions for which goals are to be set is widely expanded during an emergency period.

Figures in national-economic-budget projections are therefore subject to three main criteria. One criterion is political, social, or economic necessity or desirability. A second criterion is the likely behavior of consumers, business, and workers under stated conditions. A third criterion is consistency of the relationship among the component parts, not only for one limited period of time but for a period of sustained and balanced economic growth.

In a free-enterprise economy, particularly under more or less normal peacetime conditions, the overwhelming majority of figures are in the nature of hypothetical forecasts subject to the criterion of estimating the likely behavior of individuals and internal economic consistency. In political or economic emergency periods, a growing proportion of all transactions becomes subject to the criterion of necessity or desirability.

A five-year plan on the Russian model is essentially a government decree to be enforced by compulsion. A nation's economic budget is essentially a means of analysis and debate which can be instrumental in the development of national policies.

THE USE OF NATIONAL ECONOMIC BUDGETS FOR PUBLIC AND PRIVATE POLICY FORMULATION

National economic budgeting was developed as a tool for appraising government fiscal and economic policies, particularly for the objective of economic stabilization. It has been used recently also for evaluating defense policies. Defense programs can be tested by estimating the possible increase in total national output and the requirements for national-security programs. On this basis it is possible to appraise the adequacy of remaining resources for meeting civilian needs, for essential business investment and personal consumption. An illustration of this use can be found in the British Economic Survey for 1951 (Cmd. 8195).

CHANGES IN REAL OUTPUT AND EXPENDITURE IN 1951 COMPARED WITH THOSE IN 1950

	£ million
Increase in resources:	
Increase in national output	325
Increase in imports for current use	125
Less increase in exports and re-exports	−100
Increase in resources available for use at home	350
Required for:	
Increase in expenditure by public authorities	400
Increase in home investment	...
Consequence for consumption:	
Fall in personal consumption	50

This table indicates that for Great Britain the projected increase in government expenditures in the year 1951 will be somewhat larger than what is regarded as a feasible increase in output. Assuming that the outlays for domestic investment will remain the same as in the previous year, a moderate decline in personal consumption should follow. It is obvious that this is a very important guide in the formulation of policies that may promote an increase in national output or a limitation of business investment and personal consumption, such as tax policy, price and wage policy, and other measures that affect business investment or personal consumption.

Similar projections have been presented by the Council of Economic Advisers to the President of the United States.[9] The increase in federal expenditures for national security from the pre-Korean level to the level scheduled for 1952 is estimated at about forty billion dollars. The feasible increase in total production is smaller, so that there must be some curtailment either in government expenditures not related to national security, or in business investment, or in consumption, or in a combination of these three categories.

Assuming that it should be possible to maintain the supply of consumer goods at approximately the 1950 level, it follows that a great effort to increase production by drawing more people into the active labor force, by longer working hours, by intensified application of skills must be accomplished without allowing an increase in the standard of living of the nation as a whole during the period of rearmament. Since more workers working longer hours do receive additional wages, it follows that other people's income available for consumption must be curtailed. This again has important consequences for policies that affect wages, taxes, personal saving, and other aspects of economic stabilization.[10]

Specific policies, for instance the allocation of steel and other materials, require a finer breakdown of the estimates. The so-

[9] See *The Economics of National Defense,* Fifth Annual Report to the President by the Council of Economic Advisers, Washington, D. C., December 1950. See also 'The Economic and Political Hazards of an Inflationary Defense Economy,' materials prepared by the Staff of the Joint Committee on the Economic Report, 82nd Congress, 1st Session, Washington, D. C., 1951.

[10] [1954 Fn.] Actually the increase in national-security spending amounted to around 30 billion dollars while total production (in constant prices) rose by about 40 billion dollars. This permitted some rise in consumption and investment in spite of the increase in national-security programs.

called 'input-output' matrix of inter-industry relationships [11] provides a useful method for analyzing the detailed industry-by-industry implications of more general economic budget projections. The use of modern high-speed computing machines now makes it possible to estimate the facilities, manpower, and raw materials required in a multitude of industries for the execution of any program that is under consideration. Estimates can also be made of the time required for certain economic objectives to be reached.

Economic budget projections are of value not only for appraising government policies, but they are also of great potential value for use by private economic groups. When, for example, farm organizations press for higher prices for farm products, business groups for measures that would increase profits, or labor unions claim the need for wage increases, reference has always been made not only to the interests of that particular group but also to the economic function of farm prices, or business profits, or wages. The economic justification of such claims by the various groups is usually limited to generalities, such as that high farm incomes provide markets for the economy as a whole and thereby benefit business and workers, and vice versa. These generalities can be brought down to earth by demonstrating the effects of changes in prices and wages in quantitative terms, that is, in terms of national economic projections.

A proper relationship between wages, farm incomes, and business profits is essential for the working and expansion of the economy as a whole. In a free-enterprise economy under normal peacetime conditions there is no central authority to determine what increases in wages, or farm incomes, or business profits should take place. The relationship among these factors is hammered out through a multitude of negotiations and individual decisions, in part in the market place, in part around the bar-

[11] See 'Full Employment Patterns 1950,' *Monthly Labor Review*, Washington, D. C., U.S. Department of Labor, February and March 1947. For a general discussion, see 'Input-Output Analysis and Its Use in Peace and War Economics,' Forty-eighth meeting of the American Economic Association, *Papers and Proceedings, American Economic Review*, vol. XXXIX, no. 3, May 1949.

gaining table. It would be a great gain if labor unions and business groups would feel compelled to justify their claims in the light of the requirements of balanced economic expansion. Such procedures might bring us closer to the objective of reconciling the claims of organized groups with the promotion of economic growth and avoidance of inflationary pressures.

The formulation of business programs for investment is another example of the usefulness of economic projections. It has often been emphasized that economic stabilization would be enhanced if business would orient its investment program more toward long-run objectives than toward the short-run fluctuations in the profit outlook. For example, the power industry in the United States has begun to use long-run projections as one of the considerations in analyzing investment needs and opportunities. In some fields of investment such projections may become as useful as market analyses have already become in other fields.

We are only at the very beginning in the use of national economic projections by government and private groups in making policy decisions, but in this area lies a most promising usage of this modern tool of analysis.

National economic budget projections have been greatly promoted through several international developments. One of them is the Marshall Plan. The governments participating in the foreign-aid program of the United States decided to demonstrate, through economic projections, the use made of foreign aid in the internal reconstruction of their economies. A special research group was set up in Cambridge, England, under the leadership of Richard Stone,[12] for the purpose of developing unified forms for presenting national economic accounts. Before this work was completed, however, the Organization for European Economic Co-operation developed a simplified form for projecting for a number of years ahead the major component parts of the gross national product in the participating countries.[13]

[12] See *Income and Wealth*, Series I, International Association for Research in Income and Wealth, Cambridge, England, Spring 1951.

[13] See Richard Ruggles, *National Income Accounting and Its Relation to Economic Policy*, Economic Co-operation Administration, Paris, 1949.

Another parallel development took place in the fall of 1950 when the Economic and Social Council of the United Nations discussed the ways and means by which the members of the United Nations should implement the pledge in the Charter that all member countries will pursue, individually and severally, a full employment policy. A resolution was unanimously approved by the Council on 15 August 1950, and ratified by the General Assembly on 12 December 1950, setting up a comprehensive reporting system for all member countries. These economic reports include a statement of each country's 'economic objectives for the ensuing year or for such longer period as may be appropriate . . . accompanied, wherever practical, by a statement of quantitative goals or forecasts relating to employment, production, consumption, investment, or such other pertinent measurable economic factors as may be significant indicators of the trend of the economy. . .' The Secretariat of the United Nations receives and analyzes these statements, particularly from the aspect whether the economic objectives and policies of one country may be in conflict with those of another country. Through this Resolution, economic projections have become an established tool for international policies of the United Nations. These projections need not refer to all items in the national economic account but only to some key figures which are significant for a country. The examples given in the Resolution, namely, employment, production, consumption, and investment, relate to categories most significant for industrialized countries. For other countries, production or export of agricultural, mineral, or raw materials may be more significant. The markers that are used as guideposts for policy discussions and for appraising accomplishments must be selected by each country in the light of its economic structure.

13

The Government Budget and

the Nation's Economic Budget

(1952) *

THE budget, so to speak, is the nerve center of the public economy. Its role can be compared with that played by the market place in the private sector of the economy. In the private sector of the economy, decisions about what goods and services are to be produced, what factors of production are to be utilized, and who will receive the goods and services are determined by the actions of the people in their capacity as consumers, workers, entrepreneurs, and financiers. These actions in turn are guided through the interplay of incomes, prices, and costs, that is, the mechanism that equates supply and demand on the markets for goods, labor, and money. We there-

* 'Budget Planning: The Government Budget, the Financial Plan, and the Nation's Economic Budget,' in *Handbuch der Finanzwissenschaft*, vol. I, Tübingen, Germany, 1952 (in German).

fore characterize the private sector of the economy as the *market economy*.

In the public sphere, decisions about what goods and services are to be produced, who will receive the benefits, and who will pay for the goods and services are largely made by the political mechanism, that is, the interplay of parliamentary bodies, executive officials, and public servants in accord with what happens to be the constitutional procedures in a particular country. These constitutional procedures serve also as a channel for the social forces, including the representation of vested interests and manifestations of public opinion, that influence governmental decisions.

The budget serves as an instrument in the reaching of these decisions; it reflects the outcome of the political struggle and is the tool through which political decisions are translated into specific programs. Therefore we may properly speak of the *budget economy* as characteristic of the basic mechanism in the public economic sphere.

In the public sphere, some activities are guided at least in part through the market mechanism. This is true particularly of publicly owned, quasi-commercial enterprises such as public power works or a municipal subway. In countries that have nationalized some of their industries, the market principle may be used to a very large extent for guidance of production and investment in these industries. Nevertheless, even in this sphere of public enterprise, production 'for profit' may always be modified by political and social considerations.

The various national economies might be classified according to the relative importance of the public and the private sphere of economic operations or the use made of the budget and the market principle in the guidance of economic operations. All modern national economies are characterized by the fact that to some extent they operate under a mixture of the two principles.

Some activities essential to economic life are not suitable for operation under the market principle. This is true, first, of such

259

basic government activities as national defense, police protection, judicial administration, road construction, and care of waterways. Other activities can technically be performed for the purpose of making profits through meeting market demand, but exclusive reliance on such organization would have undesirable social consequences. Provision for education, health, and social insurance belongs in the second category. A third category of government activities is characterized by the responsibility of government to counteract certain defects in the organization and functioning of the private sector of the economy. This includes many of the regulatory activities, such as supervision of working conditions in factories, anti-monopoly measures, and the whole range of activities designed to reduce or counteract cyclical fluctuations that originate in the private sector of the economy.

The budget, then, has the role of guiding government activities in a manner that (1) is responsive to democratic control, (2) enables effective selection and execution of government programs, and (3) promotes the general welfare through private and public activities combined. It must always be remembered that the concept of general welfare itself is in flux and is conditioned by historical factors and determined by political processes that differ in various countries. Budget planning and budget execution are the main procedures through which government action can be guided so that it makes its greatest contribution to what happens to be the concept of general welfare in a particular country at a particular time.

The Essentials of the Budgetary Process

The control function of the budgetary process

Budgets and budget procedures were developed in the struggle between democratic representations and the crown. Next to the prerogative over tax legislation, the most effective means of parliamentary control was 'the power of the purse' which made it necessary for the crown to obtain parliamentary approval before it could spend money. It seemed obvious that as long as parliament had the power to determine budget appropriations, it had full control over all government operations, because virtually all government operations cost money. Thus principles of budgeting were formulated largely with the intent of leaving a minimum for discretionary action by the executive and closing all loopholes that would permit the government to use money for purposes different from those for which it was appropriated by parliament.

Budget legislation prescribed the limits within which various government agencies should operate. After the end of the budget period, the budget in the form in which it was adopted by legislation became the instrument for checking up on the agencies to determine whether or not their activities had actually stayed within the limits of the law. Thus the budget was viewed almost exclusively in the light of its suitability for setting limits for government operations and for supervising their legality. The historical principles of budgeting, therefore, were dominated by the attempt to make them a water-tight system of control.

Parliaments have never been able really to enforce adherence to the principles of strict budget control. Experience has shown, for instance, that in practically all countries, some of the executive departments have spent too much money in the first part of a fiscal year and then had to ask parliament for supplementary or deficiency appropriations to finance their operations for the rest of the year. Parliaments have then found themselves in a position in which they either had to take responsibility for discontinuing needed services or grant the agency requests for additional appropriations. Members of parliament typically feel that they are forced to grant such requests without being able fully to judge the administrative details that resulted in overspending. Thus budgetary control has to a large extent led parliament to feel frustrated and powerless vis-à-vis the growing power and complexity of the bureaucratic machine. This experience of frustration has often led to acts by which the parliament asserted its power through 'riders' attached to appropriation bills, that interfered in matters clearly belonging to the field of administrative discretion.

The affirmative role of the budgetary process

Only in recent decades has it been recognized that the purposes of legislative control through the budget can be made more effective if emphasis is shifted from the restraining to the affirmative role to be played by the budget in the formulation and execution of government programs. If the chief executive of a government has at his disposal a budget procedure that helps him in formulating and proposing to parliament an effective government program, and if methods of budget execution permit a constant follow-up on the progress or lack of progress of various government programs, then not only will all government operations be made more efficient, but also conditions for more effective parliamentary control will be created. With an effective executive budget and budget execution, definite responsibilities are established for the control of all government operations.

The late Harold D. Smith,[1] former Director of the Bureau of the Budget in the United States, formulated eight principles of budget management designed to supplement the traditional principles of budgetary control. These principles are the following:

(1) The principle of executive budget programing

This principle requires that budget formulation must be geared closely and directly to the formulation of the government program as a whole. Budgeting and programing are the two sides of the same coin.

(2) The principle of executive budget responsibility

The legislative appropriation of an amount of money is not a mandate to spend; nor does it establish a 'vested right' of an agency to use the money. The chief executive is responsible for seeing that the agency programs are brought into accord with legislative intent, and that they are executed with the greatest possible economy.

[1] Harold D. Smith, *The Management of Your Government,* New York, McGraw-Hill, 1945.

(3) The principle of budget reporting

Budget formulation and execution must be based on full financial and operating reports flowing periodically from the administrative units of the government. Budgeting without reporting is blind and arbitrary.

(4) The principle of adequate budget tools

The chief executive must have the authority and the staff to make monthly or quarterly allotments of appropriations, and to set up reserves out of appropriations which can be spent only with his approval.

(5) The principle of multiple procedures in budgeting

Although all government functions, without exception, should be reflected in the budget, the methods of budgeting should be different for functions of everyday administration, long-run construction and developmental programs, and quasi-commercial operations of the government.

(6) The principle of executive budget discretion

Effective and economical management requires appropriations for broadly defined functions of government. A detailed description of the programs to be performed should be a matter of information and general guidance rather than a specific limitation.

(7) The principle of flexibility and timing

The budget should contain provisions that permit immediate adjustment to changing economic conditions. The legislature should appropriate, for instance, funds for certain construction and developmental programs for an extended period, say five years. Timing of the rate of spending could then be modified by the executive in accord with economic necessities.

(8) The principle of two-way budget organization

Budget formulation and budget execution are not only a function of the chief executive but also require the active co-operation of the budget offices in the various agencies. These agency offices have the function of making recommendations to the central budget bureau and supervising the spending of their respective agencies. On the agency level also, budgeting and programing must be interrelated.

Some of these principles of budget management are in apparent conflict with some of the traditional principles of budgetary control. In reality they can be reconciled with each other and be made to supplement each other. It is easier for parliamentary committees to influence an administration with effective budgetary management than to influence the activities of a multitude of government agencies in which each agency head looks at his jurisdiction as his own principality.

The co-ordinating role of the budget

Modern democratic governments have a tendency to take on what has been called the 'clientele' form of government. Officials of a department of agriculture, for instance, very often regard farmers as their customers, and the farm organizations regard the department of agriculture as their domain. The same holds true with respect to labor organizations and business organizations. Under these influences it is difficult to develop a consistent government program that takes care of the legitimate claims of various groups in the population on the one hand, and that meets the needs of and does not overburden the economy as a whole on the other hand. A strong co-ordinating and integrating device which can counteract the 'clientele' tendencies in the administrative organization is needed.

In the same way, in modern democratic parliaments there is a tendency to develop 'blocs' of representatives who look after the particular interests of various groups in the population. Effective procedures of budgetary formulation, budgetary legislation, and budgetary execution appear to be the best device modern democracy has invented for reconciling the needs of the nation and the national economy as a whole with the needs of various sectors and groups.

The task of budget co-ordination must be performed, in accord with the first of the aforementioned principles of budget management, in closest relationship to the function of government program determination, particularly the determination of an integrated economic program. This raises a number of difficult problems of government staff organization. If we look at the different ways in which these functions are performed by various governments, it becomes clear that governments are still groping for a satisfactory solution of these institutional problems. Obviously, the administrative arrangements will be different under the presidential system of the United States and the cabinet system of Great Britain. In the United States the main function of executive program formulation is carried on by the Executive Office of the President, with two agencies, the Bureau of the Budget and the Council of Economic Advisers, closely co-operating. On the congressional side, also, the need for a co-ordination of the various committees engaged in budgetary, finance, and economic legislation made itself felt. The detailed arrangements are still in a state of flux.

In England, the staff work for program planning is performed both by the cabinet office and the Treasury; special committees are charged with the responsibility for co-ordinating budget and economic planning.

In many countries budget planning is still regarded mainly as a financial matter and is not yet related to the comprehensive task of government programing. In general, it is probably true that governments are not yet adequately organized for fulfilling the role they have to play in the modern economy.

The political role of the budget

Legislators and executives are not operating in a social vacuum but are exposed to all the pressure of people as individuals and in organized groups. The budget is used to balance the desire of people for more services against the desire of the taxpayers to reduce the tax load or to limit its increase.

The original political function of the budget, namely, the control of the crown by the parliament, has been largely replaced by this other kind of political control, namely, the control of claimants for additional government services through the demonstration in the budget of what additional services may mean to the taxpayer.

The present-day discussion about the so-called 'balanced budget' is in such a state of confusion because many people who refer to fiscal and economic arguments for budget balancing in reality have in mind the political function of the budget in restraint of what they regard as undue claims for additional government services. What is needed at the present time is the evolution of principles of budget conduct which, on the one hand, will meet the need for an instrument suitable for the formulation of government programs in accord with social and economic priorities and, on the other hand, will be able to demonstrate to the people the true economic costs of such programs.

The traditional budget principles, which reflect the mainly negative attitude of legislative control, are insufficient for accomplishing the objectives of program evaluation and co-ordination. Budget theory and budget practice in most countries have only recently begun to take account of these positive purposes which the budget can and must serve in the conduct of the public economy.

STRUCTURE AND CHARACTER OF THE BUDGET

Three phases of budget planning

In analyzing the structure and character of the budget, three phases of budget planning should be considered. Each of these phases is important for the use of the budget as an instrument in the determination, guidance, and control of government activities and for the broader purpose of balancing various group interests of the people.

First, the budget serves for *the appraisal and control of specific government programs.* When a plan for building a network of roads is suggested, the first question is how much is it going to cost? On the basis of the cost estimate, it becomes possible to evaluate the direct and indirect benefits in relation to cost, and to decide whether the proposal appears meritorious. Such cost estimates are needed by the executives in deciding whether or not such a recommendation should be included in the budget plan. The same cost estimates can also be used as a focus for popular debate, and for debate among the interested groups about the merits of the program. Such cost estimates are also needed for the legislators when they have to decide whether or not to adopt such a proposal. After the program has been adopted, the appropriation serves as a basis for directing the execution of the program, for checking up on progress, and for keeping it under executive and legislative control.

Budget planning involves, however, more than a number of unrelated government programs. In each situation there will be more recommendations for program consideration than can be undertaken with the available resources at any one time. Therefore, it is necessary to compare the political, social, and economic urgency of the various proposed programs, and to determine a time sequence through which a great number of undertakings can be fitted into a consistent over-all work program for the government.

Before any final decision on the program of the government as a whole can be made, it is necessary to add up the costs of all government programs which are being seriously considered and to compare this tentative total of expenditures with the available financial resources from existing and proposed tax legislation, and possibly from borrowing. Thus we proceed from program appraisal to *financial planning*. This step again is of significance for the legislators and executives who must relate legislation concerning revenues and debt management to the financial requirements of government activities; and this step again is also essential in the mobilization of group interests and public opinion. Demonstration that proposed government programs require additional taxes or additional borrowing provides effective arguments in the debate about the merits of pending recommendations.

The final phase of budget formulation relates the government budget to *actual and prospective general economic conditions*. This is the aspect of budgeting that is related to fiscal policy

267

—that is, the consideration of budgetary operations, expenditures, revenue, and debt management, in the light of their effects on the flow of funds in the national economy. Like the first two phases, this third phase of budget consideration is essential for both legislative and executive budget management in a narrower sense and for the broad political debate. If the economic analysis shows, for instance, that government programs must be expected to cause inflationary pressures, this again may mobilize the receivers of fixed incomes and other interest groups to express their views through representatives or through the various media of public opinion; or if government programs will tend to reduce existing unemployment, other groups of the population may be induced to take a position and express their preferences through any one of the available channels.

The three phases of budget consideration, namely, program appraisal, financial planning, and fiscal policy, must be interrelated. It is conceivable that the first summing-up of all meritorious recommendations for government programs may lead to a total that must be modified in the light of available financial resources or in the light of general economic conditions. In spite of the interrelationship of these three phases of budgeting, it is useful to deal with them separately because each of them requires a somewhat different structure and character of budgetary information and classification. The following sections will deal with some features of the budget structure that are related to each of these three aspects.

The budget as an instrument of program appraisal

Program appraisal first requires cost estimates. Traditionally, the estimates of expenditures were classified according to administrative units. From the point of view of legislative and executive control, it is convenient to have expenditures by organizational units, such as by number of employees and amounts to be spent on material. One organizational unit of the government, however, is often concerned with a variety of very different programs and often one complex program is administered by several agencies.

The recent Hoover Commission Report in the United States (the Commission on Organization of the Executive Branch of the Government) complained rightly that the appropriation requests in the United States budgets were broken down by administrative units and listed a tremendous amount of detail with respect to the salary of each clerk employed or to be employed in a particular agency but gave only very little information about what work was really to be performed and about what the activity of the agency was as related to the major programs of the government. It is true that for a number of years the United States budget has had a summarization of appropriation requests and estimated expenditures by functions, but this has been a statistical summary offered for informational purposes. The functional breakdown did not grow organically out of the major classification used in the detailed estimates. The Hoover Commission proposed a 'performance budget' in which for each agency details would be given by programs in descriptive language so that the executive and legislative budget examiners could relate the costs of a program to the value of the work that was to be performed. The United States budget for the fiscal year 1951 made a first step in this direction.

For an appraisal of government programs the character as well as the total amount of the proposed expenditures is of great importance. For deciding on the merits of a proposal it is important to know what part of the proposed expenditures is for purposes of 'investment' in tangible assets such as roads, dams, buildings, and what part is for purposes of maintenance or grants-in-aid to local governments. It is important to know to what extent some of these expenditures are self-liquidating, that is, the extent to which some of the costs will be defrayed by revenues, such as from charges paid by farmers for water from irrigation projects. This type of classification is related to but is not identical with the so-called capital budget.

For cost estimates of government programs, it is more important to know what expenditures will be made for the program as a whole than to know what will be spent during the next

269

year. For a decision concerning, for instance, the construction of a network of roads or a dam, a cost estimate of the project as a whole should be presented. In appraising the merits of an individual project, it is only of secondary interest to obtain estimates of the number of years needed for the construction and to know what scale of spending over a number of years is most likely. Very often appropriations are made for the initiation of a big project. The initial expenses for the first year may be very small, and all attention is focused on that initial expense. But once the first step has been taken the government is committed to the completion of the project. Looking at what the expenses for any one year are likely to be is not conducive to a judicial appraisal of the value of the project as a whole. For large developmental projects it is most desirable if the appropriation is made for the project as a whole, leaving the timing, within certain statutory limits, to executive discretion.

The budget as an instrument of financial planning

THE CASH BUDGET. While program appraisal emphasizes total costs and is concerned with liabilities incurred, financial planning must be based on estimates of cash expenditures in particular periods of time. Therefore it is not possible simply to add up the individual cost estimates and obtain a total that can then be compared with an estimate of expected revenue. The total cost estimates must be translated into estimates of periodic cash expenditures, and transactions between various government funds must be eliminated if a budget total that can be compared with expected cash revenue is to be obtained.

It is very important that a financial plan be presented for a period longer than just the ensuing fiscal year. Since revenues and expenditures in one particular year are very often influenced by temporary and non-recurrent factors, financial planning should be based on projections of cash revenue and cash expenditures covering a period of several years. Only then can it be determined whether the tax structure is sufficient to support expenditure commitments, or whether, under existing and recommended programs, there will be a surplus for debt reduction or a need for additional borrowing.

THE CAPITAL BUDGET. Some countries have adopted capital budgets with the idea that the operating budget should be financed by taxes while the capital budget might be financed by borrowing. There are arguments for and against a distinction between the operating and the capital budget. If fiscal and general economic conditions make a certain amount of borrowing by the government advisable, then it may appear desirable to demonstrate that the borrowing is to be used for productive purposes. Nobody objects to the fact that private business enterprises use outside capital acquired through the issue of stocks or obligations for financing additional plant and equipment. Setting up a capital budget demonstrates the fact that the government which borrows does no more than invest in productive capital and thus practices sound business financing. Particularly for local governments, it may be very important to convince the financial institutions lending money that the funds are being used for productive purposes, and therefore that the creditors can be assured there will be no difficulty with future debt service.

For a national government, however, there are serious doubts about the advisability of such a double budget system. The existence of a capital budget may lead to a tendency to be more generous with the allowance of expenditures that fall under the definition of capital expenditures. If, for example, capital expenditures are defined as 'self-liquidating' programs, then there may be a tendency to favor the construction of toll roads, toll bridges, and so on, and to neglect other programs, for instance, rural or city roads, or school buildings, which may be equally urgent. Furthermore, for a national government it is important to judge whether the expenditure programs contribute to the growth and productivity of the economy as a whole. Expenditures are self-liquidating in a broader sense if they result in an expanding real income and wealth, which broadens the tax base and yields higher tax returns without an increase in tax rates. It is entirely possible that viewed in this light, expenditures may be highly productive even though they cannot be classified as self-liquidating capital outlays in an accounting definition of this term.

The economic aspect of budget operations

THE RELATION OF GOVERNMENT REVENUE AND EXPENDITURES TO NATIONAL INCOME. The third phase of budgeting requires the presentation of the government budget (including extra-budgetary government transactions) in its relation to the national economy as a whole. The relation between tax revenues and national income has been estimated in many countries for practically as long as estimates of national income have been prepared. Such estimates were often used to demonstrate the 'burden' imposed on individuals and business by government. The Treaty of Versailles provided that the comparison of the relative tax burden carried by the allied nations on the one hand, and by Germany on the other hand, should be one of the factors determining the amount of reparations Germany had to pay. Though this provision stimulated much discussion and analysis of comparative tax burdens, it did not find any practical application.

Another use of the relationship between tax revenue and national income has been made in attempts to determine a limit above which a tax burden (e.g. 20 or 25 per cent) would impair necessary incentives for work or business investment and would have an inflationary effect.[2]

Experience has shown, however, that there are no fixed critical tax-burden ratios. A tolerable ratio between national income and taxes actually depends on the type of expenditures financed by taxes, on the attitude of the people toward their government, on the type of taxes used, and several other factors. An analysis of the relation between various types of government expenditures and the national income sheds more light

[2] Colin Clark, 'Public Finance and Changes in the Value of Money,' *Economic Journal*, vol. 55, London, 1945, p. 371.

on the burden of taxation than does the national income-tax ratio.

The analysis of the relation between government expenditures and national income was greatly stimulated by Adolph Wagner's thesis that in the process of industrialization the public sector assumes a growing proportion in the national economy as a whole. In the exploration of the validity of this 'law,' much empirical work was done analyzing the relation between government expenditures and national income. Such studies were made not only for individual countries over periods of time, but also on a geographically comparative basis, contrasting the relation between national income and expenditures in countries or regions with different industrial structures.

While these statistical studies of the relation between government revenues and government expenditures on the one hand, and national income on the other hand, have contributed much to our insight into the interrelation between the public and private sectors of the economy, they have not been used in any way for the direct guidance of decisions in the conduct of public finance. New attempts to use such relationships for operational purposes began with the Great Depression of the 'thirties.

THE GOVERNMENT 'NET CONTRIBUTION.' During that depression, public-finance operations were viewed by a growing number of economists as an instrument for directly influencing the general level of employment, production, and national income. Keynes, more than anyone else, contributed to the acceptance of the theory that under conditions of widespread unemployment, deficit spending by the government would lift the level of national income and employment. He developed the theory of the 'multiplier,' according to which, for instance, one billion dollars of deficit spending would raise the national income by two to three billion dollars during a given period of time.[3]

[3] John Maynard Keynes, *The General Theory of Employment, Interest, and Money,* 1936. See also the discussion in Harris: *The New Economics,* op. cit.; and Arthur Smithies, 'Federal Budgeting and Fiscal Policy,' in *A Survey of Contemporary Economics,* ed. by Howard S. Ellis, Philadelphia, Blakiston, 1948.

Though the depression forced the governments of many countries to engage in numerous programs for the support of the unemployed and of the economically distressed, such as farmers and home owners, it is doubtful whether these expenditures were, in general, motivated by the deliberate intention to raise the level of employment and income in accord with the Keynesian formula. Nevertheless, these policies were defended as both relief and recovery measures. In the United States the Treasury and the Federal Reserve Board prepared monthly estimates of the net cash outlays of the federal government—the government's 'net contribution' to the national income—in order to measure the impact of government transactions on the economy. It is now recognized that the use of the 'net contribution' was an oversimplified tool for measuring the impact of the government's budget operations on the economy. More refined tools for the guidance of fiscal policy are in the process of development.

THE NATURE OF FISCAL POLICY. There are two aspects for viewing the economic impact of government operations. Let us consider the construction of a network of roads. First, we ask—and this was the view mentioned under program appraisal—what economic benefits could be derived from the additional roads, for instance, for the marketing of farm products or for promotion of the tourist trade. Second, we ask what the effect will be of the government's hiring road-construction workers, paying wages to construction workers, buying construction equipment and material. The construction of roads affects the use of human and material resources, the flow of incomes, the creation of profits, and the inducement to invest. This example illustrates the fact that we must distinguish between the economic effect of the end product of government operations—in our case the roads—and the economic effect of paying wages and buying material in the process of building the roads.

This distinction can be applied to practically all government expenditures and revenues. The economic effect of various government programs—the 'program' effect—results, for instance, from the fact that the government (1) provides certain capital equipment, such as means of transportation or communication, needed for the operation of the economy as a whole; (2) adds to the productivity of labor by education, health measures, training, and research facilities; (3) provides needed community services, such as recreation facilities, which play a role in the standard of living of the people; and (4) influences private business decisions by various regulatory measures.

All these are examples of what we call the program effects of government expenditures. They should be distinguished from the spending effect of the same government expenditures on the allocation of labor and material resources, and on personal incomes and business profits created through the expenditures.

The specific effects of taxes on incentives to work and on consumer and business behavior should similarly be distinguished from the effect taxes have through absorption of incomes and profits, and the resulting direct and indirect effects on consumer buying, personal and business saving, and business investment.

Fiscal policy is the conduct of government expenditures, revenues, and debt management in such a way as to take fully into account the effect of these operations on the allocation of resources and the flow of funds, and thereby their influence on the levels of income, prices, employment, and production.

Thus the conduct of public finance requires, in addition to an appraisal of the merits of each expenditure program and tax measure, the preparation of estimates which demonstrate the fiscal effects of government operations and which can be used as a guide in fiscal-policy decisions. The nation's economic budget is a tabulation designed to aid in the consideration of the impact of government operations on income and expenditures of consumers and business, and on the allocation of resources. Thus it serves as the third tool for budget planning in addition to the detailed administrative budget needed for program appraisal and program control and the cash budget needed for financial planning.

THE NATION'S ECONOMIC BUDGET [4]

The nation's economic budget depicts the main economic transactions in the four major sectors of the economy, namely, consumer households, businesses, international transactions, and government; it also aids in analyzing the relation of these economic sectors to each other, particularly the interrelation between government transactions on the one hand, and consumer, business, and international transactions on the other. A table (pp. 278-9) showing the nation's economic budget for the United States in recent years illustrates such a presentation.

A short explanation of this tabulation may be useful.

This table shows the magnitudes of income and expenditures of the major economic groups, net addition to and absorption of saving by these groups, and the gross national income and the gross national product.

The gross national product or income includes all those receipts or payments arising from current production of all goods and services. This includes, for instance, as consumer personal income the wages and salaries, proprietors' and rental incomes, dividends and interest from investment in private enterprise, all of which represent claims stemming directly from production. Disposable income relating to current production consists of a total of these incomes minus the taxes paid. There are, however, other incomes which are

---

[4] There is a growing literature on national economic budgeting. This is a selective list: Grover Ensley, 'A Budget for the Nation,' *Social Research*, 10, September 1943, New York; National Planning Association, *National Budgets for Full Employment*, Washington, D. C., April 1945; U.S. Bureau of Labor Statistics, *Patterns for Full Employment in 1950*, Washington, D. C., 1945; Leon H. Keyserling, 'For a National Prosperity Budget,' *New York Times Magazine*, 9 January 1949; papers on 'Experience in the Use of Social Accounting in Public Policy,' presented by representatives of various countries at the meeting of the International Association for Research in Income and Wealth, Cambridge, England, 27 August-3 September 1949, *Income and Wealth*, Series I, ed. by Erik Lundberg, Cambridge, 1951; United Nations paper, 'The Function of Central Government,' delivered at the Second Conference of Inter-American Statistical Institute, Bogota, Colombia, 15 January 1950.

276

also available either for consumer spending or saving. These are, for instance, veterans' pensions or social-security benefit payments. These so-called transfer receipts must be included also in disposable personal income as a basis for showing what part is spent for consumer goods and what part is saved. On the other hand, these incomes should not be added to other incomes in computing the gross national product because these incomes are not derived from and do not reflect a simultaneous contribution to the production of goods or services. They are derived from government transfer expenditures. These items are shown in the table in italics and are not added in the computation of the gross national product.

Business receipts do not show all gross receipts of business but only the additions to reserves from undistributed profits, depreciation, and related allowances. Thus business receipts show only those funds that are accruing from current production and do not go through the stream of personal incomes. Business expenditures include all investments for net additions or replacements of producers' plant and equipment, inventories, and residential construction.

In the international account, United States government cash long-term loans abroad and cash subscriptions to international organizations, such as the International Monetary Fund or the International Bank, are included as receipts of the 'rest of the world.' Expenditures on the international account include the net balance of foreign payments on current account, excluding, however, that part of the export surplus financed by gifts of the United States. Private gifts (such as CARE packages) are included under consumer expenditures. Government grants are included under government expenditures.

The government account includes for federal, state, and local governments incomes and expenditures in the so-called consolidated cash account. These figures exclude all trans-

TABLE I. THE NATION'S ECONOMIC BUDGET IN THE UNITED STATES, 1948 AND 1949
(in billions of dollars)

ECONOMIC GROUP	Calendar Year 1948			Calendar Year 1949 *		
	Receipts	Expenditures	Excess of Receipts (+) or Deficit (−)	Receipts	Expenditures	Excess of Receipts (+) or Deficit (−)
CONSUMERS						
Disposable income relating to current production	175.8			177.0		
Government transfers and net interest payments	*14.9*			*15.9*		
Disposable personal income	*190.8*			*192.9*		
Expenditures for goods and services		178.8			178.5	
Personal savings (+)			+12.0			+14.4
BUSINESS						
Retained business receipts from current production	26.8			27.6		
Gross private domestic investment		45.0			36.8	
Excess of receipts (+) or investment (−)			−18.2			−9.2
INTERNATIONAL						
Government loan transfers abroad	*1.3*			*.7*		
Net foreign investment		1.9			0	
Excess of receipts (+) or investment (−)			*−.6*			*+.7*

GOVERNMENT (Federal, State, and Local)

Tax payments or liabilities	60.2		56.3	
Adjustment to cash basis	−.3		+1.2	
Cash receipts from the public	*59.9*		*57.5*	
Purchases of goods and services		36.7		43.5
Government transfers		*16.0*		*17.1*
Cash payments to the public		*52.7*		*60.6*
Excess of receipts (+) or payments (−)		*+7.2*		*−3.0*
ADJUSTMENTS				
For receipts relating to gross national product	−.4		−2.2	
Other adjustments	*0*		*−.8*	
Total: Gross national product	262.4	262.4	258.7	258.7

* Estimates based on incomplete data.

Note: Items relating to current production of goods and services are shown in regular type. Transfer payments and receipts and subtotals including them are shown in italics; they are not included in the gross national product. Detail will not necessarily add to totals because of rounding.

Source: See *The Economic Report of the President,* January 1950, p. 65.

actions from one government account to another government account, and also exclude non-cash expenditures such as the deposit of a note with a financial institution. They include all disbursements to the public from the budgetary accounts in a narrower definition, from trust accounts, and the net outlays of government corporations.

By definition, total receipts and total expenditures of the gross national product are identical. The net saving in each category and the net absorption of saving must cancel each other. As the table shows, for instance for the year 1949, personal net saving amounted to 14.4 billion dollars; business investment exceeded by 9.2 billion dollars the current accrual of undistributed business funds. The government account showed a deficit of 3 billion dollars. Thus net addition to and absorption of saving were equal, considering certain technical adjustment items.

National economic budgets have been developed in a great many countries during recent years. In the United States a full tabulation has been presented only for past periods, while a few of the most important items have been projected for future years.[5] Other countries, such as The Netherlands [6] and the Scandinavian [7] countries, have published official documents presenting targets for the national economic budget for an ensu-

[5] *The Economic Report of the President of the United States,* January 1950, p. 75f.

[6] See, for instance, *Budget of Netherlands Economy for 1949,* with comparable figures for 1948, Central Planning Bureau, The Hague, Netherlands (no date given).

[7] *Economic Survey of Denmark, National Budget for 1949* (official document). The Norwegian National Economic Budget prepared by the Royal Norwegian Ministry of Commerce is presented in the official document, St. meld. nr. 1 (1949), Nasjonalbudsjettet 1949. For Sweden, the factual analysis is presented by the Meddelanden från Konjunkturinstitutet, Serie A: 17, 'Konjunkturläget Hosten 1949,' Stockholm, 1950. The National Economic Budget is prepared by a special Governmental Committee, the National Budget Delegates, and presented in: Meddelanden från Konjunkturinstitutet, Serie B: 11, Översikt Över det Ekonomiska Läget 1950 (Nationalbudget for Ar 1950), Stockholm, 1950.

ing year similar to the presentation of government budget requirements for an ensuing year.[8]

The significance of national economic budget projections differs in various countries in accord with the character of their economic policy. In a country with a large sector of the economy nationalized or subject to detailed regulation, the nation's economic budget is a plan subject largely to government enforcement. In a country that adheres for the most part to a system which allows individuals and businesses to make their own decisions, these same projections have a different significance. Long-range national economic projections can serve, first of all, as a guide in the formulation and appraisal of long-range economic programs. Public power programs, for instance, must be related to a projection of future power needs. Or, irrigation projects must be related to future needs for agricultural products. In a similar way, the adequacy of private investment programs can be analyzed with the aid of long-term projections.

Besides these possible specific uses, economic budget projections are an essential tool for the guidance of fiscal policy.

BUDGET PLANNING FOR ECONOMIC GROWTH AND STABILITY

The three phases of budget planning—program appraisal, financial planning, and fiscal policy—must be blended into one budget plan so that government operations can make their fullest contribution to stable economic growth and enable people to derive the greatest possible benefits from the growing economic potential. Specific economic programs and financial plans must meet the requirements of a growing economy.

---

[8] For France, see 'Perspectives des Ressources et des Besoins de l'économie française au cours du premier semestre et de l'année 1948,' *Rapport présenté au Gouvernement au nom de la Commission du Bilan National,* Commissariat Général du Plan de Modernisation et d'Équipment, December 1947. For Great Britain, see *Economic Survey for 1949,* presented by the Chancellor of the Exchequer to Parliament, Cmd. 7647, London, March 1949. A survey of the plans of a number of countries is presented in *Economic Planning: The Plans of 14 Countries with Analyses of the Plans,* ed. by Seymour E. Harris, New York, Knopf, 1949.

Dogma used to have it that the budget should be balanced each year. This policy originated as a natural rule at a time when a budget deficit often meant debasement of the currency or making serious concessions, often of a degrading nature, to money lenders.

The modern sovereign state is responsible for regulating the money supply in accord with economic requirements. Neoclassicist theory wanted the state to fulfill this function through its central-bank policy. Central-bank policy was intended to encourage or discourage private borrowing so that just enough funds would be provided for a growing economy without changes in the general level of prices. Modern theory recognized the limits of central-bank policy in bringing about a desirable level of private borrowing and assigned to fiscal policy at least a supplementary role. The dogma of an annually balanced budget was found to be incompatible with this economic function of budget policy.

Recently it has been proposed that the right budget policy is the one that makes the maximum contribution to balanced economic growth. Budget policy thereby becomes part and parcel of economic policy. The recognition of this fact alone, however, does not yield practical rules of conduct for a budgetary policy.

When it was recognized that the rule of the annually balanced budget would lead to a 'perverse' budget policy in case of a recession, it was suggested that the rule should be modified to balancing the budget over the period of a full cycle. This is, however, a wholly impracticable proposal. Budget planning on the basis of the period of a business cycle requires advance knowledge of the length and amplitude of the cycle. Not even a reasonable assumption of this kind is feasible. Furthermore, this rule would require that the budget surplus during the upswing would be determined by the size of the deficits incurred during the preceding depression. No rational budgetary policy could be formulated on that basis.

Another modification of the balanced-budget rule suggested that only the operating budget should be balanced while a capital budget might be financed by borrowing. We have already discussed some reasons, pro and con, for the use of a capital budget. Though distinguishing between operational and capital expenditures certainly has great informational value, it cannot lead to a budget policy that is geared to fit into the economic situation as a whole. What rule, then, can be established that serves budgetary and economic requirements?

The dogma of an annually balanced budget at least gave some standard to which reference could be made in the debate on expenditure programs and tax policy. Do we not abandon all rules and open the door to pressure groups by saying that correct budget policy depends entirely on economic circumstances? An interesting proposal has been made by the Committee for Economic Development in the United States.[9] This proposed rule states that federal cash expenditures and revenues should be in such a relationship that a moderate cash surplus is obtained if computed under the assumption of a continuing high-employment national income. Considering that state and local governments usually finance a moderate amount of capital outlays by loans, it follows that the governments on all levels would, under this formula, show an approximate balance of cash expenditures and receipts, computed under assumed conditions of high-employment incomes. This means that cash deficits are expected and sanctioned if unemployment causes a drop in revenues below the high-employment level, if tax reductions become necessary as a means to combat a serious depression, and if relief programs or other anti-depression expenditures necessitate an increase in expenditures.

This rule implies a hypothesis concerning future economic potentials in the United States. It implies that consumer net saving, which would be forthcoming from a high-employment income, is expected to be about equal to the excess of business investment (including residential construction) and net capital exports over business's own internal accumulation of funds. The rule implies that the additional funds needed for eco-

[9] *Tax and Expenditure Policy for 1950*, Committee for Economic Development, New York, January 1950.

nomic growth without price decline will be generated through borrowing to finance private business investment and capital exports. Projections of the nation's economic budget can serve as a test for the reasonableness of this assumption.

Actually, the basic underlying assumption is subject to a serious question. Thus Professor Sumner H. Slichter,[10] for instance, concludes from his analysis of the various sources for increasing the money supply needed for a thirty-year period of economic growth in the United States: 'Hence an increase in the public debt would probably be the best way to obtain the remaining [i.e. in addition to that obtained from borrowing by private business and state and local governments] thirty billion dollars of new money. This would mean that during a thirty-year period the budget would need to be in the red, on the average, about $1 billion a year.' Here it is not intended to argue what the most reasonable assumption is in this respect either for the United States or for any other country. The point to be made is that a long-range nation's economic budget analysis should permit the establishment of a reasonable working hypothesis for a long-range budget policy. Once a budget target has been formulated on the basis of such a working hypothesis, the government is in a position to insist that demands for new expenditure commitments should be accompanied by adoption of a corresponding tax increase or that acceptance of a proposed tax reduction should be contingent on a corresponding curtailment of expenditures. This rule would not apply, of course, to increases in expenditures or tax reductions adopted as part of an anti-depression program. The rule, it should be remembered, applies to a budget computed under the assumption of a high-employment economy. Using high employment as an assumption for formulating the basic budget plan also has the advantage that hazardous economic forecasting does not need to play a primary role in budget formulation.

The rule or working hypothesis must be determined for each country and each period in accord with the economic structure

---

and basic economic policies as they are reflected in the nation's economic budget projections. In some countries there may be such a need for capital investment (e.g. for reconstruction) and prospects for such inadequate saving that a case can be made for a very substantial budget surplus as a kind of 'forced saving.' When taxes are already very high, however, a further increase to achieve a substantial budget surplus will not only limit personal consumption but may also impair work and business incentives. Tax policy must consider the incentive effects as well as the effects on funds available for consumption and investment.

Under other circumstances, it may turn out that net saving and investment will fit into a workable pattern only if some government outlays are financed by resort to borrowing, even when there is high employment. In a situation in which a workable economic relationship includes considerable government borrowing, consideration of a secondary rule is necessary. This secondary rule is that the rise in debt service should be less than the increase in the revenue yield of a given tax structure resulting from an increasing tax base, so that the rise in debt should not necessitate constantly increasing tax rates. Provided the expansionary economic policies of the government are managed in such a way as not to discourage private activity, this secondary rule should give rise to no difficulty.

Thus if the discrepancy between projected saving and projected investment is large enough to require either, on the one hand, a very drastic tax rise for creating a large surplus, or, on the other hand, a very large deficit for absorbing saving, then it becomes necessary to consider non-fiscal policies for adjusting structural relationships in the economy. Such other means include a great variety of measures (including tax policies) which affect the distribution of incomes, the propensity to save, and business investment. They may be needed to bring about structural balance between the basic factors in the economy.

The main point to be brought out here is that for each country or period there should be one relatively fixed budget target, computed under assumption of high employment, whether it is a moderate or a substantial budget surplus, a close balance, or a moderate deficit. Once a long-range budget leading to the predetermined result is outlined, any claim for additional expenditure programs or tax reduction can be countered with the argument that a change on one side of the budget must be accompanied by corresponding changes on the other side of the budget or the required result will not be obtained. For practical budget work it follows that there should always be prepared a longer-range budget plan in relation to a long-range estimate of the economic potentials and economic patterns as they are reflected in high-employment projections of the nation's economic budget.

The use of such a long-range, high-employment budget target as a basis from which to argue with claimants for additional programs or for tax reductions can serve the same political purpose as the balanced-budget dogma did in the past. In addition, it serves as a basis from which cyclical adjustments can be made for combating possible economic depressions.

Part
-V-

_____

ECONOMIC PLANNING

TOWARD STABILIZATION

14

Is Economic Planning
Compatible with Democracy?

(1937) *

I

THE answer to this question, like the answers to so many questions, depends on the meaning of the terms.[1] Whether or not economic planning is compatible with democracy depends on the interpretation of democracy and on the type of planning.

The term 'democracy' or 'democratic' is used in two different ways. Some think of a democratic society as a social order that is intended to realize certain *values*, such as individual freedom,

* 'Is Economic Planning Compatible with Democracy?' *Political and Economic Democracy,* ed. by Max Ascoli and Fritz Lehmann, New York, Norton, 1937, pp. 21-41.

[1] [1954 Fn.] Economic planning is a term used in a variety of meanings. In this essay I tried to clarify the distinction between a planned economy and planned economic policy. While I regarded an economic system which replaces the entrepreneurial function by government planning as not compatible with democracy, I believed that planned government economic policy

the dignity of man, and social justice, and give only secondary emphasis to governmental institutions held to be instrumental in the realization of these values.

Others use the term in a narrower sense. They define 'democracy' as a certain *form* of government, finding the essential criterion in a procedure for electing and replacing a government by popular vote. These democratic institutions imply the guarantee of certain individual rights, such as freedom of discussion, without which an articulation of the popular will is considered impossible.

I shall use the term democracy only in its narrower institutional sense, and the values emphasized in the social-philosophical usage of the term I shall call the humanitarian values. The two usages, of course, are closely interrelated. This relationship exists in a certain affinity between the humanitarian goal and the democratic means—corresponding to the affinity that exists between autocratic institutions and non-humanitarian goals such as nation or race as ends in themselves. The *democratic idea* consists in the belief that a social order serving humanitarian goals can best be realized under democratic institutions. And yet logically it is not impossible for humanitarian goals to be pursued also through other forms of government, or for democratic governments to pursue other than humanitarian ends.

Democratic political institutions alone certainly do not guarantee the realization of human values. Thus the early democrats fighting for these values demanded not only the replacement of autocratic regimes by popular government but at the same time the restriction of governmental power. The guarantee

is essential for a democracy to fulfill its tasks in our age of political and economic instability.

I still believe today that it would be a great mistake if we used the term 'planning' only in the meaning of a centrally planned economy. Planning is a method of intelligent human action. It would be ironical indeed if we should allow this noble concept to be monopolized by advocates of totalitarianism. H. Christian Sonne, Chairman of the Board of Trustees of the National Planning Association, expressed the thought very well when he said: 'It is our conviction that American businessmen, farmers, workers, and Government must plan to avoid a planned economy.'

of the 'rights of man,' of personal freedom and property rights, was demanded as a safeguard against the danger of an 'elective despotism.' Certainly these restrictions of governmental power were in the interests of those property-owning producers who did not enjoy a special governmental privilege, but also they were consistent with the democratic idea. The possibility of an elective despotism emerging from democratic institutions was recognized as a danger for the humanitarian values as well as for the material interests of the aspiring class. Through restriction of governmental power it was believed that harmony could be established between the humanitarian values and the democratic form of government. It was believed that individual and co-operative action, left to its own devices in family, church, and the market, would not impair the freedom and dignity of man but would secure the highest possible social justice. Thus in Western civilization the democratic idea took the form of 'liberal' democracy.

Classical ideology confined the state to the duty of watching the rules of the game; it was believed that the goals of the game, the values that make the life of man in society worth while, would be realized through social automatism. And yet it is not adequate to say that democracy in this interpretation was individualistic. The values that the early democrats fought for, such as religion, the dignity of man, or social justice, were not regarded as the direct concern of the state, but their realization depended on social rather than individual action. At that time social coherence in family, church, and business organizations existed unshaken, as a matter of course, and did not depend on the integrating power of the state. Thus the idea of liberal democracy emerged from a specific historical situation. It was a great and logical conception, but valid only under certain spiritual, social, and economic conditions.

It is not necessary for present purposes to discuss these conditions in general. But an examination of the economic conditions of a liberal democracy may help to answer the question of whether or not the *laissez-faire* attitude is still compatible with the humanitarian goals of democracy.

II

In the economic realm the restriction of governmental power is based on the *laissez-faire* theory. *Laissez faire* never became a political reality, and yet modern democratic institutions were conceived under this ideology and genuinely fitted to it. Liberal democracy was based on the belief that the freedom and dignity of man and social justice in the economic realm would be realized if the government refrained from any interference with the automatic functioning of the competitive order. A presupposition for such a theory was the existence of a great number of small competitors in every field of business. This system of non-interference was conceived in opposition to a system in which guilds regulated and limited the business activities of their members, and in opposition to one in which monopolies and corporations could operate under state privileges. It was a system supposed to give equal chances to everyone. The struggle for *laissez faire* and the unrestricted use of property rights was in harmony with the material interests of the property-owning producers striving for expansion, but at the same time it appeared to serve the humanitarian ideals of freedom, dignity, and social justice. It was the dream of a society in which the individual, striving for his interests within the general rules of the competitive game, would serve the interests of the whole; it was the dream of a society in which everyone would reach the place to which he was best fitted according to his ability and industry.

Much of this dream became reality. The achievements of the profit-seeking individuals brought an amazing increase in the material comfort of all classes of the population. Dynamic forces were unleashed which dissolved the traditional patterns of life and led to almost superhuman achievements in conquering the physical forces of the earth and air. A new vitality pervaded society. And yet, in decisive respects this dream was never realized and its outlines hardened into an 'ideology.' The opinion that the guarantee of property rights would also be the best guarantee of an equality of chances and therefore of social justice and individual freedom for all members of the society proved to be fallacious. With technical progress and large-scale production, there were new obstacles to perfect competition. The equality of opportunity was shattered, and the inequality of opportunity was aggravated by a striking lack of balance in the distribution of risk. The theory that through the marketing order the fittest would be selected and the unskillful and lazy eliminated was refuted by the facts, with ruthless disregard for liberal logic. Many of the farmers or entrepreneurs who failed during the depression, or the employees who lost their jobs, were neither inefficient nor lazy but the victims of conditions beyond their control. Business fluctuations produced an insecurity which shook the social foundations of democratic society.

The tenets of economic liberalism became suspect not only because of their social effects, but also because it was questioned whether an order of unlimited property rights can in fact guarantee the highest possible efficiency and the best conservation of natural resources. The amazing increase in the productivity of labor, as compared with former periods, could not be denied, but it was questioned whether this increase in productivity corresponded to the possibilities inherent in the technical knowledge and the skill and industry of the people. The deep and long-lasting depression of the 1930's has urged this doubt even upon some who formerly praised the automatism of the competitive system. Depressions, regarded until recently as a periodical housecleaning, of which the social costs were negligible in comparison with the advantages of economic progress, are now interpreted by many observers as a process threatening capitalistic self-destruction.

For the realization of humanitarian goals, the democratic idea can no longer rely on the automatism of an economy steered by perfect competition. There may be other arguments in favor of this economic order. It may be that any other economic order would show other defects. It may be that the unequal distribution of income and property and the unequal distribution of risk are necessary for enabling the upper class to pursue cultural goals; these aspects of capitalism are not relevant here.

But under actual conditions, a democratic society that intends to serve humanitarian goals can no longer rely on the hope that the economic mechanism by itself, without governmental participation, will secure the realization of its ideals. The conditions on which the *laissez-faire* ideology was based have changed, and therefore a policy that still clings to the attitude of non-interference is no longer a policy of liberal democracy. It might be called one of *formal* democracy—a policy that grants equality at the polls but is indifferent to inequality of chances and risk, thereby perverting the idea of a democratic order as it was envisaged by the liberal social philosophy.

Here, the idea of *economic democracy* has its place. This often used and more often misused catchword is interpreted in many ways, but I shall use it to indicate an economic order under which the democratic institutions could regain their original humanitarian meaning. Under economic conditions as they were interpreted by the liberal democrat, *laissez faire* quite logically was regarded as the supplement to political democracy necessary for realizing humanitarian goals under democratic institutions. Under conditions as they exist today, or are supposed to exist today, economic democracy is regarded by its advocates as the supplement to political democracy, through which alone it can restore its original social significance. In this way, they contend, democracy, which through technical development was deprived of its moral substance and emasculated to 'formal' democracy, can gain a new substance, can become again an institutional structure functioning in harmony with its humanitarian goals.

I shall deal here only with the measures that involve *economic planning*. Planning, of course, can be used for various purposes, for non-humanitarian as well as for humanitarian goals. There may be planning for the enrichment of a group of producers in a monopolistic position, or for the preparation of an aggressive war, but there may also be planning for the general welfare, for the conservation of natural resources, for social security, and for a smoother economic development. No one will deny that an autocratic regime, be it fascist or bolshevist, is able to apply planning in pursuing its purposes. But

294

the question is whether a democratic regime is also able to follow a policy of planning. Since the political institutions of democracy were developed under the assumption of a *laissez-faire* economic policy, does this necessarily mean that a policy departing from this attitude must destroy these democratic institutions?

III

There are many transitional stages between a *laissez-faire* policy and a policy of economic planning. A certain degree of governmental intervention has always existed. Powerful groups of industrial and agricultural producers, who identified their own interests with the national interests, have requested governmental interference. With the increasing political power of labor, governments have tried to mitigate certain social shortcomings of the capitalistic system by various means of social policy. And finally, middle-class interests have been protected against the impact of technical progress and overindebtedness by many techniques of price and credit policy. This interventionism has followed changing political expediencies; its aim has been *political* equilibrium in the democratic society rather than the shaping of the economic process according to a predetermined pattern. All the many measures of economic policy, such as tariff policy, special benefits, industrial regulation, water resources policy, government procurement policy, transportation policy, credit policy, and subsidies, have been applied while the governments still clung to an ideology of *laissez faire*.

This may be called a period of *unplanned intervention,* when governments acted in favor of big industries in some cases, of small enterprises in others, of monopolies and business associations at some times, of labor and labor associations at other times; and often all these policies were applied at the same time and in the same country by various governmental agencies. In a period of rapidly increasing economic productivity and expansion, all these inconsistencies were compensated by the economic development, and remained unobserved. The situation changed, however, when the forces of economic growth were paralyzed.

Then the necessity for a co-ordinated economic policy arose, and co-ordination means an economic policy conducted according to a plan.

Economic planning may mean two entirely different things. According to one concept it means the replacement of the whole private entrepreneurial system by socialized production and distribution, on the basis of an all-comprehensive plan. According to another concept it means planning of measures which affect the multitude of private or public enterprises by all the means of economic policy. This *planned intervention*,[2] as it may be called, is compatible with a more or less restricted sphere of private ownership and private management. It requires only that a minimum of strategic points in the economic system be occupied by public agencies.

Instead of elaborating clumsy definitions, we may illustrate the various types of planning by resort to a metaphor. Our economic system may be pictured as a torn cloth with many holes (avoiding here the baffling question of who is responsible for these holes). It is a procedure comparable to all comprehensive planning if the tailor decides that the old cloth is no longer worth repairing, throws it away, and makes a new one—regardless of the costs. Unplanned intervention may be compared with the procedure of a tailor who mends one hole here and another there, with patches of various colors, just as he finds them, without any regard to whether they match and without any imagination about how the cloth will finally look. A procedure similar to planned intervention is that of the tailor who reshapes the cloth according to a pattern he has in his mind, using as many of the old pieces as possible. This reference to a pattern seems to be the essential feature of every kind of planning, although 'pattern' does not imply that every development must be anticipated in a detailed blueprint.

Various types of planning may be further distinguished according to the realm to which the patterns refer. There is first

---

[2] [1954 Fn.] The term 'intervention' has been misused so much that 'planned economic policy' will probably express better the meaning of the text. See also Chapter 17, footnote 1, p. 334.

the type of partial planning. This may aim, for example, at the conquest or conservation of natural forces, at such goals as flood control, reforestation, soil conservation, or land reclamation. Private activities in these endeavors are insufficient because plans must be made for periods of time that far exceed the periods with which private enterprises, calculating with interest and compound interest, can reckon. Another type of partial planning emerges from the necessity of structural changes within an economy. Suppose it is necessary that there be a shift of farm population from semi-arid districts to other parts of the country, or a transformation of wheat areas into grazing land. Such changes may be left to the 'free play of natural forces'—through foreclosures, death, and the experience of generations of the uselessness of a new beginning. But this is a cruel and inefficient process to watch when the change could be guided by science and administrative practice in a way that would avoid much of the social costs in terms of human suffering and wasted natural resources.

If planning becomes necessary for certain branches of industry, the question arises whether it could be done by private business itself. But this would involve the granting of a monopolistic position to private business organizations, and unrestricted private monopolies would contradict the very meaning of the democratic idea. Co-operation between public and private agencies in partial planning is not excluded, however. On the contrary, active co-operation, wherever such co-operation is suitable, is essential for planning in a democracy.

When the pattern refers to the development of a certain district, it is possible to speak of regional planning. The outstanding example in the United States is the attempt to develop the Tennessee Valley through a co-ordination of flood control, transportation policy, resettlement, agricultural policy, measures of social hygiene, industrial policy, and educational programs. All these measures are traditional means of economic policy. The only new factor is their co-ordination according to a preconceived plan for the development of a region.

Much more complicated are those efforts of planned intervention attempting changes of one kind or another that modify the economic system as a whole. It is one of the most urgent tasks of modern economics to determine what strategic points the government must occupy if it is to be able to effect such modifications. How, for example, can a smoothing of the business cycle be brought about? There are those who believe that the mere control of monetary policy gives the key position that enables a government to smooth the economic development—if only this instrument of economic policy is used in the right way. There are others, however, who believe that money plays a more passive role, following rather than causing economic fluctuations, and that if the government is to influence the pace and the direction of economic development, monetary control must be supplemented by credit control. It can easily be shown, however, that a regulated banking system would only influence the amounts and terms of credit supply but would not determine directly the amount and rhythm of the credit demanded. A policy of influencing investments can be exercised if the government directly regulates investments in a sufficiently large number of public enterprises or public works. Probably only a coordinated policy of monetary, credit, and investment policy, combined with other measures influencing costs of production, such as wage regulation, could mitigate business fluctuations without curbing economic development.

But smoothing the business cycle is certainly not the only goal that a policy of planned economic policy requires. Other goals, such as the control of private monopolies, require additional measures which must be integrated into such an organic plan of economic policy. It is not necessary to picture here in detail the various possibilities of such a planned intervention. I wish only to make it clear that planned intervention does not, like comprehensive planning, mean wholesale nationalization or rigid regimentation of business activities but means that the government occupies and uses certain key positions from which it can exert an effective influence upon the market mechanism.

IV

The problem now is whether planning is compatible with democratic institutions. If the introduction of comprehensive planning is to be attempted, the answer seems rather simple. An attempt to transform a capitalistic society into one regulated by wholesale planning requires the transfer of all private capital into government ownership. If a majority in a democratic society should vote for such a wholesale socialization, all owners of capital would be driven into one anti-democratic front. Thus the democratic regime would be destroyed, at least for the time being, either by those who fight for expropriation or by those who are united in the defense of their property rights, because in such an alignment either group would have to abrogate the principles of political democracy in order to impose its will on the other group.

The question is different if a capitalistic society has already been transformed into a society of comprehensive planning. A securely established socialism might be compatible with democracy. But what is relevant here is that, even if a socialist system has been organized, there will be at least a transitional period of struggle and dictatorship, and no one can foresee how long this stage will last. It must last until those fighting for their property rights are radically exterminated. It may last even longer, because a dictator is unlikely to submit voluntarily to democratic control. It is possible that in an industrially advanced country the process of subduing enemies of the new regime would take a longer time than in Russia. Thus a system of comprehensive planning is not compatible with democratic institutions.

Much more complicated is the question of whether planning of the type I have called planned intervention is compatible with democracy.

Planning necessarily involves an end which the government aims to achieve. Even the moderate forms of planning, such as the co-ordination of various expedients of economic policy, must be based on a guiding principle. The multifold economic groups—farmers, exporters, workers, big business, small business —all consider their own specific interests predominant. Under a regime of desultory intervention these various interests are satisfied more or less according to the political influence they are able to exert. A planned economic policy, however, requires a principle other than a political one according to which satisfaction and sacrifices are to be distributed.

Such an all-inclusive principle exists in time of war. War preparation requires that all human and social ends be subordinated to one goal, the strengthening of the military power of the nation, and it is in accordance with this goal that favors are distributed and sacrifices imposed. Sometimes, of course, external issues are used as a mere pretext, and an autocratic state builds up a permanent 'fortification economy' in order not only to protect itself from foreign powers but also to entrench itself at home by patriotic appeal for defense or aggression. This, however, is the procedure of regimes that are totalitarian, not democratic. It is not incompatible with democratic principles for a state in time of war or genuine threat of war to organize its entire economic strength for the sake of national defense, extending its control as widely as necessary for the duration of the emergency.

But national defense, although it is certainly an integrating principle, can scarcely be considered, except perhaps in totalitarian regimes, a fundamental and enduring guide for the coordination of economic policy. Is democracy able to establish such a principle?

One answer is contained in the idea of a *liberal intervention*. There are liberals who admit that under conditions as they are the market automatism does not function satisfactorily and that governmental action is inevitable. But they believe that it is possible to re-create the conditions under which the classical scheme was conceived, and they contend that governmental action should be limited to this purpose. Thus they suggest a policy that would prevent the rise of private monopolies or would even encourage the breaking up of large enterprises which work under decreasing costs and are a potential disturbance to

300

the market equilibrium. Such a restrictive interventionism, since it envisages no other goal than the restoration of the market automatism, would seem to be compatible with the principles even of *laissez-faire* democracy. But, although this course of action would undoubtedly be feasible for the large sections of our economic system in which the small enterprise is predominant and efficient, if it were extended also to other sections in which the large-scale enterprise has proved to be superior, it would mean the abandonment of troublesome but important technical and organizational achievements.

Thus planned intervention, if it is to work with, not against, modern technical conditions, must proceed from mere restrictive measures to positive actions for establishing an economic equilibrium. But although this is a necessary goal it cannot be a constitutive goal of economic policy, because there are so many kinds of equilibria possible. If it is believed, for example, that a policy of public spending during a depression is necessary for the re-establishment of the market mechanism, this policy may be pursued as an effort toward economic equilibrium, but it would still remain to be decided how the money ought to be spent during the depression, how much should go for farmers, for the unemployed, for the construction of schoolhouses, for conservation work, and for armaments. There must be some kind of guiding principle to show which direction will be taken in reaching the goal. This is evident also in the distribution of the tax burden and in many other governmental activities.

A government that assumes the duty of such intervention cannot act under the fiction that it refrains from all evaluations; it must assume responsibility not only for the rules of the game but also to some extent for the game itself. Such a step means a departure from the principles of *laissez-faire* democracy, even in the neo-liberal form of making *laissez faire* a calculated goal of economic policy.

But does the end of *laissez faire* involve also the end of democracy? Is it true that democracy is not able to establish a goal which may serve as the leading principle for a policy of planned intervention? The Constitution of the United States established two superior goals: provision for the common defense and provision for the general welfare. Does the 'general welfare' represent a principle which could co-ordinate state activities in the economic and social fields and which could serve as a criterion of whether or not the demands of special interests are justified?

It might be objected that the general welfare is susceptible to manifold interpretations. Certainly it is no rigid standard that can be applied like a solemn commandment. It is a moving, flexible criterion, changing not only with the situation but also with the interpretation of the situation. And yet in a concrete situation the determination of what the general welfare requires is far from arbitrary. In any society there is not only a clash of various interests but also a wide sphere of common interests, and there are many achievements that will benefit an overwhelming majority of the people and will be contested only by small groups representing special interests. Especially in emergency situations the realm of common interests gains in importance as compared with the sphere of unavoidable antagonism. In a depression, for example, recovery can be regarded as a common interest. Not every opposition to measures regarded as instrumental to recovery can be interpreted as arising from another conception of general welfare, but must often stand revealed as merely the opposition of special interests to the interests of the general welfare.

Besides this realm of measures that are undebatably in the interest of the general welfare, there is a broad realm of moot measures. There was a time, for example, when the idea of elementary education as a governmental task was regarded as an encroachment upon the rights of the church and as a policy of state regimentation of the spiritual. The provision of a minimum of education by the state is today regarded as an essential element in a democratic policy. It may be that the provision of a minimum of social hygiene or of a minimum standard of housing may also eventually be regarded as an incontestable task of a government striving for the general welfare of the nation. A democratic government cannot, like an autocratic regime, force upon the nation its own program of general welfare. As far as the moot sphere is concerned, the requirements of the general welfare must be discovered and interpreted by democratic processes, with constant accommodation to changing demands.

Such a policy is a policy of compromises. General welfare in a democratic society can be pursued only within certain political limits. These limits are set by regard for the unity of the nation. Interventionism in a democratic framework may modify the use individuals make of their property rights, but it will not abolish property rights, except by taxation. In any particular instance, of course, the requirements of the general welfare are superior to such demands as the preservation of individual property; and yet if an infringement on private property is necessary in the interests of the whole, the loss must be compensated by indemnification unless the nation is to be broken up into two fronts which would destroy the basis of democracy in their struggle for ascendancy.

The execution of any such program of planned intervention will meet many obstacles, which must be discussed. But although it may be justifiable to say that planned intervention is not compatible with a *formal* democracy, which confines its duties to watching the rules of the game, it is certainly equally justifiable to say that it is not incompatible with a *substantial* democracy, which assumes responsibility for the general welfare of the society, and for the best possible realization of the humanitarian values on which democracy is based. Planned intervention cannot achieve a perfect and immediate realization of social justice, but it will not entail that violation of humanitarian values that is at least a possibility under autocratic regimes. And although consistency in the pursuit of the goal may be more difficult to secure under a democratic regime than it is under an autocratic one, the integrating power of a policy of economic democracy grows directly out of the processes of a democratic society and is not, like the co-ordination achieved by totalitarian regimes, forced on the citizens from above.

There may be situations in which the political or economic antagonism within a society reaches a stage where the democratic procedure can no longer operate. Democracy is based on a certain coherence of the society; it may be unable to function if this coherence is lost and if the state must serve as the only means of combining a multitude of individuals in an organized group. In such an extreme situation, however, the chances of a formal democracy are even smaller than are those of a substantial democracy that tries to remove gradually the reasons for social disintegration.

V

Thus it may be asserted that in principle there is no incompatibility between planned intervention and democracy, but how about the possible realization of such a policy?

A planned economic policy needs, as was said before, the use of certain key positions through which the economic system can be influenced. Is not the conquest of such key positions perhaps as impossible under democratic conditions as a wholesale nationalization? Here I see a great difference. A wholesale nationalization requires a frontal attack against all private ownership of means of production and would unite all property owners in opposition. The conquest of certain key positions, however, conflicts only with certain special interests and can be effected without expropriation. Such a policy can benefit by the diversity of capitalist interests, many of which will profit from such a planned intervention. There are many instances in which important strongholds have been taken over under democratic regimes and in which control has been assumed over a part of the economic system that was formerly left to the market automatism: democratic countries have, for example, enacted far-reaching measures concerning such key problems as agrarian reform and regulation of banks, of railways, and of other public utilities. But such measures have been achieved by democratic methods only when the majority of the population was assured that the institution of property was not attacked in general.

Nevertheless, great problems emerge from the conflict between special interests and the general welfare, and these must be solved if the policy is to succeed permanently. The private holders of the necessary key positions will certainly fight against public control with all the methods available under a democracy. By such means as propaganda and lobbies they will denounce the government's policy and stir the emotions of the population. The government must make sure that these methods are used fairly and must meet them with its own argument, for attempts toward economic democracy can survive only when public opinion is aware of and in harmony with this great task of a democratic government. The danger that democratic rights may be misused by representatives of special interests is one of the most important problems of a democracy in a period of planned intervention, but this problem is not insoluble.

Another problem that must be met by planned intervention is the existence of an administration that is able to plan. It is held by some that the democratic legislative procedure is too slow and clumsy for the quick decisions and adjustments that are necessary, that in any case the co-ordination of the various measures cannot be achieved easily under a democratic regime, and that a dictatorship is in this respect a superior form of government. There is no doubt that an autocratic administration does not need to be troubled by a wearisome co-operation with a legislative body or by any judicial supervision or constitutional limitation of governmental powers. In this respect it is certainly easier to rule as a dictator than as a democratic executive. And yet it does not follow that a dictatorship is in the long run a more efficient form of government. An autocratic government lacks correctives which in a democratic regime may be annoying but are nevertheless wholesome. A mistaken policy or a lack of conformity with popular sentiments can continue in a dictatorship for a shorter or a longer time, but then it may suddenly endanger the whole government in a much more radical reaction than will occur under a democracy when there is a change of the party in power. Even such a change of the governing party in a democracy does not necessarily mean a break in fundamental lines of the policy if there exists one stable factor—an efficient civil service. And the government should not only rely on such a civil service to execute its policy, with the general consent of public opinion, but should also, in accordance with old democratic traditions, enlist the active co-operation of the citizens themselves. Their co-operation can be used not so much for the great decision of policy, which should be reserved to the constitutional, legislative, and executive organs of the state, but for the many small duties in the daily routine of jurisdiction and administration. Such delegation of governmental functions to jurymen, to citizens' committees, to farmers', industrialists', and consumers' co-operatives, will probably succeed best in countries with a great democratic tradition.

The experiences during the last depression with some first attempts toward a policy of planned intervention have proved that the democratic machinery needs a thorough overhauling if it is to be adequate to meet this new task. This refers, on the one hand, to provision for the discretionary power needed by the executive and on the other hand to the formation of a civil service capable of executing the policy. Great administrative problems must be solved. Between centralization and decentralization, between the evils of bureaucracy and the lack of any coordination, the right way must be found. The creation of administrative bodies with a certain independence, such as the TVA, is certainly an instructive experiment; the procedure of the Agricultural Adjustment Administration may also serve as a valuable example, and on the other hand much can be learned too from the errors of the National Industrial Recovery Administration. But the problem is not only one of administrative technique. For this new task the members of the legislative and executive bodies need a profound understanding of economic and social necessities. Independence and honesty, exhaustive factual information, and courage and imagination are required.

It is impossible here to suggest in detail all the adjustments that will be needed, but one thought should be emphasized. If it is said that democracy is not yet able to cope with the task of planned intervention, I wish to answer that the capabilities indispensable for the functioning of democracy today can be developed only through activity. The democratic machinery, however, should not be overtaxed at the beginning; progress must be attempted gradually, and be in step with the improvement of the machinery.

What has been proved by these considerations? Very little. They certainly have not shown that democracy will succeed in steering the nations through this troubled age; on the contrary, they have emphasized how difficult this task is. Science can contribute only a description of the conditions under which a certain goal can be reached; whether these conditions will be fulfilled is another question, and I shall not attempt any prophecy. My only conclusion is this: democracy is not essentially incompatible with planning if planning is understood to be what I have called planned intervention and if democracy is understood as substantial democracy, that is as an institutional machinery for the realization of humanitarian values. Certain adjustments must be made, and no scientific analysis can reveal whether or not these adjustments will be attempted or whether the attempt will be successful. This depends on how far public opinion realizes the precarious world in which we live. And this in turn depends on the determination and strength of those striving for the general welfare as against special interests; and on a revitalization of the democratic idea, so that the fight for a democratic form of government, and for the individual and social values it incorporates, will be regarded as worth while by the people on whose shoulders the fate of our civilization finally rests.

15

Is Economic Security Worth the Cost?

(1939) *

I

AMONG the many things I have learned from hitch-hikers in this country belongs the significance of the question I am now going to discuss. An unemployed hitch-hiker recently asked me whether it is true that there is no longer unemployment in Germany. I confirmed this and explained to him how many people in Germany are kept busy working for the unproductive purpose of rearmament without adding to the standard of living of the population; I explained that huge spending has brought the country to the verge of inflation and necessitated a rigid regimentation of the whole economy, leading to the introduction of conscript labor and to full control of all capital investment; I told him how closely this economic control is re-

* 'Is Economic Security Worth the Cost?' pt. IV of a symposium conducted by the Graduate Faculty of Political and Social Science of the New School for Social Research on 'The Struggle for Economic Security,' *Social Research*, VI (2), May 1939, pp. 287-98.

lated to the regimentation of life in general, to the extermina-
tion of all the fundamental liberties so highly cherished in
America. I was quite certain that I had impressed my friend
by my speech. But his answer was: 'What's the use of freedom,
if I have no job and no hope of finding a job.'

I do not know how typical this experience is. Is it true that
unnoticed by the authorities on constitutional law there has been
an addition to the list of inalienable rights embodied in the
constitution? I mean the right to earn a living by one's own
work. It has been said that if an individual no longer had to
face the risk of losing his job, his right to work would be transformed into the duty to work, which is called slavery.

We speak of 'economic security.' If economic security is understood as an actionable right of the individual to own a specific job, it is incompatible with the tenets of democracy. If it
means nothing more than that the unemployed and the inva-
lids should receive relief, it is a denial of the worth of democracy. My hitch-hiker friend was not starving. He was on the relief roll. But this did not prevent him from seeing his family
life undermined, his skill deteriorating, and his life frustrated.
It is very important that American citizens and authorities watch
all activities of undemocratic organizations, but I daresay that
the existence of ten million people who are unable to earn their
living by their own work is a more serious threat to American
democracy. European democracies were not overthrown by the
unemployed, but I doubt whether Hitler would have come to
power if there had not been six million unemployed in Germany to whom he promised re-employment.

Not the guarantee of a specific job, not relief, is the issue,
but the duty of the government to promote the general welfare,
including its duty to provide opportunities for employment. This
is what we have in mind when using the ambiguous terms 'right
to work' and 'economic security.'

That dictatorial regimes have been able to provide employment opportunities, at least for the time being, is one of the
main pillars of their internal strength and to my mind is a

challenge to the democracies. But must we admit that a minimum of economic security can be accomplished only in a totalitarian regime, only in a fascist, a national socialist, or a bolshevist way of life? Must we admit that economic security can be achieved only at the cost of progress or liberty or both? Is this new claim compatible with the other rights—liberty and the pursuit of happiness—or can one of them be accomplished only at the price of the others?

II

Is not the very mention of the problem a contradiction of one of the main accomplishments of the liberal age? The kings and princes of the sixteenth, seventeenth, and eighteenth centuries were very much concerned with 'How the common people may be set to worke' (the title of a booklet published in 1530). They provided employment in subsidized industries, public works, and—workhouses. Was it not the great accomplishment of capitalism that for an enormously increasing population it created employment opportunities automatically, and without government regulation?

Some of our critics think that we put the cart before the horse. We ask what government must do in order to assure employment opportunities. They contend that economic insecurity results from the government's doing too much rather than too little. We were told that private initiative will assure full employment of all available factors of production if it is not disturbed by government interference. Some contended that in the Great Depression it was not capitalism that broke down but that it was a paralyzed, emasculated economic system—the distorted image of capitalism—disfigured by all kinds of rigidities and interference.

I am convinced that, compared with all other forms of economic organization, an ideal system of free competition has great merits. Yet in searching for a constructive policy, it does not help very much to lament the deformation of capitalism; we do not thereby restore the conditions that are essential for the working of a *laissez-faire* economy.

A good many of the rigidities in our economic system must be accepted as facts which cannot be removed by any realistic policy. Yet even if we could restore full flexibility of prices, interest, and wages, this would not remove all causes of instability and would not assure re-employment of the unemployed. Low costs of production will not lead to the construction of houses or plants if there is no reasonable expectation of an increasing demand. Only against the background of a vigorous upward trend will depressions be overcome by the market automatism. Today, if the so-called natural forces are permitted to take their course, the tendencies that make for spreading and intensifying depressions are stronger than those helping to overcome them.

It is no longer possible to regard depressions as a wholesome housecleaning which is necessary from time to time in a period of economic progress. Depressions today are a housecleaning in which the furniture is not merely cleaned but drenched and in which the water does more damage than good. As long as we do not have a fully regulated economy, we probably have some need for the services of this ugly charwoman, depression, but we must watch her carefully so that she cannot do too much damage, and we must see that we send her away as soon as her job is done. How can we get rid of this termagant?

III

There appears to be only one method by which the self-accelerating forces of the depression can be overcome—government spending. In no country has prosperity been restored by mere cost adjustments. We find a substantial amount of re-employment only in countries which embarked on a policy of spending, whether the spending was done for rearmament and had re-employment as a by-product, or whether spending was the instrument of a deliberate re-employment policy.

Is *spending* the answer to our question of how re-employment can be accomplished?

In the March (1939) issue of *Fortune* there were two articles which seemed to me very significant for the whole situation. One contained a report on a Round Table in which several businessmen discussed the problem of spending with a professor, a New Deal writer, a farmer, and an editor of *Fortune*. With one dissenting opinion, all agreed on the necessity for a spending policy, although with more or less important qualifications and reservations. In the same issue were published the results of a straw vote on the question of deficit spending. Here we find that 74 per cent of the poor were in favor of President Roosevelt. But only 18 per cent of the poor expressed their belief in deficit spending; 55 per cent voted against such a policy, and 27 per cent had no opinion.

I must say that these two findings reinforced my belief in American democracy; the acknowledgment of representative businessmen that the government has the duty to provide employment opportunities, and at the same time evidence that the masses of the population are not bribed by the policy of spending.

These poor who overwhelmingly expressed their distrust of deficit spending did not indulge in the economic question whether or not spending leads to recovery. They do not know anything about the 'leakages' of the system. But they who always have a hard time to make both ends meet, they who know that a deficit in their household budgets always breeds trouble, cannot be convinced that what is a curse in their personal affairs may be a wholesome cure if applied by the government.

This whole comparison of the household budget and the public budget is fallacious. I wonder how the same people would have answered the question if they had been asked whether or not they are in favor of government 'investments' financed by credit.

If we look upon recent discussions concerning public spending as a re-employment device, one conclusion seems to be clear. The efficacy of spending as a means of creating additional employment is no longer often denied; the records are too convincing. The criticism has shifted; it is questioned whether the wholesome effects of deficit spending can last; it is contended that this policy requires a dosing and timing which cannot be accomplished by a democratic regime; and it is said that spending undermines fiscal and political morale.

It appears to me that now, after years of experience with a spending policy, the real issues have at last become clear. Does spending, though it is the only way out, undermine democracy and lead us unwillingly into dictatorship of one type or another? Is democracy then unable to use the only existing way out?

The argument that deficit spending undermines fiscal and political morale is very serious, but it can be met by enacting an appropriate budgetary procedure and by selecting appropriate purposes for such government outlays. If this is done, the essential difference between public budgets and household budgets will become clearer, and it will be possible to satisfy the people's instinct for economy as well as the requirements of the economic situation. It seems to me that this could best be accomplished if Congress were to vote annually on a carefully prepared five-year program of public investments, a procedure similar to that provided by the Charter of the City of New York. The year-by-year *timing* of these outlays should be left to a committee representing the various departments and the Federal Reserve System and acting under the responsibility of the Chief Executive. Such a procedure would eliminate the objection that spending undermines fiscal and political morale, and would make it possible to time and dose spending in accordance with the necessities of the cyclical situation without impairing legislative control over all government outlays.

There remain, however, the objections of those who contend that spending will be effective only for a short time and must be continued indefinitely if a new recession is to be prevented. Permanent government outlays would reach the limits. More debts entail more taxes, and there are limits within which taxes can be collected by co-operation between taxpayers and government. There are limits beyond which new fields of productive government investment can be found only at the expense of fields now in private operation. These limits are certainly not rigid but they cannot be disregarded without far-reaching consequences. Therefore, a policy is needed which leads to the greatest amount of re-employment through the smallest possible amount of government outlays.

This is the idea suggested by the term 'pump priming.' It suggests that government outlays are designed to stimulate private investments so that re-employment is brought about largely by increased private activities. It is the very opposite of the policy pursued by totalitarian regimes.

IV

Thus spending alone is no panacea. If it is to be kept within the necessary limits, it must be integrated into a consistent re-employment program. We have learned from what happened in 1936-7 that public outlays cannot safely be stopped before private investments have developed sufficiently. And we have learned that private investments will not develop sufficiently if the price-cost relationship does not promise a profit in the fields where large investments are due. There are those on one side of the fence who insist that spending is *the* solution, and they do not worry, for instance, about costs which eliminate profits or drive prices up. And on the other side of the fence are those who can scarcely find names black enough for a spending policy and expect everything from a cost adjustment. Recent experience [1939] has taught the important lesson that in our economic situation both these solutions are necessary. If our discussions have aided somewhat in breaking down this fence they will have made a genuine contribution to the cause of recovery.

In view of all the rigidities in our economy of imperfect competition in business and labor, the adjustment of prices and costs cannot be expected to come entirely from the automatic working of the market. Therefore, it is the task of the government to give its support to those adjustments necessary for assuring a reasonable expectation of profits in fields where investment opportunities exist. What fields are these in which maladjustments block needed investments?

The greatest potential field for investment is housing. But here the difference between costs and the prices which the masses of the consumers can afford is fatal. Long-run city planning, adjustment of labor conditions and of prices of building materials are essential. Yet probably more important is the need to overcome the obstacles that prevent the application of modern methods of production. It appears questionable whether we can wait for the appearance of a Henry Ford who can produce on a large scale the apartment that rents for five dollars a room; this is a field in which we should allow the government to take the lead to a larger extent than it has done in the past.

Other maladjustments are the famous 'bottle-necks' which arise in the early phase of recovery and cause a temporary shortage of skilled labor and certain materials. If this situation is exploited by a rapid increase in prices and wages, the recovery will come to an early stop. To prevent an untimely increase in prices is one of the most important tasks of a recovery policy, and there are many ways of accomplishing this. One efficient means is a flexible tariff policy.

A successful wage policy probably involves greater difficulties. If a labor movement embraces all types of workers, it is in the interest of the union to increase the total wage bill rather than the wage rates of specific classes of workers. But unions competing with one another will try to obtain advantages for their members even at the expense of other workers. A strong and comprehensive labor movement whose leaders feel responsible for all workers, whether employed or unemployed, is as essential for a democratic re-employment policy as the destruction of independent unions is essential for a totalitarian policy.

Co-operation of unions, management, and the government in the interest of re-employment is probably more efficient than compulsory arbitration, which inevitably implies great difficulties for all parties concerned. The hope that such co-operation may be possible does not seem to be too utopian, since a depression is the very period in which there is no fundamental economic cleavage in the interests of management, labor, and a government bound to a policy of re-employment. It is essential

315

to create forms for such co-operation that are more stable than alternate overtures to the two groups by government officials. This leads us, however, to problems of legislative and administrative adjustments.

In short, then, re-employment of the type practiced in Nazi Germany depends entirely on government spending and on depressing private investments. In a program as outlined here, government outlays have a proper and essential place in the effort toward re-employment, but private investments, stimulated and assisted by government policy, play the greatest role.

I have no doubt that this nation may enjoy quite a number of years of prosperity based on investments in housing, railways, and utilities, if a consistent policy of this kind is followed. Yet, this does not mean that all our difficulties will thereby be overcome. The main task of policy lies in the upswing—in order to prevent or mitigate the next downswing. Economic security demands not only the creation of opportunities for the millions of unemployed but also measures designed to sustain employment.

V

The economist is in a situation similar to that of Till Eulenspiegel, who according to the story was always gay and cheerful when he climbed a mountain because he anticipated the pleasure of going down, but was sad when he went downhill because he feared the strain of climbing up again. The economist can be relatively optimistic about the absorption of unemployed in a depression. He knows what to suggest, and his only worry is whether the legislature and administration on the one hand and business and labor on the other hand will follow the prescription.

If you ask the economist what we should do in the prosperity period in order to forestall the next depression, he faces a much more difficult problem. Perhaps you may feel that it is too early to worry now about the next depression. But I do not know how often democracy can stand such severe upheavals, even if we call them 'recessions.' I am convinced that we must not wait to make plans for the next catastrophe until it engulfs us. There is a reasonable chance that this country will enjoy a number of prosperous years if the steps which have been discussed are taken. But I hope that such a sequence of prosperous years will not bring in its wake a 'new era' psychology of illusive security. We must regard the next recovery period as a breathing spell. The enactment of reform measures in a depression is psychologically and politically easier, but economically much harder, than the enactment of prophylactic measures in prosperous years. Must we admit that only a catastrophic situation can impel us to act? I earnestly hope that foreknowledge of the grave difficulties which lie ahead will be a sufficient motive for deliberation and action in time.

I have not said what measures are to my mind necessary for preventing the next depression, for I do not know any suitable formula which I could propose in a few sentences. We are, in more than one respect, living in a period of transition. Our economic organization and our governmental machinery will look different in the middle of the twentieth century from the way they looked in the nineteenth century. The analysis of the underlying causes of our present instability implies the direction in which the cure must be sought.

There seems to be a shortcut to economic security at the price of our liberty, but this shortcut leads to the security of the grave. Individuals striving for 100 per cent security undermine liberty as much as individuals and organizations pursuing their special interests without submitting to the checks enacted for the common welfare. It is, however, an even more treacherous illusion to believe that we can preserve our liberty without providing opportunities. We must reach our goal through determined action, and not by letting nature—which means human inertia, selfishness, and lobbies—take its course. The price we must pay consists of adjustments: adjustments in business organization, adjustments in our administrative machinery, and finally, adjustments in our attitudes.

317

A government policy which promotes employment opportunities is the most effective defense of the values and institutions of democracy. That the price for this goal is not too high can be testified to by none so urgently as by those who have escaped dictatorial regimes.

16

On the Road to Economic Stabilization

(1948) *

WHEN the President signed the Employment Act on 20 February 1946, he made the following statement: 'The Employment Act of 1946 is not the end of the road but rather the beginning. It is a commitment by the government to the people—a commitment to take any and all of the measures necessary for a healthy economy, one that provides opportunities for those able, willing and seeking to work. We shall all try to honor that commitment.'

Today, more than two years later, we are still at the beginning of the road. There have been opportunities for those able, willing, and seeking to work; there has indeed been full employment. It would, however, be stretching the point too far to attribute the full employment of these years to government policies under the Employment Act.

* 'On the Road to Economic Stabilization,' *Social Research*, xv (3), September 1948, pp. 265-76. This article is based on a lecture delivered at George Washington University, Washington, D. C., 20 February 1948, on the second anniversary of the signing of the Employment Act of 1946.

True, we have built the vehicles in which to travel toward economic stabilization. A Council of Economic Advisers has been established in the Executive Office of the President, and a Joint Committee on the Economic Report in Congress. These vehicles have made their first trial runs and, by skillful driving and luck, have avoided major collisions. The trial runs were not unsuccessful, but the real tests are still to come.

Equally as important as the construction of these vehicles is the fact that some progress has been made in exploring the nature of the road they will have to travel. The Employment Act consisted mainly of a policy declaration and the establishment of the two co-ordinating agencies. It prescribed their functions in a general way but gave no indication of the policies that should be followed. In this respect it was the beginning of a journey into uncharted land, and there was considerable controversy over whether the journey would lead to plenty and freedom or to ruin and serfdom.

At the time of the debate on the full-employment bill there were those who believed that without a well-co-ordinated economic policy, the country would inevitably run again into a depression with mass unemployment and mass frustration. Our free democratic institutions might not survive another experience of that sort. There were, on the other hand, those who said that economic stabilization would not be desirable because it would lead to economic stagnation or to regimentation. Some believed that, even if desirable, it would not be feasible because neither the necessary technical and statistical knowledge nor the essential policy devices are available.

It is the intention of this paper to re-examine these main economic arguments [1] in the light of the experience of the last two years. This may at least help to reformulate the crucial questions and to identify some of the fields in which intensive work

---

[1] A convenient summary of the objections can be found in *Assuring Full Employment in a Free Competitive Economy*, report of the Senate Committee on Banking and Currency, Senate Report No. 583, 79th Congress, 1st Session, September 1945.

needs to be done by the economic profession to provide the answers indispensable to the success of this great venture.

ECONOMIC PROGRESS AND ECONOMIC STABILIZATION

Opponents of the philosophy of the full-employment bill, who insisted that a policy of economic stabilization would lead to economic stagnation, asserted that depressions are the price we pay for progress. Economic progress inevitably leads to maladjustments, and depressions are the means of correcting maladjustments in a non-regulated economy.

An examination of this problem should pose two distinct questions: first, does economic progress necessarily lead to distortions in economic relationships; and second, do such distortions necessarily lead to depressions?

The experience of the last two years seems to suggest an affirmative answer to the first question. There has been remarkable economic progress, but there have also developed serious distortions in the structure of production and the distribution of purchasing power. The Economic Reports of the President point out several of these maladjustments. The postwar reconversion, modernization, and expansion of industrial plants and equipment and the demands of international reconstruction required such large amounts for domestic and international investments that consumption increased by a much smaller ratio as compared, for instance, with the prewar year 1939.[2] The Economic Report states that in order to prevent a depression the rate of consumer expenditures must increase at some future time when domestic investments and net exports begin to decline. (The possibility of a considerable increase in government expenditures for defense is not discussed.)

By calling this extraordinary increase in domestic and foreign investments a distortion or maladjustment, it is not suggested that these outlays should have been curtailed. As a matter of

[2] 'In terms of 1947 prices, annual expenditures for producers' durable equipment have increased by 170 percent, while annual consumers' expenditures have increased by only 48 percent above the prewar level,' *Economic Report of the President*, January 1948, p. 78.

fact, this increase was highly desirable. Incomes had been raised through the war effort, particularly in the lower brackets, but our productive plants and equipment were not adequate to meet the peacetime demand engendered by incomes of such size and distribution as those with which we emerged from the war. These deficiencies in our productive plant became apparent as soon as consumer spending and business outlays were released from wartime restrictions and restraints. Making up for the deficiencies and contributing to international reconstruction were therefore tasks of high economic priority after the end of the war.

It would have been folly to curb those urgent outlays in order to establish an ideal ratio between investments and consumption that could be sustained over a longer period. In saying this we have no thought of condoning a policy that failed to deal effectively with inflationary developments in the postwar years. We do say, however, that a drastic curtailment of investments or of net exports would have done more harm than good. But the investment boom brought about a relation between investment and consumption that cannot be sustained and requires future adjustments. An increase in consumption, of both absolute and relative nature, at a time when investments begin to decline, will be a major task for price and wage policy, and for tax and other fiscal policies.

The postwar investment boom was certainly the result of a very specific situation, occurring as it did after a period of rising incomes, on the one hand, and of underinvestment during depression and war, on the other. Under more normal conditions, it will be necessary to make a real effort to reduce the fluctuations in business expansion.[3] Such efforts, however, will at best only reduce, they cannot eliminate, swings in business investments. This is certainly true when investments are left to

[3] 'If the swings from expansion to contraction of private business which we have had in the past were to continue, offsetting operations would be too big to be left to "compensatory" Government policies. Economic stabilization can be achieved within our private enterprise system only if management accepts the responsibility for a more stable practice in planning its investment and operative programs.' (Council of Economic Advisers, *Second Annual Report to the President,* December 1947, p. 18.)

the free decisions of business management. It seems also to be true in countries with partial investment controls. One could cite as an example the recent British debate on the need to cut the amount of capital expenditures in relation to the portion of national resources devoted to exports and domestic consumption.[4] Even in a fully controlled economy like that of the Soviet Union, the relative emphasis on investments and consumption has been changed repeatedly. These observations refer, of course, to extraordinary situations. Yet, there will always be some peculiar reason why progress is made in uneven fashion. It would not be realistic, therefore, to assume for policy purposes that the economy of the industrial society will so expand that each component part will grow in exactly the proportion that can be permanently sustained. It is safer to assume that the various parts will move ahead unevenly, thus making periodic adjustments necessary.

In the past, maladjustments that developed during the upswing have resulted in depressions which have created further maladjustments in the process. If economic stabilization attempted only to counteract unemployment, without adjustments, it would merely perpetuate the maladjustments. The real problem is to make the needed adjustments without permitting them to degenerate into depressions and mass unemployment. Thus the task of effective economic stabilization requires that we recognize what adjustments are needed and that we develop devices to effect such adjustments and to counteract depression tendencies which might evolve in the process.

Stating the problem of economic stabilization in this way does not answer the question whether or not we shall be able to achieve it. But a more accurate identification of the task is useful for appraising the tools of economic analysis and the economic policy devices that will be needed to accomplish it.

[4] *Capital Investment in 1948,* presented by the Chancellor of the Exchequer, Cmd. 7268, London, 1947.

STABILIZATION POLICIES

Those who objected to a policy of full employment on the grounds that it would lead to economic regimentation held that continuously maintaining ample markets and plenty of jobs would result in a constant upward pressure on prices and wages, and would necessitate price and wage controls.

During the past two years, it is true, we have had full employment and we have had inflationary pressure. Of course, we have also had more than adequate purchasing power to support 'maximum employment and production' in the meaning of the Employment Act. But granting this, there still remains the possibility that a successful policy of sustained purchasing power for a high level of employment and production may result in continued inflationary pressure. The experience of the past suggests the validity of this conclusion, and yet there are factors that point toward a possible solution.

There is, first of all, the fact that in several lines of business long-run considerations and possibly also the pressure of public opinion have induced management to charge prices below what the traffic would bear. It is also encouraging that labor has become price-conscious. There have been significant voices in the labor camp acknowledging that wage increases which engender price increases are not of much value for labor as a whole. But naturally labor cannot be persuaded to forego wage demands unless it has reason to assume that there will be no general price rise.

In the light of the experience of the postwar years, there is the urgent need and the opportunity to explore some new patterns of price and wage policy. I believe that there is an alternative to permanent price and wage controls—that is, collective bargaining on the national level. It has been proposed that top national organizations of labor and management meet at least once a year to work out an agreement on general changes in wage rates which appear desirable and feasible for the coming year. This agreement would be predicated on price assumptions. If the price assumptions should prove invalid, the wage agreement would have to be reconsidered. The national wage agreement would serve for general guidance of management-labor negotiations in the various industries and regions. There are, of course, many contingent problems that require exploration, such as the role of government in national collective bargaining, the question of the relationship among various competing organizations of management and of labor, the amount of discipline within each organization necessary for making such a system effective, and how much leeway could be left to individual bargaining without impairing the purposes of the proposal.

Such a proposal would certainly require a modified stand on the part of management as well as of labor. It must be recognized that some new approach is needed if the purposes of economic stabilization are to be accomplished with a minimum of government regulation.

Critics of the full-employment bill who stated during the debates that a full-employment policy is not feasible because of a lack of suitable policy devices feared that the only device that could be used is government spending. Some of them regarded the whole measure simply as a concealed spending bill. It is true that the policy devices available for preventing threatening unemployment have not yet been tested under the Act, since the Act has been in effect only during a period of inflation. Nevertheless the experience of the postwar inflation does shed some light on this question.

Few economists would have expected a powerful inflationary pressure during a period of a substantial cash surplus in government budgets. Neither the wartime nor the postwar inflation could be effectively controlled by fiscal measures alone. Of course, sufficiently drastic fiscal measures could cope with any amount of inflation or deflation, but the cure might conceivably be as bad as the disease. It was apparent that only a combination of various devices could accomplish the objective of stabilization in a more desirable fashion.

It is certainly not by chance that in the President's Economic Report and in the Council's Report to the President the concept of 'adjustments' plays an important role. This reflects, in the first place, a concern with 'corrective' actions and, only in the second place, with 'compensating' policies. This does not mean, of course, that fiscal compensatory policy is neglected. High taxes and a budget surplus play an important role in the anti-inflation program; tax reduction and speeding up of long-delayed government programs will undoubtedly play an important role in a future program to combat a threatening or actual depression. But compensating the deflationary effects of a mal-adjustment is not enough. If that is the only policy adopted, it may even tend to perpetuate the maladjustment.

Fiscal policy, in some circumstances, may be more than a compensating device; it may be the most effective way of bringing about the needed adjustment. This is the case, for instance, when an increase in consumption is needed and a reduction in the taxes that impede consumption is feasible. In other cases the adjustment may be needed in business investment policies, in wage policies, price policies, credit policies, international policies, or in any one of a combination of other fields. Thus all kinds of economic policies may become stabilization devices, depending on the circumstances. Fiscal policies play a particular role because they are more adaptable than many other policies. They are, however, by no means the only or the ultimate instrument in the tool chest of stabilization policies.

ECONOMIC STABILIZATION AND ECONOMIC ANALYSIS

The most frequently voiced objection to the full-employment bill was that we cannot have an effective policy of stabilization unless we are able to predict economic events. This argument was raised particularly with respect to the specific formulation in the original bill that required a detailed forecast of the whole nation's economic budget—a formulation criticized from within and without the administration. The Employment Act in its final version uses more non-committal language; it requires the appraisal of 'current and foreseeable economic trends,' which is less difficult because what cannot be predicted is not foreseeable, and what is foreseeable need not be predicted.

Looking back again over the experience of the past two years, we find that economists inside and outside the government, as well as businessmen, have repeatedly been wrong in their economic predictions. Obviously we need to improve our statistical tools for making economic diagnoses. There are, however, two theoretical aspects of the problem that also require attention.

The first of these considerations concerns the fact that recent economic predictions have been based largely on the so-called national-income 'gap' analysis. In such an analysis, expected 'primary' changes in such factors as business investments, foreign purchases, government budgets, consumer backlogs, and the like are first determined. These estimates of primary changes then offer a basis for estimating secondary or induced changes in consumer incomes and expenditures and in the other categories of the nation's economic budget. This approach, with appropriate refinements, permits an estimate of expected changes in aggregate demand, which can then be compared with the expected changes in the potential supply of goods and services. If expected aggregate demand, in present prices, appears to be larger than potential supply, inflationary pressure is assumed to exist. The size of the gap is believed to permit conclusions to be drawn with regard to the expected price rise. In the absence of such a gap, no price rise is expected.

We have learned, however, that even if prospective aggregate demand is in approximate equilibrium with potential supply, we may still encounter an inflationary development. Because of specific scarcities, certain prices may rise and wage increases may follow or take place independently. Such an inflationary spiral is possible, of course, only if and as long as business can obtain funds for the additional working capital needed to carry inventories at higher prices. The price spiral in itself may then influence demand in a manner that could not be predicted by merely reviewing the various demand factors.

In the past, the economists who have used the aggregate approach, those who have studied particular price, wage, and cost movements, and those who have relied on the monetary explanation of the price level, have proceeded independently and critically of each other. The experience of the recent inflationary period suggests that these three basic types of analysis must be integrated into a comprehensive approach to the problem of price determination.

The second theoretical consideration is the difficulty that results from the fact that the behavior of businessmen seems to be atypical in many respects—'typical' being their behavior in the past and the behavior ascribed to them in our theories of the business cycle. I believe that this has been the first investment boom which over a considerable period of time was not accompanied by a boom in the stock market. There has been a significant difference between the attitudes of the production managers and those of the financiers in the American economy.

It also seems that the behavior of businessmen with respect to inventory accumulation differs from what it has been in the past in periods of price rise. Businessmen are now receiving, more so than in the past, the advice of economists, which may have contributed to their depression-consciousness. The resultant caution may have deprived some businesses of considerably larger windfall gains, but business as a whole has escaped substantial losses because of this attitude. The awareness on the part of business that a depression is possible has also mitigated speculation during the boom; the same attitude may become a hindrance when continued investments will be needed for sustained prosperity.

A now equally atypical attitude of a different nature is also evolving—namely, the conviction of some businesses that the government really 'means business' in its stabilization policy, reducing thereby the likelihood of at least long-lasting depressions and lessening the risk of inadequate markets. The latter attitude seems observable also in the feeling of job security among workers, which has its effect on the spending and saving habits of individuals.

Thus the consciousness of depression and confidence in stabilization are developing side by side. They affect the typical business behavior in different directions, and yet they are not quite so inconsistent with each other as may appear at first sight. Possible changes in business behavior and their implications for the cyclical business development should be high on the list of subjects for urgent economic study.

A better understanding of the cycle and better statistical tools should enable us to improve greatly our ability to make accurate economic forecasts. Yet, even a great improvement in this respect will not eliminate the hazards of trying to 'call the turns' in business development. The physician finds it easier to detect the existence of a physical defect or predisposition to a disease than the exact time when the defect or predisposition will gain the upper hand over the factors of resistance. Nobody would draw the conclusion, however, that a physician cannot be of help to a patient unless he can predict the exact date when the patient will be forced to take to his bed. Similarly, it is very important for a policy of economic stabilization that maladjustments in the body economic should be correctly identified. It would be desirable if we could predict the turns in the cycle because it would facilitate the most effective application of stabilization devices, but this is not essential. For the present we have to recognize that predictions are subject to considerable margins of error and should be evaluated in that light.

In basing policy recommendations on forecasts, attention should always be given to what the effect of the proposed policy would be if the economic prediction should be erroneous. It should be considered whether a policy—for instance, a contemplated tax reduction—is easily reversible or not. It should be considered which is greater in a particular situation—the risk involved in delaying a policy measure or the risk involved in possibly premature action. If we are aware of the limits and margins of error in economic prediction, the harm done by reliance on erroneous predictions can be minimized. Furthermore, the fact that our ability to predict is so limited makes it doubly necessary to explore legislative and administrative flexibilities in economic, and particularly in fiscal, policies.

As a basis for his plans, the businessman needs an unqualified economic forecast that includes forecasts of government action. A government stabilization policy, however, requires, first of all, an analysis of maladjustments and needed adjustments in economic growth. For such an analysis a qualitative and quantitative projection of economic growth and the relations of the various economic factors that may either sustain or disturb expansion is essential. Such projections (models), prepared for longer and shorter periods, should contemplate alternatives based on a variety of possible courses of government action. We must admit that economics as a science has made only the initial steps into the broad field of constructive investigations. But progress in this respect is as important as, if not more important than, the improvement in our ability to make economic forecasts.

Our economic system, as we have known it, is unstable. There are those who believe that this instability is bound to undermine its survival and that stability can be achieved only in an authoritatively controlled economy. The Employment Act is based on the philosophy that economic stability is not inconsistent with an economic system that preserves the individual freedoms essential for a democracy. Yet the Act recognizes the fact that there is no simple trick that will accomplish its objectives. The Act is only the beginning of the road. Progress without instability—that is, balanced economic expansion—requires improved legislative and administrative procedures, adjustments in the attitudes of management and labor and in the institutional patterns of their relationship, and last, but not least, a reorientiation of much of our professional thinking.

Part
-VI-

IN CONCLUSION

17

Economics Today

(1937) *

I

THE problems of economics have undergone a steady transformation during the course of history. Economics in our day deals with other subjects than did economics in the rural society of the Middle Ages. The economic problems of the eighteenth-century society of farmers and artisans were different from those of our age of corporations, credit, and rapid technical progress. There are certain general questions that are related to every economy, yet general answers to these questions are like empty frames still to be filled with pictures. Specific answers can be given only for specific economic systems. And since these specific economic systems are in a constant state of development, the economist looks on an ever-changing scene. It is essential to stop from time to time to ponder the changes that have taken place. Only in this way can the economist's consideration of present-day problems escape distortion through the applica-

* 'Economics Today,' *Social Research*, IV (2), May 1937, pp. 191-201.

tion of ideas developed by and for another historical situation. 'By and for' is said advisedly. The economist is not merely an observer detached from the stream of economic events. The great economic systems, such as mercantilism, liberalism, Marxism, or even that most recent development of economics, interventionism,[1] are all systems of economic theory, yet they are not the abstract creations of scholars floating on air above the struggle waged in the field of actual social life. These systems developed out of historical situations. Mercantilism may be called the economics of absolutism; liberalism the economics of the aspiring bourgeoisie; Marxism the economics of the proletariat in process of emancipation. And the systems in turn had an influence on historical development. Problems arise from the stream of historical events, pass through the realm of science, and in turn constitute one of the forces shaping historical development for good or evil. It is a situation similar to one that is familiar in the physical sciences: the object of study is modified by the fact that it is under observation and even by the type of observation.

It may be objected that this is confusing economic theory and economic policy. Certainly mercantilism, liberalism, and Marxism are systems of economic and social policy. But each also in-

---

[1] [1954 Fn.] There is no good term for characterizing the present state of the economy and the present task of economics in the Western world. I would not choose today the term 'interventionism,' which I used in this essay written in 1937. Interventionism stresses the fact that the modern government had to accept additional responsibilities in a predominantly free market economy. This was a one-sided view, which was influenced by the experience of the depression period. The 'new economics' must also take account of other aspects, such as the management problems of large-scale enterprise and of powerful labor organizations. We may as well admit that we have no adequate descriptive term for the 'new' economics we are talking about and toward which we are working. Calvin B. Hoover's recently coined term 'organizational economy' is preferable to 'interventionism' (see his presidential address, 66th Annual Meeting of the American Economic Association, Washington, D. C., December 1953 in *American Economic Review*, XLIV, 1, March 1954, pp. 1ff.). My present preference for this term reflects not only a change in semantics but to some extent a change in emphasis on what is the most significant criterion of the 'new economics.'

volves a certain special theoretical approach to reality. I am concerned with them here only in so far as they represent different theoretical approaches.

Before I attempt a general analysis of the historical situation of economics today, I want to illustrate the problem by a brief survey of the transformation of economic problems during the course of capitalism.

II

The idea of an *ordre naturel* was the leading principle in the establishment of economics as a modern science. What was the historical background responsible for the presentation of economic problems in this manner?

At the time of the Reformation, when the drive toward a central European authority vanished and when the decentralized feudal order fell apart, territorial monarchs were the only powers that prevented domestic anarchy and created opportunities for those excluded from making a living in the cities, where guilds monopolized and restricted opportunities. These monarchs were the only powers that could exploit the newly discovered world for domestic enrichment and that could prevent other powers from appropriating the wealth of these lands for themselves. At that time it would have been meaningless even to raise the question whether an economic system could function automatically without governmental guidance or regulation.

The monarchs, however, through subsidies and tariffs, through the importation of skilled labor, and through state monopolies, fostered business to the extent that gradually the protected merchants and industrialists became stronger than their protectors. This protection was then felt to be a handicap by the groups who wanted to make use of the newly created opportunities but did not belong to the privileged class. Under these conditions the question of whether an economic system could work without state privileges and state regulation was not merely an academic problem. It was 'the' problem of that period. The solution was provided by the discovery of the laws of the market.

The classical school certainly did not pretend to give a true picture of the economic reality of the time. Its laws have a hypothetical character, as do all laws in economics. One of the questions raised was: How would the economy work if there existed completely free competition and no state interference? Other assumptions about the state of technology and about sociological facts were taken from current reality as these writers observed it; but this one crucial assumption of non-interference of the state was taken from an imagined picture of a better society.

Economists of our day will admit that most of the classical doctrines are the logical outcome of their assumptions. They will admit also that classical writers asked an essential question. The question was vital at that time and the answer played a great role in shaping the whole period. There is no justification, however, for interpreting the classical theory as a general theory, as a theory, so to speak, of eternal validity.[2] Many of the classical assumptions do not hold for other periods. They were specific answers to specific questions in a specific historical period.

Classical economists themselves, in their search for laws of a *laissez-faire* mechanism, encountered certain difficulties. Even at that time Ricardo had to deal with the effects of technical progress on employment; and John Stuart Mill encountered the problem of unearned increments as a factor in the marketing economy, spoiling the otherwise perfect justice of the system. But these annoying facts were regarded not as the real root of the economic troubles, but as merely incidental.

Marx, and also his forerunners and successors, focused their attention on these disturbances. They disregarded the imagined order and concentrated on the existing disorder as the crucial problem. Classical economists had sought the laws that explain the working of the economic processes. Marx sought the laws

---

[2] J. M. Clark probably had in mind such undue extension of an idea when he said, 'Error is . . . truth out of place' (*Preface to Social Economics; Essays on Economic Theory and Social Problems*, New York, Farrar and Rinehart, Inc., 1936, p. 22).

that explain the disturbances in the economic balance. Is it that Marx applied a different logic? Are there really two different sciences of economics, one bourgeois and the other proletarian? As far as the economic realm is concerned, Marx merely added one assumption. Ricardo had mentioned the effects of technical progress in a chapter added only in a later edition of his main work. Marx chose as the basic assumption for his economic reasoning the superiority of large-scale production. At the time Marx wrote, large-scale production was limited to a very small field, but he based his reasoning on the assumption that this tendency would extend over the whole field of industry and agriculture. Thus he argued that more and more businessmen would be eliminated by the competition of bigger businessmen, so that an ever larger number of people would be proletarianized, until finally the expropriators would be expropriated. Marx therefore believed that the system of free competition would lead not to the greatest happiness of the greatest number, but only to the self-destruction of the capitalistic order. Once again a system of tremendous consequence. And once again the assumptions were made with deep understanding for the essentials of a historical situation.

III

It would be a mistake to infer from these examples that economic theory is nothing more than a weapon for certain political actions and that truth is only the expedient for such a course. We must remember that it is not a question of a single set of alternatives—a choice between a science as the slave of politics and science for its own sake. These opposite interpretations seem to be equally wrong. But what criteria are there for passing judgment on the value of an economic theory?

To my mind there are two. The first is verifiable, incontestable truth, agreement between the theory and the subject matter dictated by the nature of the problem. A statement that is true is true always, everywhere, and for everyone. There is no such thing as various truths for various classes, periods, or races. Truth is absolute.

337

The second criterion may be called the 'relevance' [3,4] of a theory. Relevance depends on the manner in which the question is put and consequently on the selection of the assumptions. A theory may be true but at the same time, because it is not built on a 'live hypothesis,' [5] contribute nothing toward solving the problem of a historical situation. How can we pass judgment on the relevance of a theory? Two opinions may be mentioned, which I believe should be rejected as too simple. According to one, the selection of both the problem and the assumptions is entirely subjective and arbitrary. If this position is taken, no theory can be said to have relevance from the point of view of scientific discussion. According to the other opinion, relevance means no more than a conformance of the assumptions with the observable facts; a theory is relevant if it leads directly to the grasping of existing facts. Is factual conformance the criterion of relevance? The reality of economics is dynamic. The assumption of free competition was a 'live hypothesis' at the time of Adam Smith, and the assumption of technical progress was a 'live hypothesis' at the time of Marx, but this does not mean that these assumptions were already materialized to the extent supposed in the theories based on them. The selection of these assumptions was the outcome of a specific interpretation of historical development.

[3] I cannot deal here with the logical implications of these two criteria. If we are concerned not only with the hypothetical subject matter posed by science but with the whole of a situation, then a broader concept of truth is involved, including also the criterion of relevance. Wertheimer (*Social Research*, I, May 1934, p. 135) distinguishes in this respect between truth, symbolized by a small *t*, and truth, symbolized by a capital *T*. In this latter sense truth would certainly include the criterion of relevance.

[4] [1954 Fn.] In the original article I used the term 'validity' instead of 'relevance.' I believe that relevance expresses better the meaning I had in mind. I also see that the term relevance has been used in the philosophical literature in a similar way. See for instance: Walter Fales 'Objectivity and Relevancy in Our Search for Truth,' in *Philosophy and Phenomenological Research*, XIII (2), December 1952, pp. 212ff.

[5] William James, *The Will to Believe*. The interpretation of science which I am giving here differs from pragmatism in so far as it does not allow the absolutism of truth to be questioned by emphasis on the historical determination of the relevance of our knowledge.

338

This interpretation does not arise from a mere extrapolation of the trends of the past. In social development the trend is not a 'natural' or necessary development. It may be shaped by human action, and one of the elements in its formation is the theoretical conception of economic systems. The theorist influences, mostly to a minor degree but sometimes as an important factor, the historical development that he is interpreting. Hence the social responsibility of economic theory. Hence the ethical element, the element of responsible decision that is involved in purely academic work. But such decision is not arbitrary. It arises from an understanding of what is on the 'agenda.' The most important duty of science is that it should understand the task it has to fulfill in a specific historical situation.

Nevertheless, science can never decide on its task with entire conclusiveness, because of the irrational and unpredictable elements involved in all historical development and in the evaluation of historical development. A certain element of risk always remains in any such decision. The scientist who approaches a problem can never be certain where he will end, whether he will find he is exploring a desert or fertile land, whether his findings will prove a modest contribution toward shaping the course of historical events, or whether they will be forgotten on a dusty shelf. But the scientist rooted in his today or his tomorrow will have the greatest chance of productive achievement —even though he himself can never be certain of what he has achieved.

This is perhaps an ecstatic interpretation of the role of economics and the responsibility of the scientist. There are in science, as in life generally, genuine impulses, crises, decisive turning points, as well as the routine of daily life. The daily routine in science is the process by which each solution brings in its train a fresh problem to be solved. This process contains mutual checks which guarantee by free discussion and constant verification a gradual approximation to the truth. And yet this progress is not indefinite. It continues until a crisis leads to a new way of posing the problem, thereby revising traditional assumptions. This does not mean, of course, that the new approach

339

may not make use of the traditional theories as tools. Marx used the classical doctrines even though he followed another direction of scientific research. Every new approach tends to shape the pattern of a new scientific tradition, which in turn may be followed by generations of rank and file workers in the scientific realm. But whether they are aware of it or not, their approach is intrinsically shaped by the situation and by evaluations governing at the time the basic outline of their systems was conceived. It remains a question whether economic science today has once more reached a stage at which progress can no longer be achieved by mere refinements within the traditional patterns—be they of orthodox classical or of Marxist theory—a stage at which the basic assumptions themselves must be examined anew.

IV

What can be said about the economic problems of our times? In their fundamental reasoning both classicism and Marxism abstracted themselves from the immediate action of the state. They relied on the working of economic automatism—to which the orthodox school looked for the ultimate realization of a just and efficient competitive order and from which Marxism anticipated the ultimate self-destruction of the capitalistic system. In our present economic and social situation one thing seems certain: we can wait neither for a realization of the technical and social conditions under which the orthodox theories may materialize, nor for the end of capitalistic self-destruction. The economic order has today reached a point where action will brook no delay. The question of the type of action determines the scientist's assumptions and imposes on him a share of responsibility for the historical events.

If we interpret the present stage of society as entirely disintegrated, if we believe that the patterns of social existence in family, workshop, and political organization are being dissolved, then the only valid social theory is the one that blazes a trail to a new social organization. One such answer is communism. There is much a communist may learn from classical theories. Yet, in his thinking classical theories will play quite a different

340

role from the one they play in the thinking of a liberal. For the communist the test of relevance of every economic theory lies in what it can contribute to the problems of comprehensive planning. His sets of sociological and psychological assumptions will be entirely different from the assumptions with which orthodox theory used to operate.

Different again are the economics of fascism. Fascism tries to accomplish reintegration not by a real reorganization of society but by subordinating all special interests—which, however, are not really removed thereby—to an alleged national goal. Fascist governments create a condition of international tension and then consider the national emergency arising therefrom as the co-ordinating principle for all social and economic activity. The economics of fascism is predominantly the economics of a fortification economy. Fascism too can make use of many of the elements of classical economics, as well as of the economics of communism, but it will set these elements in a different framework of sociological and political assumptions.

Communism and fascism, however, are not the only alternatives to the classical doctrine. Even though a country's traditional patterns of life may be shaken by modern industrial developments, these patterns are not necessarily destroyed. There still exists a chance to pursue a 'middle course' of reconstruction within the traditional social pattern. For those who do not believe that it is possible to remodel the capitalistic system in any way, discussion of government intervention in an economic system organized under the principles of private property and private management, seems idle talk. On the other hand, to those who still see a chance to save the humanitarian achievements of the liberal age, such questions are urgent above all others. They will demand that fundamental problems be posed in such a manner that theory may contribute to this vital task of adaption. They believe that the more energetically theory is focused on this task, the greater the chance for a country to succeed in a 'middle course.'

Science—especially ethics, political science, sociology, and economics—can contribute essential arguments on whether the problems with which economic theory is concerned in a specific situation are those that are implicit in communism, in fascism, in classicism, or in interventionism. And yet science can never reach a definite answer to this question. There will always remain, as was pointed out above, the element of risk and personal responsible decision.

If we assume that there is still a chance of pursuing the 'middle course,' what will be the path of economic science? In this remodeling of an existing system, as in the establishment of an entirely new social order, economics must be constructive. In neither case are we able to rely only on natural forces for a perfect market economy. A man-made economy and no longer the *ordre naturel* must be the starting point. Difficulties must be recognized as a challenge to action and not dismissed as incidental frictions or natural catastrophes. But the problems dealt with in constructive economics depend on the nature of the constructive goal. For a 'middle course' goal, the most urgent task is a realistic analysis of the actual functioning of economic life. Traditional theories are essential tools for grasping this reality, but they are nothing more than tools. They teach us to understand the tendencies that lead to order and those that lead to disorder in the market, but we must know also to what extent order and disorder exist. Governmental measures, often considered as a factor working, so to speak, from without the economic sphere proper, must be integrated into the realm of economic reasoning. This necessarily realistic attitude does not mean that hypothetical reasoning should be abandoned. On the contrary, constructive thinking necessarily involves an element of imagination. The economist must visualize and analyze specific possibilities of governmental measures which are to be integrated as hypotheses into his economic reasoning. Such a question as how would a marketing economy work under governmental investment policy can never be answered by mere description. But hypotheses must be constantly checked for their realistic adequacy, and observation must center on the actual working of economic life and not on some abstract construction built out of mere logic.

This observation of how economic life actually works necessarily entails a consideration of certain of its political and social aspects. Adolph Lowe [6] has shown very convincingly that there were certain sociological suppositions implicit even in classical economic doctrine. In the classical scheme, however, these suppositions were static and invariable, considered as given data. Marxism was the first great system that integrated a dynamic sociological theory into economic theory. This sociological theory was ingenious, but it was oversimplified and abstract. The sociological suppositions required of a system such as we are discussing must be realistically adequate to the immediate situation and can never be accepted as final and incapable of change.

The same holds true for psychological suppositions. For example, a theory of the business cycle is bound to include consideration of certain psychological reactions, usually introduced as the element of 'confidence.' Although experience shows that in certain phases of the cycle confidence is shaken, this fact cannot be accepted as an invariable datum. Some authors, for instance, argue that in a period of shaken confidence governmental spending cannot increase purchasing power because, in view of the lack of confidence, the deflationary tendencies will offset the additions to the purchasing power. This argument overlooks the possibility that a determined governmental policy will restore the confidence of at least some part of the business world and thereby create the proper psychological condition for a greater positive economic effect. Psychological, like sociological and political, suppositions are inescapable in economic theory, but they must be tested step by step and it must be constantly borne in mind that their validity depends on the situation from which they emerge.

In short, present-day economics must be constructive, and therefore both realistic and imaginative, integrating political, sociological, and psychological elements into the theoretical framework.

Though it is necessary for the whole theoretical structure to

---

[6] *Economics and Sociology*, London, Allen, 1935.

aim at the goal of a constructive economic policy, this element of choice refers only to the selection of the problem and the hypotheses to which it gives rise. Once the problem is stated and the hypotheses are formulated, then the answers should be entirely untrammeled by the passions from which the questions may have arisen.

The answer must be true or untrue. No argument counts except the appeal to reason and fact. The scholar in the field of the social and economic sciences is consciously or unconsciously connected with the struggle of real life because he must decide how to pose the problem and how to select the assumptions.

NOTE ON MAX WEBER'S METHODOLOGY [7]

To my mind the suggestions contained in the foregoing essay differ in three points from Max Weber's methodology.

First, Weber contends that the scholar posing the problem and selecting the assumptions establishes a relation between the subject matter of his study and the realm of values. But Weber does not believe that selection necessarily implies evaluation. For instance, the scholar dealing with the competitive order of capitalism must believe, of course, that competition is one essential feature in our social existence and therefore worthy of scientific analysis. But the scholar does not necessarily have to believe, because of this selection, that free competition ought to be enforced, or vice versa. The 'ideal type,' as Weber calls the fundamental tool of research in all historical studies, is in his opinion a working hypothesis and not a positive or negative norm. I admit this to be true only where partial theory is concerned. We constantly make use of working hypotheses, so-called 'experiments of the mind.' How would it be if . . . ? And these 'ifs' are certainly meant to be considered not as norms but as tools of logic. All such partial theories, however, are ultimately related to an all-embracing framework of assumptions within

[7] In this note I refer to Max Weber's *Objektivität sozialwissenschaftlicher und sozialpolitischer Erkenntnis,* 1904, and *Wissenschaft als Beruf,* 1919, both reprinted in Max Weber, *Gesammelte Aufsätze zur Wissenschaftslehre,* Tübingen, 1922.

344

which every partial theory has its proper place. In any scientific system as an entity, the element of evaluation is essential because of the possible effect of scholastic work on reality. Hence the social responsibility of the scholar in posing the problem and the inevitable normative element in social sciences. I am, therefore, not prepared to admit that exclusion of all evaluation (*Wertfreiheit*) is a possible postulate for the social sciences as a whole.

Second, Weber fought so passionately against evaluations in the realm of science because he believed that evaluations belong to a realm of absolute irrationality and mere subjective decision. I have tried to emphasize that rational reasoning has its proper place not only in 'pure science' but also in interpreting the task to be met in a historical situation, although I have admitted that there will always remain a certain insoluble ultimate which requires a personal decision.

Third, Weber holds that the value of scientific work rests entirely on the belief in an indefinite scientific progress. Real scientific work, he says, is motivated only by 'science for its own sake.' But I consider the vital function of science in the course of history itself to be one of the forces stimulating scholarly efforts.

18

Setting the Sights

(1954)

THE increasing importance of economics in the day-by-day operations of public and private organizations has forced a renewed
discussion of the relation between economic science and the life
of society. Three closely connected questions, in particular, concern not only the relation between economics and society but
also the limitations of economics as a science. These questions
arise from the fact that economics involved in day-by-day operations cannot avoid entanglement in value judgment; must be
realistic, which means dynamic rather than static; and must be
constructive, which means related to the objectives society attempts to realize through its economic life.

In the following essay some comments will be presented on
each of these three interrelated topics, based on the experiences
of a working economist.

MEANS AND ENDS

The economist who wants to be constructive—but who accepts
the conventional dictum that economics should be concerned

346

with analyzing means and not proposing ends—finds himself in an apparent dilemma. On the one hand, he wants to engage in economic analysis which will be useful to government officials, businessmen, labor leaders, and to all those who participate in the decisions that shape economic life. In so far as his analysis contributes to the decision-making process, he shares the responsibility for deciding on ends. On the other hand, he knows his limitations and the limitations of economics. Economics, he has been taught, is concerned with the rational use of scarce resources, that is, with means. When he takes his social responsibility seriously he is in danger of transcending the conventional limitations of his science. But when he interprets his function too narrowly he fails to make his full contribution.

Actually, the question whether the economist should concern himself only with means and should take ends as given comes from an unrealistic distinction between ends and means.

In the reality of life, ends and means are so interwoven that a clear separation seldom works. Robert D. Calkins said recently in a thoughtful paper: 'The fact that ends are so often means to higher goals, and means so often the intermediate ends of policy, requires a re-examination of the widely held notion that the economist may properly recommend the choice of means but not the choice of ends.' [1] Earning one's living is certainly a means to living, but, at the same time, it is part of our living and as such an end. It is probably more fruitful to speak in the social sciences of a hierarchy of purposes than of the dichotomy of ends and means.

By questioning whether there is a clear-cut distinction between means and ends, I do not want to suggest that the economist should disregard the limits of economics and become a crusader or reformer in his professional capacity. I only contend that some of the old boundary lines have been blurred. I doubt that workable delineations can be made by limiting the proper field

[1] *Papers and Proceedings of the Sixty-fifth Annual Meeting of the American Economic Association*, Chicago, Illinois, 27-9 December 1952, vol. XLIII, no. 2, May 1953.

of economics to means, contrasted with ends; or to facts, contrasted with norms; or to analysis, contrasted with judgment.

The interrelationship between ends and means is illustrated by a recent economic controversy. When, in the winter of 1948-9, Edwin G. Nourse, then Chairman of the President's Council of Economic Advisers, stated that a substantial rise in military expenditures (which were then running at an annual rate of about 12 billion dollars) would result in inflation or compel us to restore direct war-type controls, he made a statement apparently about means—namely, that certain devices of government control would have to be used if defense objectives were substantially increased. Still, controls (which had only recently been abandoned and for which no one had any liking at that time) were ends as well as means. They were negative ends—something to be avoided, at least in peacetime. The statement was understood as advice against a substantial rise in defense expenditures.[2]

At about the same time, Leon H. Keyserling, then Vice-chairman of the same Council, expressed the view[3] that a much higher level of defense expenditures than the then current rate would be well within the capacity of our productive system if such a rise would be desirable from the standpoint of foreign policy.

Their answers differed but were not logically inconsistent with each other. Both men addressed themselves to the question: 'What are the economic costs of a rising defense program?' On the surface it appears that both statements stayed within the limits of assaying economic costs (i.e. means), and the policy conclusions were left to be drawn by others. But why did Nourse in the one case talk about the direct controls that would be needed, and Keyserling about potential resources? Because Nourse apparently

[2] See Edwin G. Nourse, op. cit.

[3] Leon H. Keyserling made his views known to the public through various speeches and interviews. It was only after the outbreak of hostilities in Korea, at which time Mr. Keyserling had become Chairman of the Council, that these views were incorporated in official documents, such as *Economics of National Defense,* by the Council of Economic Advisers, Washington, 1950.

348

believed that the need for controls constituted the critical limit
for government programs in a peacetime situation, while Keyserling apparently believed potential resources constituted the critical limit in an international situation fraught with danger for
the peace and freedom of the world. In both instances, the choice
of the yardstick by which they elected to measure economic costs
implied an appraisal of the political urgency of the objective.
The economist, in selecting specific criteria for measuring economic costs out of a variety of possible criteria, must use at
least an assumption about the objective.

In appraising the validity of an analysis, the circumstances and
the outlook as they appeared at the time the analysis was made
have to be considered. Nourse thought that in a period of peace
—though an uneasy peace—the need for direct controls had to
be considered the critical limit for defense spending. He did not
consider an increase in taxes as a realistic possibility. Therefore,
even a moderate increase in government spending would increase
the deficit, aggravate inflationary pressure, and create a situation
in which anti-inflation controls would be needed. The potential
rise in production, emphasized by Keyserling, was not taken into
account by Nourse in appraising the immediate impact of rising
defense spending. *Ex post,* we know that with the start of fighting in Korea direct controls and tax increases could no longer
be ruled out as unacceptable. Also, the year 1949 had brought
a recession and, in spite of the recovery that started late in 1949,
there was still some slack left in the economy when the Korean
war began. The post-Korean buying boom in the fall of 1950
and spring of 1951 lifted actual production rapidly, so that what
was regarded as visionary projections in 1950 soon became reality.

Thus it happened that history validated the one set of assumptions and criteria without, however, invalidating the logic
of the other. The economist may always succeed or fail on two
accounts. His reasoning must stand the test of logic but the relevance of his findings also depends on the historical validity of
his assumptions and criteria.

Statements on the economic consequences of contemplated policies, even if of a hypothetical character, are likely to influence the decisions of policy makers. Nourse's statement reinforced the position of those who were trying to hold the budget down approximately to the then current level. Keyserling's analysis gave support to those who felt that a sizeable increase in military programs was desirable. Whether or not such statements were intended to influence policy, the economist cannot overlook their effect, particularly if he is in the public service and the public eye.[4]

Another example can be drawn from the discussions of the U.S. foreign-aid programs which have taken place since 1948. In this case, judgment about ends affects even the interpretation of so-called facts. When the domestic economic implications of these programs were analyzed, some economists pointed out that these programs—which claimed about 2 per cent of total production—could hardly be held responsible for inflation and the need for anti-inflationary measures. These economists pointed to the much larger national-security program as a whole, of which foreign aid was merely a small part. They insisted that giving a moderate amount of aid to foreign countries would not have created inflationary pressure had it not been for the very large and rising defense program.

Other analysts attributed the inflationary pressure to the foreign-aid program. If six or seven billion dollars of additional expenses are superimposed on a full-employment economy, they may indeed create inflation. This result follows from regarding foreign aid as the marginal program and considering every other public or private claim against the available resources as fixed at higher priority.

The two approaches used in analyzing the economic effects of the same program thus reflect different feelings about the need

---

[4] The author is fully conscious of the fact that some of the analyses presented in earlier chapters of this volume could be used as examples of failure in selecting the historically 'correct' assumptions. The analyses of postwar problems, written during the war, for instance, were based on the assumption that the war would lead to peace and not a period of prolonged partial mobilization and localized fighting.

for granting foreign aid—another case of a judgment about 'ends' affecting the method used in analysis.

I am not raising the question whether the different economists were right or wrong in their implied appraisals of the international situation or their explicit appraisals of the economic consequences of defense or foreign-aid programs. Nor do I raise the question of the positions which these programs should occupy in the scale of national priorities. I use these instances only to demonstrate that statements which on the surface appear to be confined to means at least in some cases actually imply a judgment about ends. From this I do not draw the conclusion that the economists acted out of character (as economists), but I wish to emphasize the great responsibility inherent in the giving of merely economic advice. If I criticize the economists for anything, then it would be for their failure to state clearly the policy judgments that are implied in these economic analyses. Making explicit such implied policy judgments might well be an essential item in a code of ethics for economists.

An economist who avoids controversial issues acts as irresponsibly as the economist who fails to reveal candidly the elements that enter his analysis. The policy maker, without advice, will either be guided by wishful thinking and disregard all economic consequences and limiting factors; or, more often, he will be guided by present observations and fail to imagine future possibilities. Decision makers who do not trust today's economists sometimes base their judgment unconsciously on yesteryear's economics.

Our emphasis on the political responsibility of the economist's work should not be understood as an underestimation of the importance of pure economic theory. There is a great need for bold and imaginative 'experiments of thought' in economics as in all other intellectual endeavors. It would be a most shortsighted view to believe that economic research work is not useful unless it has a directly visible policy application. It should be emphasized, however, that experiments of thought should be clearly characterized as such. It often happens that a scholar engaged in abstract analysis working with hypothetical assumptions

forgets the character of his own work and jumps to policy conclusions without examining the realism or lack of realism of his
assumptions. Pure economic theory, like potent medicine, needs
clear labels to protect against misuse.

ECONOMIC PERSPECTIVES

Comprehensive economic projections are one of the methods
that have recently been developed to aid in decision-making in
government, business, and labor.

If we are asked about the impact of any particular economic
event or program on the economy as a whole, conventional static
economics uses the *ceteris paribus* assumption. A wage increase,
studied under the *ceteris paribus* assumption, may appear to force
costs up, reduce profit expectations, and lead to unemployment.
In reality, it *may* coincide with technological or managerial advances which reduce costs. (These advances may be independent
of the wage rise or they may be stimulated by it.) When labor and
management discuss problems of wages and profits in a static
frame of reference, there can be nothing but conflict and at best
a truce. What one party gains the other must lose. In a dynamic
perspective, it becomes apparent that both parties have a common interest in growth, and the conflict is reduced to the question how much each party gains. Whether we study the desirability or feasibility of a government expenditure program, or a
problem of tax incidence or debt management, or almost any
other economic problem, we must relate the phenomenon under
study not to an economy that stands still but to an economy that
is in constant motion.

When, in the fall of 1950, a national-security program of possibly 50 billion dollars per year was contemplated, most economists thought it would be feasible only if consumption was se-
verely curtailed at the same time. Security expenditures were
running at about 20 billion dollars at that time and an increase of 30 billion dollars would have been necessary. Viewed,
however, in the light of an expanding economy, we see that defense expenditures were stepped up over three years by more
than 30 billion dollars without any curtailment of the level of

consumption or business investment. The increase in total production was actually almost double—measured in real terms—the increase in defense expenditures. Any *ceteris paribus* or static analysis was bound to give misleading results.

The same also applies to tax analysis. Conventional tax-burden analysis relates the increase in taxes to incomes, prices, and other economic facts as they were at the time of the imposition of the tax. Actually, during the two years following the outbreak of hostilities in Korea, incomes (even if adjusted for price rise) increased more than the amount of additional taxes. A tax analysis that has any realistic significance in such a situation must be related to changing economic data rather than be allowed to proceed on a *ceteris paribus* assumption.[5] Therefore, for most questions related to economic reality, we need a frame of reference or a perspective for dynamic analyses.

Projections are used not only as an aid in the formulation and appraisal of domestic policy or the domestic impact of foreign policy, but their use as a tool for appraising the need for assistance to foreign countries is even more widely recognized. This is true both for the European countries that receive U.S. aid and especially for the underdeveloped countries that receive assistance in one form or another. The development of methods of dynamic economic analysis by those who have been 'on the spot' has been, I believe, far ahead of the academic research work and teaching. We have only to look at the analyses and projections published, for instance, by the Council of Economic Advisers, by the Department of Commerce, and by international organizations such as the United Nations and the OEEC to appreciate the progress made in dynamic methods under the stimulus of policy-making requirements.

A frame of reference for dynamic analysis can be provided in abstract terms by a system of formulae or in concrete numerical terms by projections. An example of the first, or mathematical, approach, is J. Tinbergen's 'On the Theory of Economic

[5] See Gerhard Colm and Haskell P. Wald, 'Some Comments on Tax Burden Comparisons,' in *National Tax Journal*, v (11), March 1952.

Policy.' [6] *The American Economy in 1960—Economic Progress in a World of Tension* [7] may serve as an example of the latter type. The projections presented in that study are not predictions. They are a method of testing hypotheses in quantitative terms. They constitute a tool for exploring the pattern of economic growth that would be conducive to the maintenance of a high level of activity. Sustained high-level activity requires balance among productive capacity, output, saving, investment, and consumption. But a state of balance is not represented by only one possible combination of these factors. One could have, for instance, larger government services and lower individual consumption, or lower government services and larger individual consumption, or lower government services and a higher rate of investment in plant and equipment. In this study there were set up a number of alternative projections or models, each one of which would represent full employment some years hence, though each by a somewhat different route. By combining various features of each of these models, one set of projections which appeared most plausible to the authors was obtained.

A person who performs medical services must know something about the healthy body and about healthy growth and development before he can diagnose a disease of specific organs. In a similar way, the economist must have some concept of a balanced development of the economy as a whole as a frame of reference for the analysis of specific factors that make for instability and for the exploration of specific policies that will help achieve stable expansion.

Tinbergen said recently that in the traditional approach to economics government policies were treated as given and the economic result as the unknown to be explored. 'In the theory of economic policy these two categories interchange places; in a sense, the problem is inverted.' [8] This is a significant though oversimplified statement. Most great economists did recommend

[6] *Contributions to Economic Analysis,* vol. I, North-Holland Publishing Company, Amsterdam, 1952.
[7] Colm and Young, op. cit.
[8] Tinbergen, op. cit.

policies and did not adhere to the standard of rigorous 'pure' analysis which does take policies and attitudes as given. It is also an oversimplification that a theory of economic policy can treat the economic result as given. We speak of a 'presumably practical goal' which should be 'tentatively assumed' as given. In order to test whether a tentative goal is practical we have to analyze what changes in policies and attitudes are needed to accomplish it. If, within a given political and sociological frame of reference, the changes in policies and attitudes do not appear feasible, then the goal is not practicable. In other words, the determination of the goal and the analysis of the changes in policies and attitudes that would be needed to accomplish the goal are interdependent. This leads us back to our initial proposition that the strict division of labor between those who determine goals and those who analyze means does not work.

Nevertheless, an analysis must start with a tentative and presumably practical goal. If the analysis shows that the tentative goal is not practical, it must be modified.

In such a comprehensive approach, three types of questions must be asked: (1) What would be the economic result if present policies and attitudes were continued? (2) What economic results will best serve the general welfare as interpreted in a given society? (3) What changes in policies and attitudes—within the basic economic and political framework to which the people in a given society are committed—are necessary to accomplish or facilitate these results?

Projections can serve in such an approach as a tool for exploring desirable patterns of economic growth which would be consistent with the prevailing concept of the general welfare and with national objectives of economic policy.

GENERAL OBJECTIVES AND SPECIFIC TARGETS

People of every nation and period have certain ideas about what they expect to obtain from their economic endeavor. They have certain ideas, however vague, about national independence, national security, the standard of living, job security, freedom to manage their own affairs. These aspirations have a direct bearing on what may be called national economic objectives.

Projections of the type discussed above purport to translate these qualitative objectives into a pattern of quantitative goals. A healthy economy at some future date is depicted in terms of a limited number of aggregative figures on production, income, spending, and saving. The projected aggregates and the ratios of one to another may be thought of as general economic goals. When considered in the light of the existing pattern and existing trends, they serve to identify broad economic adjustments necessary to a balanced economic growth.

Such general goals may also be used as a frame of reference for determining specific objectives—not only by government policy makers, but by decision makers in business and labor as well. Business concerns need some frame of reference for studying the potential growth of their particular industries. They may set up sales goals which are realistic in the light of the projected growth of the total market. Such targets play an important role in investment budgeting. Labor organizations need some idea about possible technological development and about economic growth in general for deciding on a realistic strategy of wage negotiations.

The work of the so-called Paley Commission [9] is a good illustration of the establishment of specific targets within the framework of general goals. Requested by the President to study the country's raw materials needs, the Commission first projected the country's total production and its composition to 1975—then mapped out the natural-resources base required to support such production. The needed quantities of resources became specific targets, in the light of which the Commission recommended a number of policy measures for assuring their attainment.

In spite of much work done along these lines, the field of gap-bridging between the aggregative formulation of general economic goals on the one hand and specific targets for specific pol-

---

[9] *Resources for Freedom,* 5 vols., A Report to the President by the President's Materials Policy Commission, U.S. Government Printing Office, Washington, D. C., June 1952.

icies on the other is still too much neglected in economic analysis. Only specific targets can serve as guides for the formulation and appraisal of specific programs. Of course, the more specific an economic objective is, the more it is subject to uncertainty and change. Nevertheless, specific targets can be used as working hypotheses, even though their tentative character must be remembered. The main functions of targets are to help establish priorities, and to assure that various programs are developed in a manner consistent with general economic development and that these various programs are consistent with each other.

The targets can be of direct value for public policy in areas in which the government operates directly, as in the case of some types of transportation, power and water development, education, and public health services.

Setting up targets for these and similar activities is not always a matter of cold statistics alone but, in many cases, it is also a matter of judgment. Therefore, these estimates should be subject to public discussion. They really represent an attempt to translate vague notions of the general welfare into tangible, quantitative terms. As such, they will always remain tentative—subject to revision. The specific targets are based on general projections of the potential rise in productive capacity. As these projections are revised, so also are the targets which are intended to be consistent with the rates of growth of the economy and the standard of living. Specific targets depend also on technological developments. In an effort to determine the need for a road-construction program, we may work out a ratio between the rise in a physical index of production on the one hand and truck transportation on the other, and then we may use that ratio for a projection of needed road improvements. But we may make a serious mistake if we fail to take into account possible technical improvements in railroad transportation or the further development of air freight.

Therefore, specific targets must be periodically revised, taking account of revisions in general goals, technological and institutional changes, and changes in consumer preferences.

Thus, the targets should not be confused with enforceable blueprints. They are tentative guide posts for the orientation of those in private and public life who have to make decisions that reach into the future. These targets may be useful in reducing the possibility of inconsistency among the many interrelated private and public undertakings, which could result either in excessive demands on resources, in bottlenecks, or in underutilization of productive resources.

Does setting targets for private and public activities transcend the proper sphere of the economics profession? It certainly transcends economics either as a purely descriptive or a purely analytical science. It is an example of 'constructive economics' or 'welfare economics in action.' It analyzes statistics and interrelations among economic variables but becomes a tool for private and public action by projecting the results into the future. It carries the risk of error and must take this risk into account. It requires a humble attitude and an open mind ready to revise its results. Nevertheless, it is a professional service that is required by the contingent character of the modern economy which, for its successful operation, depends on intelligent—and that includes well-advised—action by public and private decision makers.

Gerhard Colm's Writings

LEGEND: B—Book
A—Article
C—Contribution
*—Article reprinted
in this volume

BEFORE 1933

GENERAL ECONOMICS

'Die Bedeutung der Stimmrechtsaktien' (The Significance of Multi-vote Shares), *Bankwissenschaft*, 2, 20, January 1926.   (A)

'Das Wesen der Kommerzialisierung und die mit ihr verbundenen Aenderungen des Londoner Paktes' (The Funding of the Reparation Payments and Related Changes in the London Agreement), *Das Reparationsproblem*, Edgar Salin, editor. Veröffentlichungen der Friedrich-List Gesellschaft, Reimar Hobbing, Berlin, 1929, 2 vols. (C)

Der Mensch im Wirtschaftlichen Kreislauf (Man in the Economic Process), J. C. B. Mohr (Paul Siebeck), Tübingen, 1930, 25 pp.   (B)

'Kapitalistische und Nichtkapitalistische Elemente in der Heutigen Deutschen Volkswirtschaft' (Capitalistic and Noncapitalistic Elements in the Present German Economy), *Kapital und Kapitalismus*, B. Harms, editor. Reimar Hobbing, Berlin, 1931, 2 vols.   (C)

359

'Der Einfluss der Sozialpolitik auf den Kapitalmarkt' (The Influence of Social Policy on the Capital Market), *Kapital und Kapitalismus*, B. Harms, editor. Reimar Hobbing, Berlin, 1931, 2 vols.   (C)

PUBLIC FINANCE

'Die Methodischen Grundlagen der International-Vergleichenden Finanzstatistik' (The Methodological Basis of International Comparative Statistics of Public Finance), *Weltwirtschaftliches Archiv*, 22, 2, 1925.   (A)

'Die Steuerliche Belastung der Englischen Wirtschaft' (The Tax Burden of the British Economy), *Weltwirtschaftliches Archiv*, 26, 1, 1927.   (A)

'Der Finanzwirtschaftliche Gesichtspunkt des Abrüstungsproblems' (The Fiscal Aspect of Disarmament), *Handbuch des Abrüstungsproblems*, Theodore Niemeyer, editor. Buchdruckerei Schmidt & Klaussig, Kiel, 1927, 85 pp.   (C)

'Ein Neuer Versuch zur International-Vergleichenden Finanzstatistik' (A New Attempt of International Comparative Statistics of Public Finance), *Allgemeines Statistisches Archiv*, 17, 1, 1927.   (A)

[With others] *Die Staatsausgaben von Grossbritanien, Frankreich, Belgien und Italien in der Vor- und Nachkriegszeit, Unterlagen zum Internationalen Finanzvergleich* (Government Expenditures of Great Britain, France, Belgium, and Italy during the Prewar and Postwar Period—Material for an International Comparison of Public Finance). Statistisches Reichsamt, 2, Einzelschriften zur Statistik des Deutschen Reichs. Reimar Hobbing, Berlin, 1927, 574 pp.   (B)

Volkswirtschaftliche Theorie der Staatsausgaben—Ein Beitrag zur Finanztheorie (Economics of Government Expenditures—A Contribution to the Theory of Public Finance), J. C. B. Mohr (Paul Siebeck), Tübingen, 1927, 83 pp.   (B)

'Der Einfluss der Steuern auf die Internationale Wettbewerbsfähigkeit' (The Influence of Taxes on the Ability to Compete in International Trade), *Beiträge zur Finanzwissenschaft, Festgabe für G. von Schanz*, J. C. B. Mohr (Paul Siebeck), Tübingen, 1928.   (C)

'Besteuerung und Rentabilität Gewerblicher Unternehmungen' (Taxation and Profitability of Business Enterprises), *Finanzarchiv*, Tübingen, 46, 1, 1929.   (A)

[Edited, with Hans Neisser] *Kapitalbildung und Steuersystem* (Capital Formation and Tax System), Veröffentlichungen der Friedrich-List Gesellschaft, vols. 3 and 4, Reimar Hobbing, Berlin, 1930.   (B)

'Zum Problem der Oeffentlichen Kapitalwirtschaft' (The Problem of the Public Capital Economy), *Finanzarchiv* (Neue Folge), Tübingen, 1, 1, 1932.   (A)

INTERNATIONAL ECONOMICS

'Ueber den Inhalt und den Erkenntniswert der Zahlungsbilanz' (The Content and Meaning of the Balance of Payments), *Weltwirtschaftliches Archiv*, 29, 1, 1929. (A)

[Co-author] *Die Deutsche Zahlungsbilanz* (The German Balance of Payments), (Enquete Ausschuss) Ausschuss zur Untersuchung der Erzeugungs- und Absatzbedingungen der deutschen Wirtschaft. I. Unterausschuss, 6. Arbeitsgruppe. E. S. Mittler & Sohn, Berlin, 1930. (C)

'England's Future Trade Policy,' *The Liverpool Trade Review*, November 1930. (A)

'Das Gesetz der Komparativen Kosten—das Gesetz der Komparativen Kaufkraft' (The Law of Comparative Costs—the Law of Comparative Purchasing Power), *Weltwirtschaftliches Archiv*, 32, 2, 1930. (A)

[With others] *Der Deutsche Aussenhandel unter der Einwirkung Weltwirtschaftlicher Strukturwandlungen* (The German International Trade under the Impact of Structural Changes in World Economics), 2 vols. Institut für Weltwirtschaft und Seeverkehr, Kiel, Enquete Ausschuss 1. Unterausschuss, 5. Arbeitsgruppe. Series vol. 20. E. S. Mittler & Sohn, Berlin, 1932, vol. 1, 367 pp.; vol. 2, 656 pp. (B)

'Die Welthandelsentwicklung und das Problem der Deutschen Ausfuhrpolitik' (The Development of World Trade and the Problem of German Export Policy), *Weltwirtschaftliches Archiv*, 36, 1, 1932. (A)

'Zahlungsbilanz' (Balance of Payments), *Handwörterbuch des Bankwesens*, M. Palyi and P. Quittner, editors. Julius Springer, Berlin, 1933. (C)

NATIONAL INCOME AND PRODUCTION

'Produktionsstatistik' (Statistics of Production), in: *Grundriss zum Studium der politischen Oekonomie*, IV Statistik, 3 Gewerbestatistik und Arbeitsstatistik, A. Hesse. Gustav Fischer, Jena, 1925, chapter I, pp. 52-74, chapter II, pp. 211-34. (C)

'Das Mehrwert-Verfahren in der Produktionsstatistik' (The Value Added Method in Statistics of Production), *Weltwirtschaftliches Archiv*, 20, 2, 1924. (A)

'Grundsätzliche Bemerkungen zum Begriff des Volkseinkommens und des Volksvermögens' (Comments on the Concepts of National Income and National Wealth), *Schriften des Vereins für Sozialpolitik*, 173, 1, 1926. (C)

[With Julius Landmann] 'Vergleichbarkeit der Vorkriegs- und Gegenwartsschätzungen der Volksvermögen und Volkseinkommen' (Comparability of Prewar and Present Estimates of National Income and Wealth), *Allgemeines Statistisches Archiv*, 22, 4, 1932. (A)

BUSINESS CYCLES

'Den Økonomiske Krise I Tyskland' (The Economic Crisis in Germany), *Økonomi og Politik*, 1931. (A)

'Wege aus der Weltwirtschaftskrise' (Ways out of the World Economic Crisis), *Die Arbeit*, 8, 11, November 1931. (A)

'Deutschland und die Weltkrise—Industrialisierung und Arbeitslosigkeit' (Germany and the World Crisis—Industrialization and Unemployment), *Schriften des Vereins für Sozialpolitik*, vol. 187, September 1932. (C)

'Gerhard Colm, Kiel,' *Der Stand und die nächste Zukunft der Konjunkturforschung—Festschrift für Arthur Spiethoff* (Status and Immediate Future of Business Cycle Research), Dunker und Humblot, Munich, 1933, pp. 56-60. (C)

'Die Krisensituation der Kapitalistischen Wirtschaft' (The Crisis of the Capitalistic Economy), *Archiv für Sozialwissenschaft*, 69, 4, 1933. (A)

'Politique Commerciale Allemande et Redressement de l'Economie,' *Revue Economique Internationale*, 25th year, vol. II, 2, May 1933. (A)

SOCIOLOGY

Beitrag zur Geschichte und Soziologie des Ruhraufstandes, 1920 (Contribution to History and Sociology of the Revolt in the Ruhr Territory, 1920), G. D. Baedeker, Essen a. d. R., 1921, 142 pp. (B)

'Die Gesellschaftlichen Grundlagen des Staatslebens der Gegenwart' (The Social Foundations of Present Political Life), *Der Deutsche Staatsbürger*, Schröder und Feldmann, editors. Stuttgart, 1924. (C)

'Die Masse—Ein Beitrag zur Systematik der Gruppen' (The Crowd—A Contribution to an Analysis of Group Formation), *Archiv für Sozialwissenschaft*, 52, 3, 1924. (A)

'Masse' (Crowd), *Handwörterbuch der Soziologie*, Alfred Vierkandt, editor. Ferdinand Enke Verlag, Stuttgart, 1931, pp. 353-60. (C)

'Die Antikapitalistische Massenbewegung und die Gegenoffensive des Liberalismus' (The Anticapitalistic Mass Movement and the Counteroffensive of Liberalism), *Zeitschrift für Politik*, 23, 4, 1933. (A)

THE TEACHING OF ECONOMICS

'Der Volkswirtschaftliche Unterricht an der Volkshochschule' (The Teaching of Economics in Schools for Adult Education), *Archiv für Erwachsenenbildung*, January 1926. (A)

'Volkswirtschaftlicher Unterricht für Laien' (Economic Education for Laymen), *Die Polizei*, 23, 23, December 1926. (A)

1933-1954

PUBLIC FINANCE AND FISCAL POLICY

* 'The Ideal Tax System,' *Social Research,* 1, p. 319ff., 1934.   (A)
'Unearned Increment,' *Encyclopedia of the Social Sciences,* The Macmillan Co., New York, 1935, vol. 15, pp. 144-7.   (C)
'War Finance,' ibid. pp. 347-52.   (C)
'Adolph Wagner,' ibid. p. 320.   (C)
'Methods of Financing Unemployment Compensation,' *Social Research,* 2, p. 148ff., 1935.   (A)
* 'Theory of Public Expenditures,' *Annals of the American Academy of Political and Social Science,* 183, 1, 1936.   (A)
'Public Expenditures and Economic Structure in the United States,' *Social Research,* 3, p. 57ff., 1936.   (A)
* [With Fritz Lehmann] 'Public Spending and Recovery in the United States,' *Social Research,* 3, p. 129ff., 1936.   (A)
'European Public Finance in the World Crisis,' *Taxation and Public Policy,* Paul Studenski, editor. Richard R. Smith, New York, 1936, pp. 141-50.   (A)
'Probleme der Finanzsoziologie' (Problems of a Sociology of Public Finance), *Reine und Angewandte Soziologie—Festgabe für Ferdinand Tönnies,* Hans Buske Verlag, Leipzig, 1936, pp. 106-12.   (C)
'Comments on Extraordinary Budgets,' *Social Research,* 5, p. 168ff., 1938.   (A)
'Significant Tax Legislation in Foreign Countries,' *Proceedings of the National Tax Association,* 31st Annual Conference. National Tax Association, Columbia, S. C., 1938, p. 526ff.   (C)
'The Revenue Act of 1938,' *Social Research,* 5, p. 255ff., 1938.   (A)
[With Fritz Lehmann] *Economic Consequences of Recent American Tax Policy,* The Graduate Faculty of Political and Social Science, New School for Social Research (Supplement 1 to *Social Research*), New York, 1938, 108 pp.   (B)
'The Basis of Federal Fiscal Policy,' *Taxes,* 17, 338, 1939.   (A)
[Co-author] 'Final Report of the Committee on Federal Taxation of Corporations,' *Proceedings of the National Tax Association,* 32nd Annual Conference on Taxation, 1939, 12th Session. National Tax Association, Columbia, S. C., 1940, p. 534ff.   (C)
'Recent Developments in Corporation Taxes in Foreign Countries,' *Proceedings . . .* op. cit., Supplement to Appendix No. 1, pp. 582-93.   (C)
'Tax Policy and Capital Formation,' *Capital Formation and Its Elements,* National Industrial Conference Board, New York, 1939, p. 73ff.   (C)

'War Finance,' *War in Our Time,* by the Graduate Faculty of the New School for Social Research, Hans Speier and Alfred Kähler, editors. W. W. Norton & Co., New York, 1939, p. 192ff.   (C)

* 'Full Employment Through Tax Policy?' *Social Research,* 7, p. 447ff., 1940.   (A)

'Fiscal Policy and Recovery,' *Proceedings of the National Tax Association,* 33rd Conference on Taxation. National Tax Association, Columbia, S. C., 1940, pp. 89-96.   (C)

[With H. Tarasov] *Who Pays the Taxes?—Allocation of Federal, State, and Local Taxes to Consumer Income Brackets,* Temporary National Economic Committee, Investigation of Concentration of Economic Power, Monograph No. 3. Superintendent of Documents, Washington 25, D. C., 1940, 55 pp.   (B)

'Conflicting Theories of Corporate Income Taxation,' *Law and Contemporary Problems,* Duke University, 7, 281, 1940.   (A)

'The Cost of Arming America,' *The Annals of the American Academy of Political and Social Science,* 214, pp. 2-13, 1941.   (A)

'National Income and Defense Financing,' *Conference on Research in Income and Wealth,* Papers on National Income, Defense and National Income, Part II. National Bureau of Economic Research, New York, 1941.   (C)

* [With the assistance of Gerald M. Alter] 'Washington Fiscal Policy— Its War and Postwar Aims,' *Fortune,* 26, 4, 1942.   (A)

'Federal Budgeting and the National Fiscal Policy,' *Budgeting—An Instrument of Planning and Management,* Cathryn Seckler-Hudson, editor. American University, Washington, D. C., 1944, unit II (Processed).   (C)

* 'Fiscal Policy in Economic Reconstruction,' *Economic Reconstruction,* Seymour E. Harris, editor. McGraw-Hill Book Co., New York, 1945, pp. 253-74.   (C)

[With Joseph M. Dodge and Raymond W. Goldsmith] *A Plan for the Liquidation of War Finance and the Financial Rehabilitation of Germany,* U.S. Department of the Army, Office of Military Government, Berlin, Germany, 1946 (Processed, declassified document).   (B)

'Keynes' Influence on U.S. Fiscal Policy,' *The New Economics,* Seymour E. Harris, editor. Alfred A. Knopf, New York, 1947, pp. 450-67.   (C)

* 'Why Public Finance?' *National Tax Journal,* 1, p. 193ff., 1948.   (A)

* 'Public Finance in the National Income,' *Bulletin of the Central Bank of Venezuela,* Caracas, Venezuela, Nos. 59 and 60, January and February 1950. Translated into German: *Allgemeines Statistisches Archiv,* Munich, Germany, 1951.   (A)

[With Haskell P. Wald] 'Some Comments on Tax Burden Comparisons,' *National Tax Journal,* March 1952.   (A)

* 'Haushaltplanung, Staatsbudget, Finanzplan und Nationalbudget' (Budget Planning: The Government Budget, the Financial Plan, and the Nation's Economic Budget), *Handbuch der Finanzwissenschaft,* Tübingen, Germany, 1952, vol. I, pp. 519-36.   (C)

'Tax Policy for Economic Progress and Stability,' *Conference on Taxation,* Committee on Economic Policy, Congress of Industrial Organizations, 16 October 1953, pp. 3-6.   (C)

[With the assistance of Marilyn Young] *Can We Afford Additional Programs for National Security?* A National Planning Association Special Committee Report, Planning Pamphlet No. 84. National Planning Association, Washington, D. C., October 1953, 70 pp.   (B)

* 'Fiscal Policy and the Federal Budget,' *Income Stabilization for a Developing Democracy—A Study of the Politics and Economics of High Employment without Inflation,* Max F. Millikan, editor. Yale University Press, New Haven, 1953, chapter V, pp. 213-59.   (C)

'Don't Throw the Baby Out with the Bath—Comments on Recent Articles on Progressive Income and Corporate Income Taxes,' *Finanzarchiv* (Neue Folge), Tübingen, 1953, 14, 3, pp. 525-30.   (C)

'Taxation and Consumption,' Statement before the *Joint Committee on the Economic Report of the President,* Hearings, 83rd Congress, Second Session, 1-18 February 1954. Superintendent of Documents, Washington 25, D. C., 1954, p. 432ff.   (C)

* 'The Corporation and the Corporate Income Tax in the American Economy,' 1953. Paper presented on The Role of Corporate Taxation at the American Economic Association Annual Meeting, 1953. *The American Economic Review,* May 1954, vol. 44, 2.   (C)

NATIONAL ECONOMIC BUDGETS AND NATIONAL INCOME

'Production: Statistics,' *Encyclopedia of the Social Sciences,* vol. 12. The Macmillan Co., New York, 1934, pp. 467-72.   (C)

'Public Revenue and Public Expenditures in National Income,' *Studies in Income and Wealth.* Conference on Research in Income and Wealth, National Bureau of Economic Research, New York, 1937, vol. I, part V, pp. 175-228; 240-49.   (C)

'On the Measurement of National Wealth,' ibid. 1938, vol. II, part I, pp. 65-72.   (C)

'Income and the Measurement of the Relative Capacities of the States,' ibid. 1939, vol. III, part VII, pp. 450ff.   (C)

'From Estimates of National Income to Projections of the Nation's Budget,' *Social Research,* 12, pp. 350-69, 1945.   (C)

'The Nation's Economic Budget—A Tool of Full Employment Policy,' *Studies in Income and Wealth.* Conference on Research in Income and Wealth, National Bureau of Economic Research, New York, 1947, vol. 10, part 2, pp. 85-93. (C)

'The Government Budget and the Nation's Economic Budget,' *Openbare Financien* (Netherlands), 3, 5, 1948. (A)

'The Nation's Economic Budget and the Government,' *Annals of the American Academy of Political and Social Sciences,* 266, pp. 32-40, 1949. (A)

'Comments on Prof. Laufenburger's Article "L'Elargissement du Concept du Budget," ' *Finanzarchiv* (Neue Folge), Tübingen, 1950, 12, 2, pp. 296-9. (A)

* 'National Economic Budgets,' *Bulletin of the Central Bank of Venezuela,* Caracas, Venezuela, May-June 1951, pp. 13-20. (A)

'Experience in the Use of Social Accounting in Public Policy in the United States,' Paper for Meeting of the International Association for Research in Income and Wealth, Cambridge, England, 27 August-3 September 1949. *Income and Wealth,* series 1, Bowes & Bowes, Cambridge, England, 1951 (Appendix prepared by Mrs. Mary W. Smelker), pp. 98-111. (C)

'Comments on Lowe's "Structural Model." ' (With reference to Adolph Lowe's 'A Structural Model of Production,' in *Social Research,* 19, 135, 1952). *Social Research,* 19, 501, 1952. (A)

'Comments on "Concepts and Assumptions in Long-Term Projections of National Product," ' by Simon Kuznets. *Long-Range Economic Projection,* Studies in Income and Wealth, National Bureau of Economic Research, New York, 1954, vol. 16, pp. 38-42. (C)

'Entwicklungen in Konjunkturforschung und Konjunkturpolitik in den Vereinigten Staaten von Amerika' (Developments in Business Cycle Analysis and Policy in the United States), *Kieler Vorträge* No. 6 (Neue Folge), Fritz Baade, editor. Institut für Weltwirtschaft an der Universität Kiel, 1954. (B)

ECONOMIC PLANNING AND ECONOMIC STABILIZATION

'Why the Papen Plan for Industrial Recovery Failed,' *Social Research,* 1, p. 83ff., 1934. (A)

'Economic Limitations of Government Control,' *Government Control of the Economic Order—A Symposium,* Benjamin E. Lippincott, editor. University of Minnesota Press, Minneapolis, Minn., 1935, pp. 18-30. (C)

'Die Krisenbekämpfung in den Vereinigten Staaten unter Roosevelt's "New Deal." ' (The Battle Against the Depression under Roosevelt's New Deal), *Gewerkschaftliche Rundschau für die Schweiz,* April 1936. (A)

* 'Economics Today,' *Social Research,* 4, p. 191ff., 1937. (A)

* 'Is Economic Planning Compatible with Democracy?' *Political and Economic Democracy*, Fritz Lehmann and Max Ascoli, editors. W. W. Norton & Co., Inc., New York, 1937, pp. 21-41. (C)
* 'Is Economic Security Worth the Cost?' *Social Research*, 4, p. 287ff., 1939. (A)
'Comments on W. I. King: "Are We Suffering from Economic Maturity?"' *Journal of Political Economy*, 48, p. 114ff., 1940. (A)
* 'Maintaining High-Level Production and Employment: Technical Requirements,' *The American Political Science Review*, 39, 1126, 1945. (A)
* 'On the Road to Economic Stabilization,' *Social Research*, 15, p. 265ff., 1948. (A)
[With the assistance of Marilyn Young] *The American Economy in 1960—Economic Progress in a World of Tension*, A National Planning Association Staff Report, Planning Pamphlet No. 81. National Planning Association, Washington, D. C., December 1952, 166 pp. (B)
'Government Planning—How Much Do We Need? If We Need It, Where Should We Draw the Line?' *New Perspectives in Economics for Top Management*. Paper presented at the New York University Management Institute, Division of General Education, 9 December 1953. (C)
'A Depression? It All Depends . . . ,' *The Reporter*, 17 February 1953. (A)
'Our Standard of Living by 1960,' *Challenge Magazine*, May 1953; also, *Advertiser's Digest*, 18, 9, 1953. (A)
'The Shape of Things to Come,' *Looking Ahead* (National Planning Association Monthly), 1, 1, 1953. (A)
'Council of Economic Advisers—A New Start,' ibid. 1, 6, 1953. (A)
'The Economic Outlook for 1954,' ibid. 1, 10, 1954. (A)
'The Importance of Selling to Our National Economy,' *Opportunity*, 62, 4, February 1954. (A)
'Comments on the President's Economic Report of January 1954,' A Symposium on the Economic Report of the President and Related Documents, *The Review of Economics and Statistics*, Seymour E. Harris, editor. Harvard University Press, 1954, vol. 26, 3, pp. 254-8. (A)
[Co-author] *'Opportunities for Economic Expansion,'* A National Planning Association Steering Committee Report, Planning Pamphlet No. 87. National Planning Association, Washington, D. C., July 1954, 24 pp. (B)

Index

Budget procedure (Cont.)
for financial planning, 208-9, 267, 270-72
and forecasting, 284
for program control, 208
for program formulation, 208, 266-7, 268-70
Business cycle, *see* Budget, Business investments, Fiscal policy, Government expenditures, Public borrowing, Tax policy
Business cycle policy, *see* Fiscal policy, Government expenditures, Tax policy
Business expenses and taxation, 102
Business investment
aided by economic projections, 256, 356
and confidence, 132-3
and consumption, 252
in depression, 122, 130-31
in national economic accounts, 279
in postwar period, 158, 183
regularization of, 107-8, 214-15
Business psychology in the economic cycle, 132, 328

Calkins, R. D., 347
Cameralism, 6
Central bank policy, 152, 174, 282
Clark, C., 272n.
Clark, J. M., 115, 116, 117, 336n.
Classical economics, 6, 49, 174-5, 291, 336, 340, 343
and democracy, 292-4
Classical theory of recovery, 128
Colm, G., 39n., 53n., 54n., 71n., 79n., 185n., 203n., 214n., 223n., 237n., 240n., 244n., 353n., 354n.
Committee for Economic Development, 17n., 18-19, 196n., 202n., 283
Communism, economics of, 340-41; *see also* Marxism
Consumer income and expenditures in national economic accounts, 184, 227, 276-7
Consumption and investment, sustainable relationship, 251-2

Corporation
an economic and social entity, 89
public and private, 104-6
Council of Economic Advisers, 15n., 213n., 217, 219, 254, 265, 320, 322n., 325, 353

Deficits, *see* Budget
Democracy
and classical economics, 292-4
defined, 290
institutions and humanitarian values, democratic, 290-91
Dupuit, J., 13n.

Economic democracy, defined, 294
Economic dynamics, 153, 245, 352-4
Economic forecasts, 180, 206-7, 244, 245-6, 329
Economic goals and targets, 356-8
Economic models
defined, 185, 244
full employment, 156-7, 158, 166-7, 169-71
use of, 244
Economic planning
and the business cycle, 297-8
defined, 289n., 294-5
and democracy, 289, 299-307
and general welfare, 302-3
and *laissez-faire*, 295-7
vs. planned economy, 289-90n.
regional, 297
Economic progress and maladjustments, 321-3
Economic projections, 181-6, 245-6, 355
criteria of, 252
defined, 243
and economic forecasts, 354
and economic policy, 253-5
and national economic objectives, 247-52, 356
for 1948-9, 277-8
for 1950, 157-8, 167, 170
in other countries, 250, 280
and private enterprise, 255-6
Economic security, 308-18
and democracy, 309